LECTURES ON ECONOMIC GROWTH

ROBERT E. LUCAS, JR.

LECTURES ON
ECONOMIC GROWTH

HARVARD UNIVERSITY PRESS

Cambridge, Massachusetts, and London, England

First Harvard University Press paperback edition, 2004

Library of Congress Cataloging-in-Publication Data

Lucas, Robert E.
   Lectures on economic growth / Robert E. Lucas, Jr.
      p. cm.
   Includes bibliographical references and index.
   ISBN 0-674-00627-5 (cloth)
   ISBN 0-674-01601-7 (pbk.)
   1. Economic development. I. Title.

HD75 .L824 2002
338.9—dc21   2001045263

To Nancy

CONTENTS

ACKNOWLEDGMENTS

In the course of writing and giving a series of lectures over a fifteen-year period, I have accumulated many debts, intellectual and personal. To begin at the most general level, I am grateful for the many conversations I have had over the years with Edward Prescott, Sherwin Rosen, and Nancy Stokey. All of them have influenced my thinking on economic growth, to the point where I can no longer be sure I can tell their ideas from my own.

"On the Mechanics of Economic Development," Chapter 1 of this volume, was written for the Marshall Lectures, given at Cambridge University in 1985. Versions of this lecture were later given as the David Horowitz Lectures in Jersusalem and Tel Aviv, the W. A. Mackintosh Lecture at Queens University, the Carl Snyder Memorial Lecture at the University of California at Santa Barbara, the Chung-Hua Lecture in Taipei, the Nancy Schwartz Lecture at Northwestern University, and the Lionel McKenzie Lecture at the University of Rochester.

Nancy Stokey gave detailed and very helpful criticism of an early draft of "Mechanics." Arnold Harberger, Jane Jacobs, Akiva Offenbacher, Theodore Schultz, and Robert Solow gave useful comments. Richard Manning was an able assistant. Robert King and Charles Plosser encouraged me to publish the lectures in the *Journal of Monetary Economics*, and Chapter 1 of this volume is the version that appeared there.

Chapter 3, "Making a Miracle," was given as the 1991 Fisher-Schultz Lecture at the European meetings of the Econometric Society. Jose Scheinkman, Theodore Schultz, Nancy Stokey, and Alwyn Young provided helpful discussion and criticism, as did the referees for *Econometrica*.

Chapter 5, "The Industrial Revolution: Past and Future," the last and longest chapter of this book, is a revision of the Kuznets Lectures that I gave at Yale University in 1997. I thank Paul Schultz, T. N. Srinivasan,

Robert Evenson, and other Yale friends for hospitality and criticism on that occasion. David Weil provided a thoughtful and stimulating discussion when I presented some of this material at a conference at the Technion in Haifa. I also benefited from presentation and discussion of some of this material at the University of Pennsylvania, Northwestern University, UCLA, and at lectures in Seoul, Buenos Aires, Rosario, and Santiago de Chile.

Joel Mokyr read the entire manuscript of "The Industrial Revolution: Past and Future," and his detailed comments led to several improvements. Ivan Werning also provided extremely useful comments on many aspects of the chapter, some (but certainly not all) of which are explicitly acknowledged there. Comments of Fernando Alvarez, D. Gale Johnson, Alvin Marty, and Raj Saah were also very helpful. Above all, this chapter reflects the influence of many discussions of economics and demography with Robert Tamura.

The data set described in the Appendix of Chapter 5 is the work of three very able Chicago students over a period of several years. Vimut Vanitcharearnthum and I first put together a set of time series for world GDP and population for classroom use over ten years ago, starting with the Penn World Table and working back in time from other sources. This data set was extended and refined by Krishna Kumar and Enric Fernandez. The data appendix was compiled from their voluminous notes. I thank Alison Krueger, another excellent Chicago student, for her care in preparing the index.

This is the point at which custom requires me to thank my typist—but word processing has transformed me into a professional-quality mathematical typist, and this is a task I enjoy much too much to give up to anyone else. Instead, I must thank my secretary, Shirley Ogrodowski, for doing everything else in our office superlatively well, and letting me bang away at the computer for long stretches of uninterrupted time.

The Kuznets Lectures—Chapter 5—have not been previously published. Chapter 1 is reprinted from the *Journal of Monetary Economics* with the permission of North-Holland Publishing Company. Chapters 2 and 4 are reprinted from the *American Economic Review* and the *Journal of Economic Perspectives*, both with the permission of the American Economic Association. Chapter 3 is reprinted from *Econometrica* with the permission of the Econometric Society.

I thank Michael Aronson of Harvard University Press for his encouragement and patience, and Mary Ellen Geer for her assistance in putting the manuscript into shape.

The chapters in this book began as lectures, given over a decade and a half. There are many things I would do differently if I were writing an up-to-date monograph, and a vast amount of related literature has since arisen that would need to be considered. So to my fellow students of economic growth whose contributions have been neglected or given too brief a treatment in this volume of mine: Thanks in advance for forgiving my scholarly lapses. I hope one of you will be stimulated to write the definitive monograph that this book, obviously, is not.

This book contains my writing on economic growth and development, from the Marshall Lectures that I gave in 1985 to the 1997 Kuznets Lectures, published here for the first time. The general theme of the collection is the attempt to adapt modern growth theory, originally developed to describe the behavior of the industrialized economies, to obtain a unified understanding of rich and poor economies alike in a world of vast income and growth rate differences.

The methods used in this inquiry are theoretical. A series of mathematically explicit models are constructed to exhibit certain kinds of observed behavior: sustained income growth, sustained or increasing inequality, trade-related growth episodes, the demographic transition. From repeated attempts to produce realistic behavior from simulated models, I have learned a great deal about the way the process of economic development works. This book is a record of that learning process.

The chapters themselves have substantive introductions. There is no need to repeat or summarize them here. In this introduction I will simply try to describe how they came to be written, explain some of my reasons for choosing to focus each of them as I did, and deal with some issues that I wish I had handled better the first time around.

1

"On the Mechanics of Economic Development" (Chapter 1 of this volume) was written for the 1985 Marshall Lectures at Cambridge University. My week in Cambridge was part of a month-long trip that included weeks in England, Israel, Finland, and France. This was my first visit to any of these four countries, and indeed my first trip of more than a day or two outside the United States. In Finland I gave the Yrjö Jahnsson Lectures, later published as *Models of Business Cycles*. In Israel I gave the David Horowitz Lectures, basically a repeat of the Marshall Lectures. In France I spoke at the University of Paris, Dauphine, and at the evening seminar series chaired by Edmund Malinvaud.

None of these hosts had asked me to speak on economic growth and development. I was expected to speak on rational expectations and macroeconomics, as I did in Finland. But the Jahnsson Lectures had proved difficult to write—I was in the process of adjusting my thinking on business cycles to the shock of Kydland and Prescott's work—and I did not look forward to the prospect of spending the latter half of my career trying to hang on to what I had done in the first half. The invitation from Cambridge came well in advance, so I had plenty of time. Why not use the opportunity to try something new?[1]

Though I had never written on growth or development, I had been interested in these topics for as long as I could remember. How can an economist not be interested in the wealth of nations? I had taught an undergraduate elective course in development economics at Carnegie-Mellon, and again at Chicago: an excuse to look at some data, read some papers, and work out some models, without the responsibility for covering the literature that teaching a graduate course entails. The question I asked myself and my students in these classes was whether one could use modern growth theory—as exemplified by Robert Solow's (1956) paper—to think about the behavior of poor countries as well as rich ones.

The modern theory of growth, which originated in the 1960s and has continued to be developed in new, interesting ways, provides a tractable and empirically fairly successful account of twentieth-century growth in the United States and the post–World War II growth of Japan and much of Europe. Growth theory has matured into a successful basis for applied economics, in the sense that it provides an agreed-upon framework for quantitative studies of taxation, monetary policy, and social insurance. The basic idea of "On the Mechanics of Economic Development," articulated in its initial sections, was to see if modern growth theory could also be adapted for use as a theory of economic development.

---

1. I was concerned that people at Cambridge would be disappointed if I spoke about something other than business cycles and rational expectations, and remember writing to Frank Hahn about this. To deal with it, the people at Cambridge set up an open-ended question-and-answer session for me in addition to the Marshall Lectures.

Adaptation of some kind was evidently necessary: The balanced paths of growth theory, with constant income growth and the assumed absence of population pressures, obviously do not fit all of economic history or even all of the behavior that can be seen in today's world. The theory is, and was designed to be, a model of the behavior in the recent past of a subset of highly successful societies. The strategy I adopted in "Mechanics" was to take the fact that the industrial revolution had occurred in some societies as an unexplained given, and to try to think about the economics of the relations between economies in which sustained growth was under way and economies that remained stagnant.

There is a difficulty that any theory about these relations must face, arising from the tendency toward income equalization predicted by economic theory. The law of diminishing returns tells us that any resource is most valuable where it is relatively scarce. An immediate consequence is that resources will move, where possible, until the relative quantities of resources are equalized across locations. Labor will move so as to equate workers per unit of land (of equal quality) in different locations. Capital or labor or both will move so as to equate capital-labor ratios in different locations. The law of diminishing returns gives a reasonable explanation both of why there are so many people per square mile in the lush plain of Bengal, compared to the tundra of northern Canada, and also of why living standards are about the same in these two places.

If the law of diminishing returns is a helpful construct in explaining the allocation of labor and land in pre-industrial societies, it seems hard to square with the way reproducible capital has been allocated to labor during the industrial revolution of the last two centuries. How did economic growth create so much inequality in the returns to resources—to labor in particular—in different parts of the world? If new technological ideas improved the productivity of workers in nineteenth-century England, why did these ideas not spread rapidly to other economies, improving productivity there? Or if the new technology was embodied in new machines or in expert Englishmen, why did these machines and experts not go abroad, to be combined in production with inexpensive foreign labor rather than with expensive English workers?

These are not just hypothetical examples. The diffusion through imitation of ideas and the enormous flows of people and capital around the world have been observed in all times, and continue to occur today. But it is evident that these flows, implied by diminishing returns, were not nearly large enough to distribute the productivity gains of the industrial revolution evenly across different parts of the world. The question of why this was so is raised in Section 3 of "Mechanics." I elaborated on it in the essay "Why Doesn't Capital Flow from Rich to Poor Countries?" also included in this volume (Chapter 2).

Indeed, since the onset of the industrial revolution the most rapid growth has often occurred in areas where growth had been most rapid in the past, creating gaps between living standards in the richest and poorest economies that are now on the order of 25 to 1. This growing inequality in capital accumulation of all kinds—human as well as physical—suggests the importance of *increasing* returns, of a force that makes the return to at least some kinds of investment higher the more investment has already taken place. But how can we simultaneously maintain the importance of both diminishing and increasing returns? And how can the importance of increasing returns be squared with the fact that large-scale enterprises are not always, or even typically, more successful economically than smaller ones?

Paul Romer (1986a, 1986b) worked out an explicit model of a growing economy that reconciled the opposing forces of increasing and diminishing returns, and did so in a way that generated sustained production growth and was at the same time consistent with market equilibrium of many, competing producers. The economics of Romer's model are closely related to the ideas of Allyn Young (1928), but his development of these ideas is entirely new. In the theory, goods are produced with a single kind of capital—Romer called it "knowledge capital"—and each producer's output depends both on his own stock of this capital and on the stock held by other firms. Aggregating over producers, production in the economy as a whole is subject to increasing returns: Every 10 percent increase in the *total* stock of knowledge capital leads to an output increase of *more than* 10 percent. But an individual producer, who has no control over the economy's total stock of capital, faces diminishing returns to increases in his own capital. Thus the fact of increasing inequality among the economies of the world is reconciled with the absence of a tendency to monopolization within each economy.

Romer's formulation opened up new possibilities for the understanding of income inequality across societies. If we think of a world with two Romer-like economies, each at a different level of income, it must be that the richer of the two economies has a higher level of "knowledge capital." The social or economy-wide return to capital need not be lower in the richer economy, though, because both economies are subject to increasing returns to their aggregate capital stocks. Then why doesn't capital flow to the richer economy, and why don't capitalists in both economies consolidate their holdings in larger units? Because both economies are subject to diminishing returns at the level of the individual enterprise.

Section 4 of my "On the Mechanics of Economic Development" constructs a model designed to deal with the problem posed by diminishing returns along the lines proposed by Romer. In doing this, I found it more convenient to make use of a model of Uzawa (1965) in which there is both physical and human capital but returns, private and social, depend only on the ratio of these two stocks.[2] The theory replaces the increasing returns assumed by Romer with a kind of constant returns, yielding a system which is easier to analyze than Romer's (it has a constant asymptotic growth rate, not an increasing one) but which circumvents the problems of diminishing returns in a similar way.

The human capital model I used involves an external effect of human capital, patterned on the external effect of knowledge capital that Romer introduced. But in my analysis, this external effect is not needed to ensure the existence of a competitive equilibrium the way it is in Romer's model. If this effect is removed, the model continues to be internally consistent and is in fact even easier to analyze.[3] In this human capital model, balanced paths exist and have the property that each country's relative income position is dictated by its initial situation. Initial inequality persists. This prediction survives trade in capital goods, in the sense that when every economy is on its balanced path, the return to physical capital is equalized across economies at different income levels. Diminishing returns to individual investments do not imply income-equalizing capital flows.

If there were no external human capital effects in that model, then a second prediction would be that the return to labor at any given skill

---

2. Razin (1972) is an interesting, earlier application of Uzawa's model.

3. Rebelo (1990) stripped the model down to its simplest one-capital-good "Ak" form. Caballe and Santos (1993) provide an elegant analysis of the off-balanced-path dynamics of an Uzawa model without a production externality. This has yet to be done for the model whose balanced path is constructed in "Mechanics" (Chapter 1).

level would be equalized: This just follows from constant returns to scale. But while we do not observe capital flows in the world economy that are anything like the flows predicted by the theory without external effects, we do observe enormous pressures for immigration from poor to rich countries. Capital and labor flows are not just mirror images of each other: A given collection of capital and labor produces more in a rich country than in a poor one.

The view is sometimes advanced that it is a virtue of the constant returns model that it does not need an externality to guarantee the existence of an equilibrium, as though postulating an external effect were the last resort of a poor theorist. But the existence of important external effects of investments in human capital—in knowledge—has long been viewed as an evident and important aspect of reality. When Romer incorporated such an effect in his growth theory, it was not only to ensure the existence of a competitive equilibrium but also to introduce an important element of realism. I think it serves the same purpose in the Arrow (1962) model.

For anyone who sees economic growth as driven by ideas, by increases in "the stock of useful knowledge," the most basic reason for emphasizing external effects must be the classic observation that much of the return to an idea—virtually all of it for a really important idea—accrues to people other than the originator. If ideas are the engine of growth and if an excess of social over private returns is an essential feature of the production of ideas, then we want to go out of our way to introduce external effects into growth theory, not try to do without them.

Some authors write as though treating exogenous technical change as an engine of growth eliminates the need to appeal to external effects, and restores the equivalence of optimal and competitive equilibrium allocations. As long as the "exogenous technical change" that drives the economy under study originates from activities outside that economy, this argument works and, as we know, it can be technically useful in characterizing equilibrium behavior. But it is a partial equilibrium argument that simply evades the question of the source of the technical change. If the growth of knowledge is external to an economy under study, then it must be internal to some other economy, the economy where the new knowledge was produced. Somewhere in the world, someone took the effort to create new knowledge and received at most a fraction of the return from this investment. In growth theory, "exogenous technological change" is just a euphemism for "unanalyzed production externalities."

2

The most spectacular growth successes of the postwar world have been associated with growth in international trade. This is the single empirical generalization that strikes everyone who is trying to understand economic growth in the last 50 years. Countries like Japan, South Korea, Taiwan, Hong Kong, and Singapore began producing goods they had never made before and exporting them to the United States, successfully competing with American and European producers who had the advantages of decades of experience. At the other extreme, the Communist countries that cut themselves off from trade with the West stagnated, as did India and many Latin American economies that used tariff walls to protect inefficient domestic producers from outside competition. These observations seem to provide further confirmation of the usual economic arguments in favor of free trade, arguments that seem to me as true and as relevant now as they were when Hume and Smith first articulated them.

But classic trade theory does not really help in understanding the connections between trade and growth that we see in the postwar period. One problem is that while some of the Asian successes—in Taiwan and Hong Kong—were associated with liberal trade policy, others—Japan, Korea, and Singapore—occurred in heavily managed environments, under policies that Smith would certainly have criticized as mercantilist. (I agree with Smith that the mercantilist economies would have fared even better without managed trade, but this view is obviously not a straightforward statement of the facts.) A second, more important, barrier to the application of the theory of gains-from-trade to postwar growth is that quantitative versions of the theory do not yield estimated benefits of tariff reduction that are of the right order of magnitude to account for the growth miracles. South Korean incomes doubled every 10 years in the 30 years after 1960. Even if we assume that Korean trade barriers were completely removed in 1960, a wild exaggeration, the best current trade models would predict perhaps a 20 percent increase in production over 30 years. Nothing to be sneezed at, to be sure: These models support a compelling case for the importance of free trade. What they do *not* provide, though, is a theoretical link between free trade and economic growth that is both rapid and sustained.

The model of growth in Section 4 of "Mechanics" does not have a place for catch-up growth, growth "miracles," in which countries at the bottom of the income distribution enter into a phase of rapid growth and begin to close the income gap between themselves and the richest economies. The model was designed to explain the persistence of inequality in a way that is consistent with diminishing returns, and like Romer's it has the feature that initial differences are maintained into the indefinite future.

In Section 5 of "Mechanics" I worked out the evolution of national incomes in a two-good world, a modified version of Krugman's (1987) model. The key assumption of this model is that the production of one of the two goods results in productivity-improving learning, while production of the other good does not. To keep the microeconomics simple, the learning effect was assumed to be external to the producer but internal to the country. The attraction of the model is that it connects trade volumes, and perhaps the nature of the goods that are traded as well, with knowledge acquisition: learning. If growth is mainly a matter of accumulating human capital and if trade and growth are closely related, then we need a theory that makes this connection. In this particular model, though, the dynamics work to intensify static comparative advantages over time, and incomes become ever more unequal. The theory works in the wrong direction to explain catch-up growth.

My 1991 Fisher-Schultz Lecture, "Making a Miracle" (Chapter 3 of this volume), contains two more attempts to link trade and growth. Section 2 was stimulated by Parente and Prescott's (1994) observation that a constant returns, human capital model can also be interpreted as predicting growing rather than constant income inequality across countries. For suppose, they argued, that we drop the assumption that production is entirely deterministic and add random shocks to production in that model, shocks that are not perfectly correlated across countries. Then the model, so modified, predicts that income in each country will follow random-walk-like behavior and thus that income variance across countries will grow without bound.

This prediction reflects the model's economic assumption that each country's engine of growth is its own stock of human capital, and that the external benefits of each country's human capital accrue only to producers within that country. This assumption runs counter to our sense that growth in world productivity reflects growth in a single state variable, something like Kuznets's worldwide "stock of useful knowledge."

Once we see this, it is easy to modify the human capital model in a reasonable way so that it predicts convergence to common income levels or, with stochastic shocks, to a limiting distribution with finite variance. This is sketched in Section 2 of my lecture, where I assume that some of the spillover effects of human capital accumulation in any one country are worldwide. Such a modification—not quite worked out in "Making a Miracle," where savings rates and human capital accumulation rates are taken as givens—completely preserves the desirable features of the human capital model while converting a prediction of income divergence into a prediction of convergence at any desired rate.[4]

But the catch-up growth we have observed since the nineteenth century is typically not a smooth reduction of income differentials at a common rate between any pair of countries. If this were all there was to it, the inequality we observe would never have arisen in the first place! What we see at any time is some economies "taking off," in W. W. Rostow's famous image, rapidly industrializing and closing the income gap with the leaders in a few decades, while other economies remain stagnant, on the outside looking in. The annual income convergence rate of about .02 that Barro and Sala-i-Martin (1992) estimated from postwar data is an average of a few much higher rates with a lot of zeros.

The simulation in my paper "Some Macroeconomics for the Twenty-first Century" (Chapter 4 of this volume) provides an explicit example of world growth with these features, one that exhibits the simultaneous occurrence of divergence and catch-up growth. In this model, as in the model sketched in Section 2 of "Making a Miracle," productivity-related knowledge is pictured as though it floated across national boundaries, like acid rain or volcanic ash. But the evidence on trade and growth suggests that the rate of diffusion of technology depends on economic interactions—on trade. To understand how this connection works, and thus to understand the extreme variability of development experience and the policies that lead to successful development, we need to get deeper into the nature of knowledge spillovers.

The models of Stokey (1988, 1991a) and Young (1991) that relate trade to learning-by-doing seem to have closer ties to evidence and more promise

---

4. Tamura (1991) had also proposed a model of international human capital spillovers, designed to account for aspects of the diffusion of the industrial revolution.

for growth theory than do Krugman's model and my adaptation of it. In the model of Stokey (1988), for example, there are an infinite number of producible goods, unambiguously ordered from lowest quality, to next lowest, and so on, *ad infinitum*. Economic growth in this setting means gaining the ability to produce better and better goods. As this occurs, new goods are added, old goods are dropped, and both welfare and national product (if correctly measured) grow. The general idea is to capture the fact that economic growth is poorly described as the production of more and more of the same stuff. A more specific objective is to find a setting in which one can analyze what Vernon (1966) described as a product cycle: A new good is invented and initially produced in an advanced country. Its manufacture then moves to a lower-wage economy, then to an even lower-wage economy, and so on. In the process, the poor economies acquire the manufacturing skills that were initially available only in the rich economy.

When I began work on "Making a Miracle," I had hoped to construct a model based on learning-by-doing that could generate growth rates as miraculously high as the postwar East Asian economic successes. The experience in American shipbuilding during World War II that Leonard Rapping (1965) had studied many years earlier stimulated this hope.[5] I began with a description of a technology—close to that proposed by Stokey—in which learning rates are determined by the way the workforce is distributed over goods with different learning potentials. My exposition makes it clear that a trade-off is involved in growth based on learning: A society that is continually taking on new tasks never gets really good at doing anything. Something more is needed to describe rapid, catch-up growth.[6]

My version of a learning-by-doing model got as far as a description of a technology that would make the trade-offs clear, but not as far as a model of equilibrium behavior based on such a technology. If learning models of technological change are useful in thinking about growth, then we will evidently need a theory of market equilibrium that describes the way firms with such learning technologies interact. Stokey and Young deal with this issue as Krugman and I did, by treating on-the-job learning as purely external: Everyone benefits equally. The convenience of this assumption is

---

5. Thompson (2001) argues that Rapping overestimated the learning effect.

6. Nakajima (1999) contains a promising approach to the problem of explaining catch-up growth, building on the model of Young (1993).

that there will be a competitive industry equilibrium. But one would like to have the ability to analyze situations in which at least some of the returns to learning-by-doing are captured by the individual producers.

There is a complementary way of thinking about the economics of knowledge diffusion, based on models of research and development in monopolistically competitive settings.[7] In these models, the activities of invention and imitation are given detailed descriptions, and the division of the returns to knowledge creation is analyzed rather than simply assumed. Because of its tractability, the Dixit-Stiglitz (1977) model of product variety plays a workhorse role in this literature.

In Romer (1990) and Grossman and Helpman (1991a, 1991b), for example, "blueprints" for new Dixit-Stiglitz products are produced in a distinct research activity, the private return to which is the monopoly rent on the exclusive right to produce any newly discovered good. A by-product—an external effect—of this research activity is an addition to a stock of publicly shared "knowledge capital." More knowledge capital, in turn, increases the effectiveness of all research activities. The details of such a model can be so arranged as to produce endogenous growth at a constant rate, just as in an Uzawa-type model. In contrast to the external effect of knowledge (human capital, in my terminology) on the *level* of production that I assumed in "Mechanics," the external effect that Romer and Grossman and Helpman studied works on the rate of change.

The specifics of models based on these ideas lead one to think about historical evidence on particular inventions and the processes that produced them in a way that aggregative modeling does not. The fact that these models have many distinct goods makes it possible to use them to think about international trade in new, realistic ways. The monopolistically competitive setting in which the analysis is conducted lets one think rigorously about inventive activities that have both private and social returns. These are all important virtues. As yet, however, these models have not led to theories of catch-up growth or economic miracles. Something important is still missing in our thinking about the connections between trade and growth.

Surely Romer, Grossman and Helpman, and others are right that an important part of knowledge creation or human capital accumulation takes place in business firms. Some of the accumulation of production-related

---

7. See Romer (1990), Grossman and Helpman (1991a, 1991b), Aghion and Howitt (1992).

knowledge takes place in schools, but no one who thinks about it will treat schools as the only place. The rapidly growing economies of East Asia had well-schooled workforces relative to many slower-growing neighbors, but schooling differences are not of the right order of magnitude to account for the observed differences in growth rates. Most of the knowledge growth in these economies has to have taken place on the job. Of course, this is true in the developed countries, too: T. W. Schultz (1962) estimated that something like half of U.S. human capital growth took place at work, using the Mincer (1962) estimates based on the estimated effects of experience on earnings. All of this knowledge accumulation has private benefit: Otherwise, no one would take the time to do it, and Mincer would not have been able to estimate it. Most of it, I would say, has external effects, too.

If one uses the term "human capital" as a synonym for "schooling," as Grossman and Helpman and many others do, then obviously one needs to add another state variable, say "knowledge capital" or "blueprints," to a model that is to have any chance of fitting data on growth. An aggregative model must have *all* sources of productivity growth represented somewhere. The real issue is one of aggregation: How many distinct state variables do we need? I think of "human capital" as a comprehensive stock of all knowledge, as in Romer's (1986a) model, and in this single state variable setting it is straightforward to analyze both internal and external effects in a competitive equilibrium setting. One can argue over what to call this state variable, but the substantive questions are: What can be gained by disaggregating into two or more knowledge-related variables? Which distinctions are helpful to draw on in carrying out such a disaggregation?

The idea underlying the models of Romer (1990) and Grossman and Helpman (1991a, 1991b) is not simply that human capital or knowledge accumulation takes place in firms and yields both internal and external returns, but that one can identify distinct activities—goods production—the returns to which are internal, and other activities—blueprint production—the returns to which are purely external. Since no one would undertake the latter type of activity under competition, one needs to assume that new blueprints carry monopoly rights to production in order that any be produced. There must indeed be large differences in the ratio of external to private returns across different human capital-accumulating activities, and this fact naturally leads to attempts to isolate activities—research, development, invention—that lead to knowledge increases that are hard to keep private, and to model such activities as being different in kind from those with large private returns. This idea has certainly led to interesting economics, but the distinction seems overdrawn to me.

One way to think about human capital externalities or knowledge spillovers is based on the cultures of high science. In these cultures, today, new findings—blueprints, if you like—are transmitted around the world almost instantaneously, and become shared knowledge wherever people skilled enough to interpret them are working. In this situation, new findings may not seem a likely source for local productivity differentials, and even a century and a half ago, when ideas were transmitted only by mail and telegraph, communication times hardly seem a significant factor.

But even if scientific findings are quickly transmitted, trained people are needed to realize their possibilities for production. Physics journals can be sent from Germany to the United States in a couple of weeks, and this has been so for more than a century, yet physics training in the United States remained far behind until European-trained physicists migrated here in the 1930s. Somehow, one doesn't learn physics from reading journals in isolation: One needs to be part of a physics community, interacting on a daily basis. This observation is surely not limited to physics. Activity on any scientific or artistic frontier, and even decent training of students, tends generally to be concentrated in a few places.

In any case, most productivity-related ideas are far from high science and are transmitted among practitioners, with little or nothing published. Civil engineers learn basic facts and principles in school, but the only way to learn how a modern skyscraper or an interstate highway is built is to work for a construction company and learn from those who are doing it. Starbucks trains its *baristas* not just to master the company lingo for the incredible variety of coffee drinks it offers but even to deal with customers cheerfully. The idea that it will help business to smile at customers is not patentable or publishable, but whenever someone remembers and implements it, it shows up in profits and in total factor productivity as well. Starbucks's design and training policies came from somewhere and have, in turn, been widely and profitably imitated (even improved upon), but they have also made fortunes for the company's owners.

Considerations like these may explain why the distinction between goods-producing activities and knowledge-producing activities has enjoyed such limited empirical success. They also explain why I think models of learning-by-doing—models in which the production of goods and the production of knowledge are tied together—are closer to reality than models at the other extreme. Such models also seem to me to have more promise for understanding the connections between trade and growth. If automobile-producing expertise is mainly accumulated by firms that make a lot of cars, then those firms need to find a lot of car buyers. It seems to be harder than I thought it would be to construct tractable models centered on such dynamic scale economies (in Krugman's terminology), but it is a problem that may need to be solved before models of growth miracles can be constructed.

3

In most of my thinking on economic growth, I have followed the modern growth theory tradition in treating population growth as a side issue. In the introduction to "On the Mechanics of Economic Development" I noted the potential importance of ideas in Barro and Becker (1988, 1989), an integrated treatment of the fertility and savings decisions, but did not make use of them. Tamura (1988) and Becker, Murphy, and Tamura (1990) later integrated the fertility and human capital accumulation decisions, producing a model in which equilibrium undergoes a transition from a situation of low and constant per capita incomes to one that exhibits "Ak" behavior with income growth at a constant rate. In Becker, Murphy, and Tamura, the demographic transition and the onset of sustained income growth appeared as a single event, with changes in fertility and production growth simultaneously determined. Neither variable could be taken as given in studying the determinants of the other.

These ideas were new to me, and their potential importance to an understanding of the onset and continuation of the industrial revolution was obvious. I decided to use Yale's invitation to give the Kuznets Lectures as an excuse to think about the role of the demography in economic growth.

One of the most rewarding aspects of this effort was the engagement with Ricardo's *Principles*, and my mathematical exposition of Ricardian theory may be the most successful part of the lectures. I came to appreciate the empirical power of the Malthusian-Ricardian model: its ability to account for the similarity in real incomes across different societies and the stability of living standards over time in the face of ongoing technological change.[8] From this starting point, the problem becomes one of explaining how the industrial revolution overcame the force for stagnation in living standards that the classical model captured, or how, for the first time in history, in some societies, technological change became the source of sustained growth in living standards and not of population growth only.

The approach to demography that I took in the Kuznets Lectures is based on the quantity-quality trade-off that Becker (1960) introduced many years ago, motivated by the cross-sectional observation that although the number of children may decline as families get richer, the resources devoted to children continue to increase. Becker, Murphy, and Tamura (1990) constructed an aggregate model on the basis of this trade-off. In their model, a small displacement from an initial position of income stagnation can induce an economy to shift from quantity of children to quality, to shift onto an equilibrium path with reduced fertility and perpetual growth. The limitation of the model is that the low-level steady state is not really Malthusian: Neither land nor resources more generally play any role in the theory.

To describe the transition from Malthusian stagnation to sustained income growth, we need—it seems to me—at least two state variables: human capital and population (or population per unit of land). Becker, Murphy, and Tamura have one: human capital. There is a complementary model due to Hansen and Prescott (1998)[9] in which population is the single state variable, and living standards are reduced when more people work a fixed amount of land. In their model, the transition occurs when the use of a second, non-land-using technology becomes economic. The approach I took in the Kuznets Lectures is a kind of merger of these two models.

4

The central idea in all the essays in this volume is that the successful transformation from an economy of traditional agriculture to a modern, growing economy depends crucially on an increase in the rate of accumulation of

---

8. I suppose I had inherited George Stigler's (1952) view of the Malthusian-Ricardian theory as an unsuccessful theory, grossly inconsistent with the facts. And so it turned out to be, but the theory was a good enough fit to the data that were available to these writers in 1800.

9. See also Doepke (2000).

human capital. As have Schultz and Becker and others before me, I have tried to show how this idea, embodied in aggregative models of economic growth, produces behavior that conforms better to the facts of economic development than the behavior predicted by models centered on other visions of the engine of growth. Yet the sources and perhaps even the character of this increase in human capital growth remain somewhat ill understood, a *deus ex machina*, an invisible cause to which important visible effects are attributed.

But what is visible depends on where one looks. Look, for example, at V. S. Naipaul's great novel of economic development, *A House for Mr. Biswas*. The novel begins with the story of Mohun Biswas's birth and death, all within its first 40 pages. He is born in rural Trinidad, a grandson of immigrants who had come from India as indentured servants. As a small boy, his ambition is to become a herder of cattle like his older brothers. At his death, he is an unemployed journalist in Port-of-Spain, living in a ramshackle house, with no assets to support his wife and large family after he is gone. What life within such limits is to sustain the reader for the novel's remaining 540 pages? Yet measured by the cultural distance between Mr. Biswas's parents and his children, his life is a story of amazing progress. By the end of Biswas's life, his oldest son, Anand—Naipaul's own fictional counterpart—is a scholarship student at Oxford. Between Anand and Mohun Biswas's parents is the entire 25-to-1 difference between living standards in India and living standards in Western Europe and the United States.

Biswas himself is no Horatio Alger figure. His talents are modest, and his willingness to ingratiate himself with those who might advance his career is nonexistent. He passes from one mediocre, limited job to another. But his unwillingness to accept the limits of each current situation as permanent, to make the best of it, turns out to be his strength. Through all his misfortunes and setbacks Mr. Biswas is able to maintain the sense of himself as a man with possibilities, with options, a man who is in a position to set limits on what he will put up with. And equally important, he lives in a society that will let him survive with this attitude. An African slave with these attitudes, working the same sugar cane fields as Biswas's father and brothers did, would have been beaten to death, or starved as an outcast. So too might have been his own grandfather. But in the Trinidad of the interwar and World War II periods, options *were* available. A man with a little literacy could move from rural to small town to Port-of-Spain jobs, jobs where he could interact with people who could teach him a little more. Somehow Biswas survives, marries, supports a family after a fashion, and succeeds in passing on to some of his children this sense of living in a world with possibilities, a world that can reward those who accept the challenges it offers.

We know from direct experience that the passage in two generations from traditional agricultural society to the modern world that *A House for Mr. Biswas* describes is not a singular one. In my neighborhood in Chicago I bring my shirts to a laundry operated by a Korean woman, recently arrived, whose English is barely adequate to enable her to conduct her business. Her shop is open from 7 to 7, six days a week. As I enter, her 3-year-old daughter is seated on the counter, being drilled in arithmetic—which she is very good at and clearly enjoys enormously. Fifteen years from now this girl will be beginning her studies at Chicago or Caltech, alongside the children of professors and Mayflower descendants.

The mathematics and science that this girl will study and perhaps contribute to were not created by the efforts of her and her family, just as the culture in which V. S. Naipaul was immersed when he arrived at Oxford was not the product of his and his father's effort. These are parts of the body of knowledge that is generally available for access by suitably prepared people, "free to the people" as Andrew Carnegie had engraved over the entrances to the public libraries he built. The growth of what Kuznets called "the stock of useful knowledge" is, as everyone agrees, an essential factor in the industrial revolution. Without the existence of this stock, the efforts of families like the Naipauls would add up to nothing, or next to nothing.

Without in any way disputing this point, I am making a complementary point: Growth in the stock of useful knowledge does not generate sustained improvement in living standards unless it raises the return to investing in human capital in most families. This condition is a statement about the nature of the stock of knowledge that is required, about the kind of knowledge that is "useful." But more centrally, it is a statement about the nature of the society. For income growth to occur in a society, a large fraction of people must experience changes in the possible lives they imagine for themselves and their children, and these new visions of possible futures must have enough force to lead them to change the way they behave, the number of children they have, and the hopes they invest in these children: the way they allocate their time. In the words of a more recent title of Naipaul's, economic development requires "a million mutinies."

For someone born into a traditional agricultural society, these decisions— what occupation to follow, what training to acquire, when and whom to marry, how many children to try to have and how to raise them— have already been made. It is not that there is nothing to think and argue about—Mr. Biswas's in-laws argued over which sister gave her children the best beatings!—but that none of the possibilities being argued over leads anywhere new.

This situation cannot be changed by new knowledge, by the arrival of a blueprint. A blueprint that showed how to raise yields per acre in Jamaica to the levels of yields in Java would have a dramatic initial effect on Jamaican farm output, but as Malthus and Ricardo showed two centuries ago, a new equilibrium would be established with larger production and population and no increase in average farm income: High yield per acre is the reason that Java is the most densely populated agricultural area on earth, but it has no connection with sustained growth in living standards. In the end, the blueprint changes *nothing* in the lives and the life-decisions of those who work on the farms. It creates no new possibilities for individual families.

In a successfully developing society, new options continually present themselves and everyone sees examples of people who have responded creatively to them. Within a generation, those who are bound by tradition can come to seem quaint, even ridiculous, and they lose their ability to influence their children by example or to constrain them economically. The people who respond to the new possibilities that development creates are also the ones who make sustained development possible. Their decisions to take new risks and obtain new skills make new possibilities available for those around them. Their decisions to have fewer children and to try to prepare those children to exploit the opportunities of the modern world increase the fraction of people in the next generation who can contribute to the invention of new ways of doing things.

In economically successful societies, today, these are all familiar features of the lives of ordinary people. In pre-industrial societies, all of these features are rare, confined if present at all to small elites. If these observations are central to an understanding of economic growth, as I believe they are, then we want to work toward aggregative models of growth that focus on them. The models analyzed in these lectures are all attempts to contribute to this end.

ON THE MECHANICS
OF ECONOMIC DEVELOPMENT

1. Introduction

By the problem of economic development I mean simply the problem of accounting for the observed pattern, across countries and across time, in levels and rates of growth of per capita income. This may seem too narrow a definition, and perhaps it is, but thinking about income patterns will necessarily involve us in thinking about many other aspects of societies too, so I would suggest that we withhold judgment on the scope of this definition until we have a clearer idea of where it leads us.

The main features of levels and rates of growth of national incomes are well enough known to all economists, but I want to begin with a few numbers, in order to set a quantitative tone and to keep us from getting mired in the wrong kind of details. Unless stated otherwise, all figures are from the World Bank's *World Development Report* of 1983.

The diversity across countries in measured per capita income levels is literally too great to be believed. Compared to the 1980 average for what the World Bank calls the "industrial market economies" (Ireland up through Switzerland) of U.S. $10,000, India's per capita income is $240, Haiti's is $270, and so on for the rest of the very poorest countries. This is a difference of a factor of 40 in living standards! These latter figures are too low to sustain life in, say, England or the United States, so they cannot be taken at face value and I will avoid hanging too much on their exact magnitudes. But I do not think anyone will argue that there is not enormous diversity in living standards.[1]

---

1. The income estimates reported in Summers and Heston (1984) are more satisfactory than those in the *World Development Reports*. In 1975 U.S. dollars, these authors estimate 1980 U.S. real GDP per capita at $8000, and for the industrialized economies as a group, $5900. The comparable figures for India and Haiti are $460 and

Rates of growth of real per capita GNP are also diverse, even over sustained periods. For the period 1960–1980 we observe, for example: India, 1.4 percent per year; Egypt, 3.4 percent; South Korea, 7.0 percent; Japan, 7.1 percent; the United States, 2.3 percent; the industrial economies averaged 3.6 percent. To obtain from growth rates the number of years it takes for incomes to double, divide these numbers into 69 (the log of 2 times 100). Then Indian incomes will double every 50 years; Korean every 10. An Indian will, on average, be twice as well off as his grandfather; a Korean 32 times. These differences are at least as striking as differences in income levels, and in some respects more trustworthy, since within-country income comparisons are easier to draw than across-country comparisons.

I have not calculated a correlation across countries between income levels and rates of growth, but it would not be far from zero. (The poorest countries tend to have the lowest growth; the wealthiest next; the "middle-income" countries highest.) The generalizations that strike the eye have to do with variability within these broad groups: the rich countries show little diversity (Japan excepted—otherwise it would not have been classed as a rich country in 1980 at all). Within the poor countries (low and middle income) there is enormous variability.[2]

Within the advanced countries, growth rates tend to be very stable over long periods of time, provided one averages over periods long enough to eliminate business-cycle effects (or corrects for short-term fluctuations in some other way). For poorer countries, however, there are many examples of sudden, large changes in growth rates, both up and down. Some of these changes are no doubt due to political or military disruption: Angola's total GDP growth fell from 4.8 in the 1960s to −9.2 in the 1970s; Iran's fell from 11.3 to 2.5, comparing the same two periods. I do not think we need

---

$500, respectively. Income differences of a factor of 16 are certainly smaller, and I think more accurate, then a factor of 40, but they can still be fairly described as exhibiting "enormous diversity."

2. Baumol (1986) summarizes evidence, mainly from Maddison (1982), indicating apparent convergence during this century to a common path of the income levels of the wealthiest countries. But De Long (1988) shows that this effect is entirely due to "selection bias": If one examines the countries with the highest income levels at the *beginning* of the century (as opposed to currently, as in Maddison's "sample"), the data show apparent *divergence*!

to look to economic theory for an account of either of *these* declines. There are also some striking examples of sharp increases in growth rates. The four East Asian "miracles" of South Korea, Taiwan, Hong Kong, and Singapore are the most familiar: for the 1960–1980 period, per capita income in these economies grew at rates of 7.0, 6.5, 6.8, and 7.5, respectively, compared to much lower rates in the 1950s and earlier.[3] Between the 1960s and the 1970s, Indonesia's GDP growth increased from 3.9 to 7.5; Syria's from 4.6 to 10.0.

I do not see how one can look at figures like these without seeing them as representing *possibilities*. Is there some action a government of India could take that would lead the Indian economy to grow like Indonesia's or Egypt's? If so, *what*, exactly? If not, what is it about the "nature of India" that makes it so? The consequences for human welfare involved in questions like these are simply staggering: Once one starts to think about them, it is hard to think about anything else.

This is what we need a theory of economic development *for*: to provide some kind of framework for organizing facts like these, for judging which represent opportunities and which necessities. But the term "theory" is used in so many different ways, even within economics, that it is important to clarify what I mean by it early on to avoid misunderstanding. I prefer to use the term "theory" in a very narrow sense, to refer to an explicit dynamic system, something that can be put on a computer and *run*. This is what I mean by the "mechanics" of economic development—the construction of a mechanical, artificial world, populated by the interacting robots that economics typically studies, that is capable of exhibiting behavior the gross features of which resemble those of the actual world that I have just described. This chapter will be occupied with one such construction, and it will take some work: It is easy to set out models of economic growth based on reasonable-looking axioms that predict the cessation of growth in a few decades, or that predict the rapid convergence of the living standards of different economies to a common level, or that otherwise produce logically possible outcomes that bear no resemblance to the outcomes produced

---

3. The World Bank no longer transmits data for Taiwan. The figure 6.5 in the text is from Harberger (1984, table 1, p. 9).

According to Summers and Heston (1984), Taiwan's per capita GDP growth rate in the 1950s was 3.6. South Korea's was 1.7 from 1953 to 1960.

by actual economic systems. On the other hand, there is no doubt that there must be mechanics other than the ones I will describe that would fit the facts about as well as mine. This is why I have titled this chapter "*On* the Mechanics . . . " rather than simply "*The* Mechanics of Economic Development." At some point, then, the study of development will need to involve working out the implications of competing theories for data other than those they were constructed to fit, and testing these implications against observation. But this is getting far ahead of the story I have to tell, which will involve leaving many important questions open even at the purely theoretical level and will touch upon questions of empirical testing hardly at all.

My plan is as follows. I will begin with an application of a now-standard neoclassical model to the study of twentieth-century U.S. growth, closely following the work of Robert Solow, Edward Denison, and many others. I will then ask, somewhat unfairly, whether this model *as it stands* is an adequate model of economic development, concluding that it is not. Next, I will consider two adaptations of this standard model to include the effects of human capital accumulation. The first retains the one-sector character of the original model and focuses on the interaction of physical and human capital accumulation. The second examines a two-good system that admits specialized human capital of different kinds and offers interesting possibilities for the interaction of trade and development. Finally, I will turn to a discussion of what has been arrived at and what is yet to be done.

In general, I will be focusing on various aspects of what economists, using the term very broadly, call the "technology." I will be abstracting altogether from the economics of demography, taking population growth as a given throughout. This is a serious omission, for which I can only offer the excuse that a serious discussion of demographic issues would be at least as difficult as the issues I will be discussing, and I have neither the time nor the knowledge to do both. I hope the interactions between these topics are not such that they cannot usefully be considered separately, at least in a preliminary way.[4]

---

4. Becker and Barro (1988) is the first attempt known to me to analyze fertility and capital accumulation decisions *simultaneously* within a general equilibrium framework. Tamura (1986) contains further results along this line.

I will also be abstracting from all monetary matters, treating all exchange as though it involved goods-for-goods. In general, I believe that the importance of financial matters is very badly overemphasized in popular and even much professional discussion and so am not inclined to be apologetic for going to the other extreme. Yet insofar as the development of financial institutions is a limiting factor in development more generally conceived, I will be falsifying the picture, and I have no clear idea as to how badly. But one cannot theorize about everything at once.

2. Neoclassical Growth Theory: Review

The example, or model, of a successful theory that I will try to build on is the theory of economic growth that Robert Solow and Edward Denison developed and applied to twentieth-century U.S. experience. This theory will serve as a basis for further discussion in three ways: as an example of the *form* that I believe useful aggregative theories must take; as an opportunity to explain exactly what theories of this form can tell us that other kinds of theories cannot; and as a possible theory of economic development. In this third capacity, the theory will be seen to fail badly, but also suggestively. Following up on these suggestions will occupy the remainder of this chapter.

Both Solow and Denison were attempting to account for the main features of U.S. economic growth, not to provide a theory of economic development, and their work was directed at a very different set of observations from the cross-country comparisons I cited in my introductory section. The most useful summary is provided in Denison's 1961 monograph, *The Sources of Economic Growth in the United States*. Unless otherwise mentioned, this is the source for the figures I will cite next.

During the 1909–1957 period covered in Denison's study, U.S. real output grew at an annual rate of 2.9 percent, employed man-hours at 1.3 percent, and capital stock at 2.4 percent. The remarkable feature of these figures, as compared to those cited earlier, is their *stability* over time. Even if one takes as a starting point the trough of the Great Depression (1933), output growth to 1957 averages only 5 percent. If business-cycle effects are removed in any reasonable way (say, by using peak-to-peak growth rates), U.S. output growth is within half a percentage point of 3 percent annually for any sizable subperiod for which we have data.

Solow (1956) was able to account for this stability, and also for some of the relative magnitudes of these growth rates, with a very simple but also easily refinable model.[5] There are many variations of this model in print. I will set out a particularly simple one that is chosen also to serve some later purposes. I will do so without much comment on its assumed structure: There is no point in arguing over a model's assumptions until one is clear on what questions it will be used to answer.

We consider a closed economy with competitive markets, with identical, rational agents and a constant returns technology. At date t there are $N(t)$ persons or, equivalently, man-hours devoted to production. The exogenously given rate of growth of $N(t)$ is λ. Real, per capita consumption is a stream $c(t)$, $t \geq 0$, of units of a single good. Preferences over (per capita) consumption streams are given by

$$(1) \qquad \int_0^\infty e^{-\rho t} \frac{1}{1-\sigma} \left[c(t)^{1-\sigma} - 1 \right] N(t) \, dt,$$

where the discount rate ρ and the coefficient of (relative) risk aversion σ are both positive.[6]

Production per capita of the one good is divided into consumption $c(t)$ and capital accumulation. If we let $K(t)$ denote the total stock of capital, and $\dot{K}(t)$ its rate of change, then total output is $N(t)c(t) + \dot{K}(t)$. (Here $\dot{K}(t)$ is net investment and total output $N(t)c(t) + \dot{K}(t)$ is identified with net national product.) Production is assumed to depend on the level of capital and labor inputs and on the level $A(t)$ of the "technology," according to

$$(2) \qquad N(t)c(t) + \dot{K}(t) = A(t)K(t)^\beta N(t)^{1-\beta},$$

where $0 < \beta < 1$ and where the exogenously given rate of technical change, $\dot{A}/A$, is $\mu > 0$.

---

5. Solow's 1956 paper stimulated a vast literature in the 1960s, exploring many variations on the original one-sector structure. See Burmeister and Dobell (1970) for an excellent introduction and survey. By putting a relatively simple version to empirical use, as I shall shortly do, I do not intend a negative comment on this body of research. On the contrary, it is exactly this kind of theoretical experimentation with alternative assumptions that is needed to give one the confidence that working with a particular, simple parameterization may, for the specific purpose at hand, be adequate.

6. The inverse σ^{-1} of the coefficient of risk aversion is sometimes called the intertemporal elasticity of substitution. Since all the models considered in this chapter are deterministic, this latter terminology might be more suitable.

The resource allocation problem faced by this economy is simply to choose a time path $c(t)$ for per capita consumption. Given a path $c(t)$ and an initial capital stock $K(0)$, the technology (2) then implies a time path $K(t)$ for capital. The paths $A(t)$ and $N(t)$ are given exogenously. One way to think about this allocation problem is to think of choosing $c(t)$ at each date, given the values of $K(t)$, $A(t)$, and $N(t)$ that have been attained by that date. Evidently, it will not be optimal to choose $c(t)$ to maximize current-period utility, $N(t)[1/(1-\sigma)][c(t)-1]^{1-\sigma}$, for the choice that achieves this is to set net investment $\dot{K}(t)$ equal to zero (or, if feasible, negative): One needs to set some *value* or *price* on increments to capital. A central construct in the study of *optimal* allocations, allocations that maximize utility (1) subject to the technology (2), is the *current-value Hamiltonian II* defined by

$$H(K, \theta, c, t) = \frac{N}{1-\sigma}[c^{1-\sigma} - 1] + \theta[AK^{\beta}N^{1-\beta} - Nc],$$

which is just the sum of current-period utility and (from (2)) the rate of increase of capital, the latter valued at the "price" $\theta(t)$. An optimal allocation must maximize the expression H at each date t, provided the price $\theta(t)$ is correctly chosen.

The first-order condition for maximizing H with respect to c is

(3) $c^{-\sigma} = \theta,$

which is to say that goods must be so allocated at each date as to be equally valuable, on the margin, used either as consumption or as investment. It is known that the price $\theta(t)$ must satisfy

$$\dot{\theta}(t) = \rho\theta(t) - \frac{\partial}{\partial K}H(K(t), \theta(t), c(t), t)$$

(4) $$= \left[\rho - \beta A(t)N(t)^{1-\beta}K(t)^{\beta-1}\right]\theta(t)$$

at each date t if the solution $c(t)$ to (3) is to yield an optimal *path* $(c(t))_{t=0}^{\infty}$.

Now if (3) is used to express $c(t)$ as a function $\theta(t)$, and this function $\theta^{-1/\sigma}$ is substituted in place of $c(t)$ in (2) and (4), these two equations are a pair of first-order differential equations in $K(t)$ and its "price" $\theta(t)$. Solving this system, there will be a one-parameter family of paths $(K(t), \theta(t))$, satisfying the given initial condition on $K(0)$. The *unique* member of this family that satisfies the transversality condition:

(5) $\lim_{t\to\infty} e^{-\rho t}\theta(t)K(t) = 0$

is the optimal path. I am hoping that this application of Pontryagin's Maximum Principle, essentially taken from David Cass (1965), is familiar to most readers. I will be applying these same ideas repeatedly in what follows.

For this particular model, with convex preferences and technology and with no external effects of any kind, it is also known and not at all surprising that the *optimal* program characterized by (2), (3), (4), and (5) is also the unique *competitive equilibrium* program, provided either that all trading is consummated in advance, Arrow–Debreu style, *or* (and this is the interpretation I favor) that consumers and firms have rational expectations about future prices. In this deterministic context, rational expectations just means perfect foresight. For my purposes, it is this equilibrium interpretation that is most interesting: I intend to use the model as a positive theory of U.S. economic growth.

In order to do this, we will need to work out the predictions of the model in more detail, which involves solving the differential equation system so we can see what the equilibrium time paths look like and compare them to observations like Denison's. Rather than carry this analysis through to completion, I will work out the properties of a *particular* solution to the system and then just indicate briefly how the rest of the answer can be found in Cass's paper.

Let us construct from (2), (3), and (4) the system's *balanced growth path*: the particular solution $(K(t), \theta(t), c(t))$ such that the rates of growth of each of these variables is constant. (I have never been sure exactly what it is that is "balanced" along such a path, but we need a term for solutions with this constant growth rate property and this is as good as any.) Let κ denote the rate of growth of per capita consumption, $\dot{c}(t)/c(t)$, on a balanced growth path. Then from (3), we have $\dot{\theta}(t)/\theta(t) = -\sigma\kappa$. Then from (4), we must have

(6) $\quad \beta A(t)N(t)^{1-\beta}K(t)^{\beta-1} = \rho + \sigma\kappa.$

That is, along the balanced path, the marginal product of capital must equal the constant value $\rho + \sigma\kappa$. With this Cobb–Douglas technology, the marginal product of capital is proportional to the average product, so that dividing (2) through by $K(t)$ and applying (6) we obtain

(7) $\quad \dfrac{N(t)c(t)}{K(t)} + \dfrac{\dot{K}(t)}{K(t)} = A(t)K(t)^{\beta-1}N(t)^{1-\beta} = \dfrac{\rho + \sigma\kappa}{\beta}.$

By definition of a balanced path, $\dot{K}(t)/K(t)$ is constant so (7) implies that $N(t)c(t)/K(t)$ is constant or, differentiating, that

$$(8) \qquad \frac{\dot{K}(t)}{K(t)} = \frac{\dot{N}(t)}{N(t)} + \frac{\dot{c}(t)}{c(t)} = \kappa + \lambda.$$

Thus per capita consumption and per capita capital grow at the common rate κ. To *solve* for this common rate, differentiate either (6) or (7) to obtain

$$(9) \qquad \kappa = \frac{\mu}{1 - \beta}.$$

Then (7) may be solved to obtain the constant, balanced consumption-capital ratio $N(t)c(t)/K(t)$ or, what is equivalent and slightly easier to interpret, the constant, balanced net savings rate s defined by

$$(10) \qquad s = \frac{\dot{K}(t)}{N(t)c(t) + \dot{K}(t)} = \frac{\beta(\kappa + \lambda)}{\rho + \sigma\kappa}.$$

Hence along a balanced path, the rate of growth of per capita magnitudes is simply proportional to the given rate of technical change, μ, where the constant of proportionality is the inverse of labor's share, $1 - \beta$. The rate of time preference ρ and the degree of risk aversion σ have no bearing on this long-run growth rate. Low time preference ρ and low risk aversion σ induce a high savings rate s, and high savings is, in turn, associated with relatively high output *levels* on a balanced path. A thrifty society will, in the long run, be wealthier than an impatient one, but it will not grow faster.

In order that the balanced path characterized by (9) and (10) satisfy the transversality condition (5), it is necessary that $\rho + \sigma\kappa > \kappa + \lambda$. (From (10), one sees that this is the same as requiring the savings rate to be less than capital's share.) Under this condition, an economy that begins on the balanced path will find it optimal to stay there. What of economies that begin *off* the balanced path—surely the normal case? Cass showed—and this is exactly why the balanced path is interesting to us— that for *any* initial capital $K(0) > 0$, the optimal capital-consumption path $(K(t), c(t))$ will converge to the balanced path asymptotically. That is, the balanced path will be a good approximation to any actual path most of the time.

Now given the taste and technology parameters (ρ, σ, λ, β, and μ), (9) and (10) can be solved for the asymptotic growth rate κ of capital, consumption and real output, and the savings rate s that they imply. Moreover, it would be straightforward to calculate numerically the approach to the balanced path from any initial capital level $K(0)$. This is the exercise that an idealized planner would go through.

Our interest in the model is positive, not normative, so we want to go in the opposite direction and try to infer the underlying preferences and technology from what we can observe. I will outline this, taking the balanced path as the model's prediction for the behavior of the U.S. economy during the entire (1909–1957) period covered by Denison's study.[7] From this point of view, Denison's estimates provide a value of 0.013 for λ, and two values, 0.029 and 0.024, for $\kappa + \lambda$, depending on whether we use output or capital growth rates (which the model predicts to be equal). In the tradition of statistical inference, let us average to get $\kappa + \lambda = 0.027$. The theory predicts that $1 - \beta$ should equal labor's share in national income, about 0.75 in the United States, averaging over the entire 1909–1957 period. The savings rate (net investment over NNP) is fairly constant at 0.10. Then (9) implies an estimate of 0.0105 for μ. Equation (10) implies that the preference parameters ρ and σ satisfy

$$\rho + (0.014)\sigma = 0.0675.$$

(The parameters ρ and σ are not separately identified along a smooth consumption path, so this is as far as we can go with the sample averages I have provided.)

These are the parameter values that give the theoretical model its best fit to the U.S. data. How good a fit *is* it? Either output growth is underpredicted or capital growth overpredicted, as remarked earlier (and in the theory of growth, half a percentage point is a *large* discrepancy). There are interesting secular changes in man-hours per household that the model assumes away, and labor's share is secularly rising (in all growing economies), not constant as assumed. There is, in short, much room for improvement, even in accounting for the secular changes the model was designed to fit, and indeed, a fuller review of the literature would reveal interesting progress

---

7. With the parameter values described in this paragraph, the half-life of the approximate linear system associated with this model is about eleven years.

on these and many other fronts.[8] A model as explicit as this one, by the very nakedness of its simplifying assumptions, invites criticism and suggests refinements to itself. This is exactly why we prefer explicitness, or why I think we ought to.

Even granted its limitations, the simple neoclassical model has made basic contributions to our thinking about economic growth. Qualitatively, it emphasizes a distinction between "growth effects"—changes in parameters that alter growth rates along balanced paths—and "level effects"—changes that raise or lower balanced growth paths without affecting their slope—that is fundamental in thinking about policy changes. Solow's 1956 conclusion that changes in savings rates are level effects (which transposes in the present context to the conclusion that changes in the discount rate, ρ, are level effects) was startling at the time, and remains widely and very unfortunately neglected today. The influential idea that changes in the tax structure that make savings more attractive can have large, sustained effects on an economy's growth rate sounds so reasonable, and it may even be true, but it is a clear implication of the theory we have that it is not.

Even sophisticated discussions of economic growth can often be confusing as to what are thought to be level effects and what growth effects. Thus Krueger (1983) and Harberger (1984), in their recent, very useful surveys of the growth experiences of poor countries, both identify inefficient barriers to trade as a limitation on growth, and their removal as a key explanation of several rapid growth episodes. The facts that Krueger and Harberger summarize are not in dispute, but under the neoclassical model just reviewed one would not expect the removal of inefficient trade barriers to induce sustained increases in growth rates. Removal of trade barriers is, on this theory, a level effect, analogous to the one-time shifting upward in production possibilities, and not a growth effect. Of course, level effects can be drawn out through time through adjustment costs of various kinds, but not so as to produce increases in growth rates that are both large and

---

8. In particular, there is much evidence that capital stock growth, as measured by Denison, understates true capital growth because of the failure to correct price deflators for quality improvements. See, for example, Griliches and Jorgenson (1967) or Gordon (1971). These errors may well account for all of the 0.005 discrepancy noted in the text (or more!).

Boxall (1986) develops a modification of the Solow–Cass model in which labor supply is variable, and which has the potential (at least) to account for long-run changes in man-hours.

sustained. Thus the removal of an inefficiency that reduced output by five percent (an enormous effect) spread out over 10 years is simply a one-half of one percent annual growth rate stimulus. Inefficiencies are important and their removal certainly desirable, but the familiar ones are level effects, not growth effects. (This is exactly why it is not paradoxical that centrally planned economies, with allocative inefficiencies of legendary proportions, grow about as fast as market economies.) The empirical connections between trade policies and economic growth that Krueger and Harberger document are of evident importance, but they seem to me to pose a real paradox in light of the neoclassical theory we have, not a confirmation of it.

The main contributions of the neoclassical framework, far more important than its contributions to the clarity of purely qualitative discussions, stem from its ability to *quantify* the effects of various influences on growth. Denison's monograph lists dozens of policy changes, some fanciful and many others seriously proposed at the time he wrote, associating with each of them rough upper bounds on their likely effects on U.S. growth.[9] In the main, the theory adds little to what common sense would tell us about the *direction* of each effect—it is easy enough to guess which changes stimulate production, hence savings, and hence (at least for a time) economic growth. Yet most such changes, quantified, have *trivial* effects: The growth rate of an entire economy is not an easy thing to move around.

Economic growth, being a summary measure of all the activities of an entire society, necessarily depends, in some way, on everything that goes on in a society. Societies differ in many easily observed ways, and it is easy to identify various economic and cultural peculiarities and imagine that they are keys to growth performance. For this, as Jacobs (1984) rightly observes, we do not need economic theory: "Perceptive tourists will do as well." The role of theory is not to catalogue the obvious, but to help us to sort out effects that are crucial, quantitatively, from those that can be set aside. Solow's and Denison's work shows how this can be done in studying the growth of the U.S. economy, and the growth of other advanced economies

---

9. Denison (1961, chap. 24). My favorite example is number 4 in this "menu of choices available to increase the growth rate": "0.03 points [i.e., 0.03 of one percentage point] maximum potential . . . Eliminate all crime and rehabilitate all criminals." This example and many others in this chapter are pointed rebukes to those in the 1960s who tried to advance their favorite (and often worthy) causes by claiming ties to economic growth.

as well. I take success at this level to be a worthy objective for the theory of economic development.

3. Neoclassical Growth Theory: Assessment

It seems to be universally agreed that the model I have just reviewed is not a theory of economic development. Indeed, I suppose this is why we think of "growth" and "development" as distinct fields, with growth theory defined as those aspects of economic growth we have some understanding of, and development defined as those we don't. I do not disagree with this judgment, but a more specific idea of exactly where the model falls short will be useful in thinking about alternatives.

If we were to attempt to use the Solow–Denison framework to account for the diversity in income levels and rates of growth that we observe in the world today, we would begin, theoretically, by imagining a world consisting of many economies of the sort I have just described, assuming something about the way they interact, working out the dynamics of this new model, and comparing them to observations. This is actually much easier than it sounds (there isn't much to the theory of international trade when everyone produces the same, single good!), so let us think it through.

The key assumptions involve factor mobility: Are people and capital free to move? It is easiest to start with the assumption of *no* mobility, since then we can treat each country as an isolated system, exactly like the one we have just worked out. In this case, the model predicts that countries with the same preferences and technology will converge to identical levels of income and asymptotic rates of growth. Since this prediction does not accord at all well with what we observe, if we want to fit the theory to observed cross-country variations, we will need to postulate appropriate variations in the parameters (ρ, σ, λ, β, and μ) and/or assume that countries differ according to their initial technology levels, $A(0)$. Or we can obtain additional theoretical flexibility by treating countries as differently situated relative to their steady-state paths. Let me review these possibilities briefly.

Population growth, λ, and income shares going to labor, $1 - \beta$, do of course differ across countries, but neither varies in such a way as to provide an account of income differentials. Countries with rapid population growth are not systematically poorer than countries with slow-growing populations, as the theory predicts, either cross-sectionally today or historically. There are, certainly, interesting empirical connections between economic variables (narrowly defined) and birth and death rates, but I am fully persuaded by the work of Becker (1960) and others that these connections are best understood as arising from the way decisions to maintain life and to initiate it *respond* to economic conditions. Similarly, poor countries have lower labor shares than wealthy countries, indicating to me that elasticities of substitution in production are below unity (contrary to the Cobb-Douglas assumption I am using in these examples), but the prediction (9) that poorer countries should therefore grow more rapidly is not confirmed by experience.

The parameters ρ and σ are, as observed earlier, not separately identified, but if their joint values differed over countries in such a way as to account for income differences, poor countries would have systematically much higher (risk-corrected) interest rates than rich countries. Even if this were true, I would be inclined to seek other explanations. Looking ahead, we would like also to be able to account for sudden large changes in growth rates of individual countries. Do we want a theory that focuses attention on spontaneous shifts in people's discount rates or degree of risk aversion? Such theories are hard to refute, but I will leave it to others to work this side of the street.

Consideration of off-steady-state behavior would open up some new possibilities, possibly bringing the theory into better conformity with observation, but I do not view this route as at all promising. Away from steady states, (9) need not hold and capital and output growth rates need not be either equal or constant, but it still follows from the technology (2) that output growth (g_{yt}, say) and capital growth (g_{kt}, say), both per capita, obey

$$g_{yt} = \beta g_{kt} + \mu.$$

But g_{yt} and g_{kt} can both be measured, and it is well established that for no value of β that is close to observed capital shares is it the case that $g_{yt} - \beta g_{kt}$ is even approximately uniform across countries. Here "Denison's Law" works against us: the insensitivity of growth rates to variations in the model's underlying parameters, as reviewed earlier, makes it hard to use the theory to account for large variations across countries or across time. To conclude that even large changes in "thriftiness" would not induce large changes in U.S. growth rates is really the same as concluding that differences in Japanese and U.S. thriftiness cannot account for much of the difference in these two economies' growth rates. By assigning so great a role to "technology" as a source of growth, the theory is obliged to assign correspondingly minor roles to everything else, and thus has very little ability to account for the wide diversity in growth rates that we observe.

Consider, then, variations across countries in technology—its level and rate of change. This seems to me to be the one factor isolated by the neoclassical model that has the potential to account for wide differences in income levels and growth rates. This point of departure certainly does accord with everyday usage. We say that Japan is technologically more advanced than China, or that Korea is undergoing unusually rapid technical change, and such statements seem to mean something (and I think they do). But they cannot mean that the "stock of useful knowledge" (in Kuznets's (1959) terminology) is higher in Japan than in China, or that it is growing more rapidly in Korea than elsewhere. "Human knowledge" is just human, not Japanese or Chinese or Korean. I think when we talk in this way about differences in technology across countries we are not talking about knowledge in general, but about the knowledge of particular people, or perhaps particular subcultures of people. If so, then while it is not exactly wrong to describe these differences by an exogenous, exponential term like $A(t)$, neither is it useful to do so. We want a formalism that leads us to think about individual decisions to acquire knowledge, and about the consequences of these decisions for productivity. The body of theory that does this is called the theory of *human capital*, and I am going to draw extensively on this theory in the remainder of this chapter. For the moment, however, I simply want to impose the terminological convention that technology—its level and rate of change—will be used to refer to something common to all countries, something pure or disembodied, something whose determinants are outside the bounds of our current inquiry.

In the absence of differences in pure technology, then, and under the assumption of no factor mobility, the neoclassical model predicts a strong tendency to income equality and equality in growth rates, tendencies we can observe within countries and, perhaps, within the wealthiest countries taken as a group, but which simply cannot be seen in the world at large. When factor mobility is permitted, this prediction is very powerfully reinforced. Factors of production, capital or labor or both, will flow to the highest returns, which is to say where each is relatively scarce. Capital-labor ratios will move rapidly to equality, and with them factor prices. Indeed, these predictions survive differences in preference parameters and population growth rates. In the model as stated, it makes no difference whether labor moves to join capital or the other way around. (Indeed, we know that with a many-good technology, factor price equalization can be achieved without mobility in *either* factor of production.)

The eighteenth- and nineteenth-century histories of the Americas, Australia, and South and East Africa provide illustrations of the strength of these forces for equality, and of the ability of even simple neoclassical models to account for important economic events. If we replace the labor–capital technology of the Solow model with a land–labor technology of the same form, and treat labor as the mobile factor and land as the immobile, we obtain a model that predicts exactly the immigration flows that occurred and for exactly the reason—factor price differentials—that motivated these historical flows. Though this simple deterministic model abstracts from considerations of risk and many other elements that surely played a role in actual migration decisions, this abstraction is evidently not a fatal one.

In the twentieth century, of course, immigration has been largely shut off, so it is not surprising that this land–labor model, with labor mobile, no longer gives an adequate account of actual movements in factors and factor prices. What *is* surprising, it seems to me, is that capital movements do not perform the same functions. Within the United States, for example, we have seen southern labor move north to produce automobiles. We have also seen textile mills move from New England south (to move a factory, one lets it run down and builds its replacement somewhere else) to achieve this same end of combining capital with relatively low wage labor. Economically, it makes no difference which factor is mobile, so long as one is.

Why, then, should the closing down of international labor mobility have slowed down, or even have much affected, the tendencies toward factor price equalization predicted by neoclassical theory, tendencies that have proved to be so powerful historically? If it is profitable to move a textile mill from New England to South Carolina, why is it not more profitable still to move it to Mexico? The fact that we do see *some* capital movement toward low-income countries is not an adequate answer to this question, for the theory predicts that *all* new investment should be so located until such time as return and real wage differentials are erased. Indeed, why did these capital movements not take place during the colonial age, under political and military arrangements that eliminated (or long postponed) the "political risk" that is so frequently cited as a factor working against capital mobility? I do not have a satisfactory answer to this question, but it seems to me to be a major—perhaps *the* major—discrepancy between the predictions of neoclassical theory and the patterns of trade we observe. Dealing with this issue is surely a minimal requirement for a theory of economic development.

4. Human Capital and Growth

To this point, I have reviewed an example of the neoclassical model of growth, compared it with certain facts of U.S. economic history, and indicated why I want to use this theory as a kind of model, or image, of what I think is possible and useful for a theory of economic development. I have also described what seem to me two central reasons why this theory is not, as it stands, a useful theory of economic development: its apparent inability to account for observed diversity across countries and its strong and evidently counterfactual prediction that international trade should induce rapid movement toward equality in capital–labor ratios and factor prices. These observations set the stage for what I would like to do in the rest of this chapter.

Rather than take on both problems at once, I will begin by considering an alternative, or at least a complementary, engine of growth to the technological change that serves this purpose in the Solow model, retaining for the moment the other features of that model (in particular, its closed character). I will do this by adding what Schultz (1963) and Becker (1964) call *human capital* to the model, doing so in a way that is very close technically to similarly motivated models of Arrow (1962), Uzawa (1965), and Romer (1986a and b).

By an individual's human capital I will mean, for the purposes of this section, simply his general skill level, so that a worker with human capital $h(t)$ is the productive equivalent of two workers with $\frac{1}{2}h(t)$ each, or a half-time worker with $2h(t)$. The theory of human capital focuses on the fact that the way an individual allocates his time over various activities in the current period affects his productivity, or his $h(t)$ level, in future periods. Introducing human capital into the model, then, involves spelling out both the way human capital levels affect current production and the way the current time allocation affects the accumulation of human capital. Depending on one's objectives, there are many ways to formulate both these aspects of the "technology." Let us begin with the following, simple assumptions.

Suppose there are N workers in total, with skill levels h ranging from 0 to infinity. Let there be $N(h)$ workers with skill level h, so that $N = \int_0^\infty N(h)\, dh$. Suppose a worker with skill h devotes the fraction $u(h)$ of his non-leisure time to current production, and the remaining $1 - u(h)$ to human capital accumulation. Then the effective workforce in production— the analogue to $N(t)$ in equation (2)—is the sum $N^e = \int_0^\infty u(h)N(h)h\, dh$ of the skill-weighted man-hours devoted to current production. Thus if output as a function of total capital K and effective labor N^e is $F(K, N^e)$, the hourly wage of a worker at skill h is $F_N(K, N^e)h$ and his total earnings are $F_N(K, N^e)hu(h)$.

In addition to the effects of an individual's human capital on his own productivity—what I will call the *internal effect* of human capital—I want to consider an *external effect*. Specifically, let the *average* level of skill or human capital, defined by

$$h_a = \frac{\int_0^\infty hN(h)\, dh}{\int_0^\infty N(h)\, dh},$$

also contribute to the productivity of all factors of production (in a way that I will spell out shortly). I call this h_a effect external, because though everyone's productivity benefits from it, no individual human capital accumulation decision can have an appreciable effect on h_a, so no one will take it into account in deciding how to allocate his time.

Now it will simplify the analysis considerably to follow the preceding analysis and treat all workers in the economy as being identical. In this case, if all workers have skill level h and all choose the time allocation u, the effective workforce is just $N^e = uhN$, and the average skill level h_a is just h. Even so, I will continue to use the notation h_a for the latter, to emphasize the distinction between internal and external effects. Then the description (2) of the technology of goods production is replaced by

$$(11) \quad N(t)c(t) + \dot{K}(t) = AK(t)^\beta [u(t)h(t)N(t)]^{1-\beta} h_a(t)^\gamma,$$

where the term $h_a(t)^\gamma$ is intended to capture the external effects of human capital, and where the technology level A is now assumed to be constant.

To complete the model, the effort $1 - u(t)$ devoted to the accumulation of human capital must be linked to the rate of change in its level, $h(t)$. Everything hinges on exactly how this is done. Let us begin by postulating a technology relating the growth of human capital, $\dot{h}(t)$, to the level already attained and the effort devoted to acquiring more, say:

(12) $\dot{h}(t) = h(t)^{\zeta} G(1 - u(t))$,

where G is increasing, with $G(0) = 0$. Now if we take $\zeta < 1$ in this formulation, so that there is diminishing returns to the accumulation of human capital, it is easy to see that human capital cannot serve as an alternative engine of growth to the technology term $A(t)$. To see this, note that, since $u(t) \geq 0$, equation (12) implies that

$$\frac{\dot{h}(t)}{h(t)} \leq h(t)^{\zeta-1} G(1),$$

so that $\dot{h}(t)/h(t)$ must eventually tend to zero as $h(t)$ grows no matter how much effort is devoted to accumulating it. This formulation would simply complicate the original Solow model without offering any genuinely new possibilities.

Uzawa (1965) worked out a model very similar to this one (he assumed $\gamma = 0$ and $U(c) = c$) under the assumption that the right-hand side of (12) is *linear* in $u(t)$ ($\zeta = 1$). The striking feature of his solution, and the feature that recommends his formulation to us, is that it exhibits sustained per capita income growth from endogenous human capital accumulation alone: no external "engine of growth" is required.

Uzawa's linearity assumption might appear to be a dead-end (for our present purposes) because we seem to see diminishing returns in observed, individual patterns of human capital accumulation: people accumulate it rapidly early in life, then less rapidly, then not at all—as though each additional percentage increment were harder to gain than the preceding one. But an alternative explanation for *this* observation is simply that an individual's lifetime is finite, so that the return to increments falls with time. Rosen (1976) showed that a technology like (12), with $\zeta = 1$, is consistent with the evidence we have on individual earnings. I will adapt the Uzawa–Rosen formulation here, assuming for simplicity that the function G is linear:

(13) $\dot{h}(t) = h(t)\delta[1 - u(t)]$.

According to (13), if no effort is devoted to human capital accumulation, ($u(t) = 1$), then none accumulates. If all effort is devoted to this purpose,

$(u(t) = 0)$, $h(t)$ grows at its maximal rate δ. In between these extremes, there are *no* diminishing returns to the stock $h(t)$: A given *percentage* increase in $h(t)$ requires the same effort, no matter what level of $h(t)$ has already been attained.

It is a digression I will not pursue, but it would take some work to go from a human capital technology of the form (13), applied to each finite-lived individual (as in Rosen's theory), to this same technology applied to an entire infinitely-lived typical household or family. For example, if each individual acquired human capital as in Rosen's model but if *none* of this capital were passed on to younger generations, the household's stock would (with a fixed demography) stay constant. To obtain (13) for a family, one needs to assume both that each individual's capital follows this equation *and* that the initial level each new member begins with is proportional to (not equal to!) the level already attained by older members of the family. This is simply one instance of a general fact that I will emphasize again and again: that human capital accumulation is a *social* activity, involving *groups* of people in a way that has no counterpart in the accumulation of physical capital.

Aside from these changes in the technology, expressed in (11) and (13) to incorporate human capital and its accumulation, the model to be discussed is identical to the Solow model. The system is closed, population grows at the fixed rate λ, and the typical household has the preferences shown in (1). Let us proceed to the analysis of this new model.[10]

In the presence of the external effect $h_a(t)^\gamma$, it will not be the case that optimal growth paths and competitive equilibrium paths coincide. Hence we cannot construct the equilibrium by studying the same hypothetical planning problem used to study Solow's model. But by following Romer's analysis of a very similar model, we can obtain the optimal and equilibrium paths separately, and compare them. This is what I will now do.

By an *optimal* path, I will mean a choice of $K(t)$, $h(t)$, $H_a(t)$, $c(t)$, and $u(t)$ that maximizes utility (1) subject to (11) and (13), *and* subject to the constraint $h(t) = h_a(t)$ for all t. This is a problem similar in general

---

10. The model discussed in this section (in contrast to the model of Section 2) has not been fully analyzed in the literature. The text gives a self-contained derivation of the main features of balanced paths. The treatment of behavior off balanced paths is largely conjecture, based on parallels with Uzawa (1965) and Romer (1986a and b).

structure to the one we reviewed in Section 2, and I will turn to it in a moment.

By an *equilibrium* path, I mean something more complicated. First, take a path $h_a(t)$, $t \geq 0$, to be given, like the exogenous technology path $A(t)$ in the Solow model. Given $h_a(t)$, consider the problem that the private sector, consisting of atomistic households and firms, would solve if each agent *expected* the average level of human capital to follow the path $h_a(t)$. That is, consider the problem of choosing $h(t)$, $k(t)$, $c(t)$, and $u(t)$ so as to maximize (1) subject to (11) and (13), taking $h_a(t)$ as exogenously determined. When the solution path $h(t)$ for this problem coincides with the given path $h_a(t)$—so that actual and expected behavior are the same—we say that the system is in equilibrium.[11]

The current-value Hamiltonian for the optimal problem, with "prices" $\theta_1(t)$ and $\theta_2(t)$ used to value increments to physical and human capital respectively, is

$$
\begin{aligned}
&H(K, h, \theta_1, \theta_2, c, u, t) \\
&= \frac{N}{1 - \sigma}(c^{1-\sigma} - 1) + \theta_1[AK^\beta(uNh)^{1-\beta}h^\gamma - Nc] \\
&\quad + \theta_2[\delta h(1 - u)].
\end{aligned}
$$

In this model, there are two decision variables—consumption, $c(t)$, and the time devoted to production, $u(t)$—and these are (in an optimal program) selected so as to maximize H. The first-order conditions for this problem are thus:

$$
(14) \quad c^{-\sigma} = \theta_1
$$

and

$$
(15) \quad \theta_1(1 - \beta)AK^\beta(uNh)^{-\beta}Nh^{1+\gamma} = \theta_2\delta h.
$$

On the margin, goods must be equally valuable in their two uses—consumption and capital accumulation (equation 14)—and time must be equally valuable in its two uses—production and human capital accumulation (equation 15).

---

11. This formulation of equilibrium behavior in the presence of external effects is taken from Arrow (1962) and Romer (1986a and b). Romer actually carries out the study of the fixed-point problem in a space of $h(t)$, $t \geq 0$, paths. Here I follow Arrow and confine explicit analysis to balanced paths only.

The rates of change of the prices θ_1 and θ_2 of the two kinds of capital are given by

(16) $\quad \dot{\theta}_1 = \rho\theta_1 - \theta_1\beta AK^{\beta-1}(uNh)^{1-\beta}h^\gamma,$

(17) $\quad \dot{\theta}_2 = \rho\theta_2 - \theta_1(1 - \beta + \gamma)AK^\beta(uN)^{1-\beta}h^{-\beta+\gamma} - \theta_2\delta(1 - u).$

Then equations (11) and (13) and (14)–(17), together with two transversality conditions that I will not state here, implicitly describe the optimal evolution of $K(t)$ and $h(t)$ from any initial mix of these two kinds of capital.

In the *equilibrium*, the private sector "solves" a control problem of essentially this same form, but with the term $h_a(t)^\gamma$ in (11) taken as given. Market clearing then requires that $h_a(t) = h(t)$ for all t, so that (11), (13), (14), (15), and (16) are necessary conditions for equilibrium as well as for optimal paths. But equation (17) no longer holds: It is precisely in the valuation of human capital that optimal and equilibrium allocations differ. For the private sector, in equilibrium, (17) is replaced by

$$\dot{\theta}_2 = \rho\theta_2 - \theta_1(1 - \beta)AK^\beta(uN)^{1-\beta}h^{-\beta}h_a^\gamma - \theta_2\delta(1 - u).$$

Since market clearing implies $h(t) = h_a(t)$ for all t, this can be written as

(18) $\quad \dot{\theta}_2 = \rho\theta_2 - \theta_1(1 - \beta)AK^\beta(uN)^{1-\beta}h^{-\beta+\gamma} - \theta_2\delta(1 - u).$

Note that, if $\gamma = 0$, (17) and (18) are the same. It is the presence of the external effect $\gamma > 0$ that creates a divergence between the social valuation formula (17) and the private valuation (18).

As with the simpler Solow model, the easiest way to characterize both optimal and equilibrium paths is to begin by seeking balanced growth solutions of both systems: solutions on which consumption and both kinds of capital are growing at constant percentage rates, the prices of the two kinds of capital are declining at constant rates, and the time allocation variable $u(t)$ is constant. Let us start by considering features that optimal and equilibrium paths have in common (by setting aside equations 17 and 18).

Let κ denote $\dot{c}(t)/c(t)$, as before, so that (14) and (16) again imply the marginal productivity of capital condition:

(19) $\quad \beta AK(t)^{\beta-1}(u(t)h(t)N(t))^{1-\beta}h(t)^\gamma = \rho + \sigma\kappa,$

which is the analogue to condition (6). As in the earlier model, it is easy to verify that $K(t)$ must grow at the rate $\kappa + \lambda$ and that the savings rate

s is constant, on a balanced path, at the value given by (10). For the derivation of these facts concerning physical capital accumulation, it is immaterial whether $h(t)$ is a matter of choice or an exogenous force as was technological change in the earlier model.

Now if we let $v = \dot{h}(t)/h(t)$ on a balanced path, it is clear from (13) that

(20) $\quad v = \delta(1 - u)$,

and from differentiating (19) that κ, the common growth rate of consumption and per capita capital, is

(21) $\quad \kappa = \left(\dfrac{1 - \beta + \gamma}{1 - \beta}\right) v.$

Thus with $h(t)$ growing at the fixed rate v, $(1 - \beta + \gamma)v$ plays the role of the exogenous rate of technological change μ in the earlier model.

Turning to the determinants of the rate of growth v of human capital, one sees from differentiating both first-order conditions (14) and (15) and substituting for $\dot{\theta}_1/\theta_1$ that

(22) $\quad \dfrac{\dot{\theta}_2}{\theta_2} = (\beta - \sigma)\kappa - (\beta - \gamma)v + \lambda.$

At this point, the analyses of the efficient and equilibrium paths diverge. Focusing first on the efficient path, use (17) and (15) to obtain

(23) $\quad \dfrac{\dot{\theta}_2}{\theta_2} = \rho - \delta - \dfrac{\gamma}{1 - \beta}\delta u.$

Now substitute for u from (20), eliminate $\dot{\theta}_2/\theta_2$ between (22) and (23), and solve for v in terms of κ. Then eliminating κ between this equation and (21) gives the solution for the *efficient* rate of human capital growth, which I will call v^*:

(24) $\quad v^* = \sigma^{-1}\left[\delta - \dfrac{1 - \beta}{1 - \beta + \gamma}(\rho - \lambda)\right].$

Along an equilibrium balanced path (18) holds in place of (17), so that in place of (23) we have

(25) $\quad \dfrac{\dot{\theta}_2}{\theta_2} = \rho - \delta.$

Then by the same procedure used to derive the efficient growth rate v^* from (23), we can obtain from (25) the equilibrium growth rate v:

(26) $\quad v = [\sigma(1 - \beta + \gamma) - \gamma]^{-1}[(1 - \beta)(\delta - (\rho - \lambda))].$

(For the formulas (24) and (26) to apply, the rates v and v^* must not exceed the maximum feasible rate δ. This restriction can be seen to require

(27) $\quad \sigma \geq 1 - \dfrac{1 - \beta}{1 - \beta + \gamma} \dfrac{\rho - \lambda}{\delta},$

so the model cannot apply at levels of risk aversion that are too low (that is, if the intertemporal substitutability of consumption is too high).[12] When (27) holds with equality, $v = v^* = \delta$; when the inequality is strict, $v^* > v$, as one would expect.)

Equations (24) and (26) give, respectively, the efficient and the competitive equilibrium growth rates of human capital along a balanced path. In either case, this growth increases with the effectiveness δ of investment in human capital and declines with increases in the discount rate ρ. (Here at last is a connection between thriftiness and growth!) In either case, (21) gives the corresponding rate of growth of physical capital, per capita. Notice that the theory predicts sustained growth whether or not the external effect γ is positive. If $\gamma = 0$, $\kappa = v$, while if $\gamma > 0$, $\kappa > v$, so that the external effect induces more rapid physical than human capital growth.

For the case $\sigma = 1$, the difference between efficient and equilibrium human capital growth rates is, subtracting (26) from (24),

$$v^* - v = \frac{\gamma}{1 - \beta + \gamma}(\rho - \lambda).$$

Thus the inefficiency is small when either the external effect is small ($\gamma \simeq 0$) or the discount rate is low ($\rho - \lambda \simeq 0$).

Equations (21), (24), and (26) describe the asymptotic rates of change of both kinds of capital, under both efficient and equilibrium regimes. What can be said about the *levels* of these variables? As in the original model, this information is implicit in the marginal productivity condition

---

12. If utility is too nearly linear (σ is too near zero) and if δ is high enough, consumers will keep postponing consumption forever. (This does not occur in Uzawa's model, even though he assumes $\sigma = 0$, because he introduces diminishing returns to $1 - u(t)$ in his version of (13).)

for capital, equation (19). In the original model, this condition—or rather its analogue, equation (6)—determined a unique long-run value of the normalized variable $z(t) = e^{-(\kappa+\lambda)t}K(t)$. In the present, two-capital model, this condition defines a curve linking the *two* normalized variables $z_1(t) = e^{-(\kappa+\lambda)t}K(t)$ and $z_2(t) = e^{-\nu t}h(t)$. Inserting these variables into (19) in place of $K(t)$ and $h(t)$ and applying the formula (21) for κ, we obtain

$$(28) \quad (\beta A N_0^{1-\beta} u^{1-\beta}) z_1^{\beta-1} z_2^{1-\beta+\gamma} = \rho + \sigma\kappa.$$

It is a fact that *all* pairs (z_1, z_2) satisfying (28) correspond to balanced paths. Let us ask first what this locus of (normalized) capital combinations looks like, and second what this means for the dynamics of the system.

Figure 1.1 shows the curve defined by equation (28). With no external effect ($\gamma = 0$) it is a straight line through the origin; otherwise ($\gamma > 0$) it is convex. The position of the curve depends on u and κ, which from (20) and (21) can be expressed as functions of ν. Using this fact one can see that increases in ν shift the curve to the right. Thus an efficient economy, on a balanced path, will have a higher level of human capital (z_2) for any given level of physical capital (z_1), since $\nu^* > \nu$.

The dynamics of this system are not as well understood as those of the one-good model, but I would conjecture that for any initial configuration

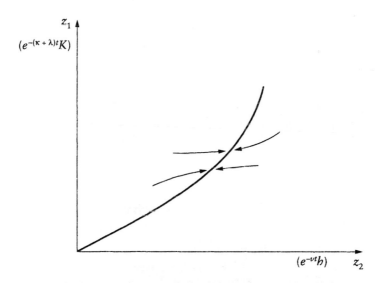

Figure 1.1 Possible human and physical capital paths

$(K(0), h(0))$ of the two kinds of capital, the solution paths (of either the efficient or the equilibrium system) $(z_1(t), z_2(t))$ will converge to *some* point on the curve in Figure 1.1, but that this asymptotic position will depend on the initial position. The arrows in Figure 1.1 illustrate some possible trajectories. Under these dynamics, then, an economy beginning with low levels of human and physical capital will remain *permanently* below an initially better endowed economy.

The curve in Figure 1.1 is *defined* as the locus of long-run capital pairs (K, h) such that the marginal product of capital has the common value $\rho + \sigma \kappa$ given by the right side of (19). Along this curve, then, returns to capital are constant and also constant over time even though capital stocks of both kinds are growing. In the absence of the external effect γ, it will also be true that the real wage rate for labor of a given skill level (the marginal product of labor) is constant along the curve in Figure 1.1. This may be verified simply by calculating the marginal product of labor from (11) and making the appropriate substitutions.

In the general case, where $\gamma \geq 0$, the real wage increases as one moves up the curve in Figure 1.1. Along this curve, we have the elasticity formula

$$\frac{K}{w} \frac{\partial w}{\partial K} = \frac{(1 + \beta)\gamma}{1 - \beta + \gamma},$$

so that wealthier countries have higher wages than poorer ones for labor of any given skill. (Of course, workers in wealthy countries are typically also more skilled than workers in poor countries.) In all countries, wages at each skill level grow at the rate

$$\omega = \frac{\gamma}{1 - \beta} \nu.$$

Then taking skill growth into account as well, wages grow at

$$\omega + \nu = \frac{1 - \beta + \gamma}{1 - \beta} \nu = \kappa,$$

or at a rate equal to the growth rate in the per capita stock of physical capital.

The version of the model I propose to fit to, or estimate from, U.S. time series is the equilibrium solution (21), (26), and (10). As in the discussion of Solow's version λ, κ, β, and s are estimated, from Denison (1961), at 0.013, 0.014, 0.25, and 0.1, respectively. Denison also provides an estimate of 0.009 for the annual growth rate of human capital over his period, an estimate based mainly on the changing composition of the workforce by levels of education and on observations on the relative earnings of differently schooled workers. I will use this 0.009 figure as an estimate of v, which amounts to assuming that human capital is accumulated to the point where its private return equals its social (and private) cost. (Since schooling is heavily subsidized in the United States, this assumption may seem way off, but surely most of the subsidy is directed at early schooling that would be acquired by virtually everyone anyway, and so does not affect the margins relevant for my calculations.) Then the idea is to use (10), (21), and (26) to estimate ρ, σ, γ, and δ.

As was the case in the Solow model, ρ and σ cannot separately be identified along steady-state paths, but equation (10) (which can be derived for this model in exactly the same way as I derived it for the model of Section 2) implies $\rho + \sigma\kappa = 0.0675$. Equation (21) implies $\gamma = 0.417$. Combining equations (21) and (26) yields a relationship involving γ, v, β, δ, λ, and $\rho + \sigma\kappa$, but not ρ or σ separately. This relationship yields an estimate for δ of 0.05. The implied fraction of time devoted to goods production is then, from (20), $u = 0.82$.

Given these parameter estimates, the *efficient* rate of human capital growth can be calculated, as a function of σ, from (24). It is: $v^* = 0.009 + 0.0146/\sigma$. Table 1.1 gives some values of this function and the associated values of u^* and $\kappa^* = (1.556)v^*$. Under log utility ($\sigma = 1$), then, the U.S. economy "ought" to devote nearly three times as much effort to human capital accumulations as it does, and "ought" to enjoy growth in per capita consumption about two full percentage points higher than it has had in the past.

One could as easily fit this model to U.S. data under the assumption that *all* returns to human capital are internal, or that $\gamma = 0$. In this case v, v^*, and κ have the common value, from (21), (24), and (26), $\sigma^{-1}[\delta - (\rho - \lambda)]$, and the *ratio* of physical to human capital will converge to a value that is

Table 1.1

σ	v^*	u^*	κ^*
1	0.024	0.52	0.037
2	0.016	0.68	0.025
3	0.014	0.72	0.022

independent of initial conditions (the curve in Figure 1.1 will be a straight line). Identifying this common growth rate with Denison's 0.014 estimate for κ implies a u value of 0.72, or that 28 percent of effective workers' time is spent in human capital accumulation. Accepting Denison's estimate of a 0.009 growth rate of human capital due to schooling, this would leave 0.005 to be attributed to other forms, say on-the-job training that is distinct from productive activities.

What can be concluded from these exercises? Normatively, it seems to me, very little: The model I have just described has *exactly* the same ability to fit U.S. data as does the Solow model, in which equilibrium and efficient growth rates coincide. Moreover, it is clear that the two models can be merged (by re-introducing exogenous technical change into equation 11) to yield a whole class of intermediate models that also fit data in this same rough sense. I am simply generating new possibilities, in the hope of obtaining a theoretical account of cross-country *differences* in income levels and growth rates. Since the model just examined is consistent with the *permanent* maintenance of per capita income differentials of any size (though not with differences in growth rates), some progress toward this objective has been made. But before returning to empirical issues in more detail, I would like to generate another, quite different, example of a system in which human capital plays a central role.

5. Learning-by-Doing and Comparative Advantage

The model I have just worked through treats the decision to accumulate human capital as equivalent to a decision to withdraw effort from production—to go to school, say. As many economists have observed, on-the-job training or learning-by-doing appear to be at least as important as schooling in the formation of human capital. It would not be difficult to incorporate such effects into the previous model, but it is easier to think about one thing at a time, so I will just set out an example of a system (again, for the moment, closed) in which *all* human capital accumulation is learning-by-doing. Doing this will involve thinking about economies with many consumption goods, which will open up interesting new possibilities for interactions between international trade and economic growth.[13]

---

13. The formulation of learning used in this section is taken from Krugman (1987).

Let there be two consumption goods, c_1 and c_2, and no physical capital. For simplicity, let population be constant. The ith good is produced with the Ricardian technology:

$$(29) \quad c_i(t) = h_i(t)u_i(t)N(t), \qquad i = 1, 2,$$

where $h_i(t)$ is human capital specialized to the production of good i and $u_i(t)$ is the fraction of the workforce devoted to producing good i (so $u_i \geq 0$ and $u_1 + u_2 = 1$). Of course, it would not be at all difficult to incorporate physical capital into this model, with (29) replaced by something like (11) for each good i. Later on, I will conjecture the behavior of such a hybrid model, but it will be simpler for now to abstract from capital.

In order to let $h_i(t)$ be interpreted as a result of learning-by-doing, assume that the growth of $h_i(t)$ increases with the effort $u_i(t)$ devoted to producing good i (as opposed to increasing with the effort *withdrawn* from production). A simple way to do this is

$$(30) \quad \dot{h}_i(t) = h_i(t)\delta_i u_i(t).$$

To be specific, assume that $\delta_1 > \delta_2$, so that good 1 is taken to be the "high-technology" good. For the sake of discussion, assume at one extreme that the effects of $h_i(t)$ in (29) and (30) are entirely external: production and skill accumulation for each good depend on the average skill level in that industry only.

As was the case in (13), the equation for human capital accumulation in the model discussed earlier, (30) seems to violate the diminishing returns we observe in studies of productivity growth for particular products. Learning-by-doing in any particular activity occurs rapidly at first, then more slowly, then not at all. Yet as in the preceding discussion, if we simply incorporate diminishing returns into (30), human capital will lose its status as an engine of growth (and hence its interest for the present discussion). What I want equation (30) to stand for, then, is an environment in which new goods are continually being introduced, with diminishing returns to learning on each of them separately, and with human capital specialized to old goods being inherited in some way by new goods. In other words, one would like to consider the inheritance of human capital within families of goods as well as within families of people.[14]

---

14. Stokey (1988) formulates a model of learning on an infinite family of produced and potentially producible goods that captures exactly these features.

Under these assumptions of no physical capital accumulation and purely external human capital accumulation, the individual consumer has no intertemporal trade-offs to decide on, so all we need to know about his preferences is his current-period utility function. I will assume a constant elasticity of substitution form:

$$(31) \quad U(c_1, c_2) = [\alpha_1 c_1^{-\rho} + \alpha_2 c_2^{-\rho}]^{-1/\rho},$$

where $\alpha_i \geq 0$, $\alpha_1 + \alpha_2 = 1$, $\rho > -1$, and $\sigma = 1/(1 + \rho)$ is the elasticity of substitution between c_1 and c_2. (Note that the parameters ρ and σ represent completely different aspects of preferences in this section from those they represented in Sections 2–4.) With technology and preferences given by (29)–(31), I will first work out the equilibrium under autarky and then turn to international trade considerations.

Take the first good as numeraire, and let $(1, q)$ be the equilibrium prices in a closed economy. Then q must equal the marginal rate of substitution in consumption, or

$$q = \frac{U_2(c_1, c_2)}{U_1(c_1, c_2)} = \frac{\alpha_2}{\alpha_1} \left(\frac{c_2}{c_1} \right)^{-(1+\rho)}.$$

Solving for the consumption ratio,

$$(32) \quad \frac{c_2}{c_1} = \left(\frac{\alpha_2}{\alpha_1} \right)^{\sigma} q^{-\sigma}.$$

Hence both goods will be produced, so that (29) plus profit maximization implies that relative prices are dictated by the human capital endowments: $q = h_1/h_2$. Then (29) and (32) together give the equilibrium workforce allocation as a function of these endowments,

$$\frac{c_2}{c_1} = \frac{u_2 h_2}{u_1 h_1} = \left(\frac{\alpha_2}{\alpha_1} \right)^{\sigma} \left(\frac{h_2}{h_1} \right)^{\sigma},$$

or

$$(33) \quad \frac{1 - u_1}{u_1} = \left(\frac{\alpha_2}{\alpha_1} \right)^{\sigma} \left(\frac{h_2}{h_1} \right)^{\sigma - 1}.$$

The dynamics of this closed economy are then determined by inserting this information into equation (30). Solving first for the autarchy price path, $q(t) = h_1(t)/h_2(t)$, we have

$$\frac{1}{q}\frac{dq}{dt} = \frac{1}{h_1}\frac{dh_1}{dt} - \frac{1}{h_2}\frac{dh_2}{dt} = \delta_1 u_1 - \delta_2(1 - u_1),$$

or

(34) $$\frac{1}{q}\frac{dq}{dt} = (\delta_1 + \delta_2)\left[1 + \left(\frac{\alpha_2}{\alpha_1}\right)^\sigma q^{1-\sigma}\right]^{-1} - \delta_2.$$

Solving this first-order equation for $q(t) = h_1(t)/h_2(t)$, given the initial endowments $h_1(0)$ and $h_2(0)$, determines the workforce allocation at each date (from equation 33) and hence, from (30), the paths of $h_1(t)$ and $h_2(t)$ separately.

It will come as no surprise to trade theorists that the analysis of (34) breaks down into three cases, depending on the elasticity of substitution σ between the two goods. I will argue below, on the basis of trade considerations, that the interesting case for us is when $\sigma > 1$, so that c_1 and c_2 are assumed to be good substitutes. But in order to make this case, we need all three possibilities in front of us. Refer to Figure 1.2.

The figure is drawn for the case $\sigma > 1$, in which case the function $[1 + (\alpha_2/\alpha_1)^\sigma q^{1-\sigma}]^{-1}$ has the depicted upward slope. To the left of q^*,

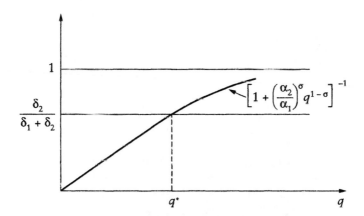

Figure 1.2 Equilibrium price determination

$dq/dt < 0$, so $q(t)$ tends to 0. To the right, $dq/dt > 0$, so $q(t)$ grows without bound. Thus the system in autarchy converges to specialization in one of the two goods (unless $q(0) = q^*$). The choice of *which* good to specialize in is dictated by initial conditions. If we are initially good at producing c_1 (if $q(0) > q^*$), we produce a lot of it, get relatively better and better at producing more of it, eventually, since c_1 and c_2 are good substitutes, producing vanishingly small amounts of c_2.

If the goods are poor substitutes, $\sigma < 1$, the curve in Figure 1.2 slopes down and q^* becomes a *stable* stationary point. At this point, the workforce is so allocated as to equate $\delta_1 u_1$ and $\delta_2 u_2$.

In the borderline case of $\sigma = 1$, the curve is flat. The workforce is initially allocated as dictated by the demand weights, $u_i = \alpha_i$, $i = 1, 2$, and this allocation is maintained forever. The autarchy price grows (or shrinks) at the constant rate $(1/q)(dq/dt) = \alpha_1\delta_1 - \alpha_2\delta_2$ forever.

As we learn how to produce computers more and more cheaply, then, we can substitute in their favor and consume more calculations and fewer potatoes, or we can use this benefit to release resources from computer production so as to consume more potatoes as well. The choice we take, not surprisingly, depends on whether these two goods are good substitutes or poor ones.

As was the case with the human capital model of the preceding section, it is obvious that the equilibrium paths we have just calculated will *not* be efficient. Since learning effects are assumed to be external, agents do not take them into account. If they did, they would allocate labor toward the high δ_i good, relative to an equilibrium allocation, so as to take advantage of its higher growth potential.

Thus, except for the absence of physical capital, this closed economy model captures very much the same economics as does the preceding one. In both cases, the accumulation of human capital involves a sacrifice of current utility. In the first model, this sacrifice takes the form of a decrease in current consumption. In the second, it takes the form of a less desirable *mix* of current consumption goods than could be obtained with slower human capital growth. In both models the equilibrium growth rate falls short of the efficient rate and yields lower welfare. A subsidy to schooling would improve matters in the first model. In the second, in language that is current in the United States, an "industrial policy" focused on "picking winners" (that is, subsidizing the production of high $\alpha_i\delta_i$ goods) would be called for. In the model, "picking winners" is easy. If only it were so in reality!

The introduction of international trade into this second model leads to possibilities that I think are of real interest, though I have only begun to think them through analytically. The simplest kind of world to think about is one with perfectly free trade in the two final goods and with a continuum of small countries, since in that case prices in all countries will equal world prices $(1, p)$, say, and each country will take p as given. Figure 1.3 gives a snapshot of this world at a single point in time. The contour lines in this figure are intended to depict a joint distribution of countries by their initial human capital endowments. A country is a point (h_1, h_2), and the distribution indicates the concentration of countries at various endowment levels.

At a given world price p, countries above the indicated line are producers of good 2, since for them $h_1/h_2 < p$ and they maximize the value of their production by specializing in this good. Countries below the line specialize in producing good 1, for the same reason. Then for each p one can calculate world supply of good 1 by summing (or integrating) the h_1 values below this price line, and the world supply of good 2 by summing the h_2 values

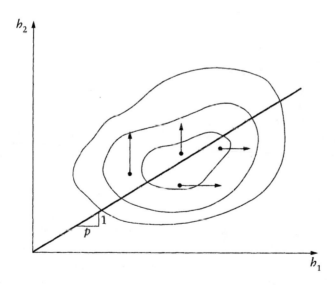

Figure 1.3 Evolution of skills

above the line. Clearly, the supply of good 2 is an increasing function of p and that of good 1 a decreasing function, so that the ratio c_2/c_1 of total quantities supplied increases as p increases.

Now world relative demand, with identical homothetic preferences, is just the same decreasing function of p that described each country's demand in the autarchic case: $c_2/c_1 = (\alpha_2/\alpha_1)^\sigma p^{-\sigma}$. Hence this static model determines the equilibrium world relative price p uniquely. Let us turn to the dynamics.

Those countries above the price line in Figure 1.3 are producing only good 2, so their h_1 endowments remain fixed while their h_2 endowments grow at the rate δ_2. Each country below the price line will produce only good 1, so that its h_2 is constant while h_1 grows at the rate δ_1. Thus each country's (h_1, h_2) coordinates are changing as indicated by the arrows in Figure 1.3, altering the distribution of endowments that determines goods supplies over time. These movements obviously intensify the comparative advantages that led each country to specialize in the first place. On the other hand, as the endowment distribution changes, so does the equilibrium price p. Is it possible that these price movements will induce any country to switch its specialization from one good to the other?

A little reflection suggests that if anyone switches, it will have to be a producer of the high-δ good: good 1. The terms of trade are moving against good 1 (in the absence of switching) since its supply is growing faster. The issue again turns on the degree of substitutability between the two goods. If σ is low, the terms of trade may deteriorate so fast that a marginal good 1 producer may switch to producing good 2: he is getting relatively better at producing good 1, but not fast enough. The inequality that rules this possibility out is

$$(35) \quad \sigma \geq 1 - \frac{\delta_2}{\delta_1}.$$

I have already said that I think $\sigma > 1$ is the interesting case, so I want to accept (35) for the rest of the discussion.

Under (35)—that is, with no producer switching—we can read the dynamics of prices right off the relative demand schedule:

$$(36) \quad \frac{1}{p}\frac{dp}{dt} = \frac{\delta_1 - \delta_2}{\sigma}.$$

With relative price movements determined, the growth rates of real output in all countries are also determined. Measured in units of good 1, output of the good 1 producers grows at the rate δ_1. Output of the good 2 producers, also measured in units of good 1, grows at the rate $\delta_2 + (1/p)(dp/dt) = \delta_2 + (\delta_1 - \delta_2)/\sigma$. In general, then, countries in equilibrium will undergo constant but not equal growth rates of real output.

Which countries will grow fastest? The condition that producers of the high-δ good, good 1, will have faster real growth is just

$$\delta_1 > \delta_2 + \frac{\delta_1 - \delta_2}{\sigma},$$

which is equivalent to the condition: $\sigma > 1$. That is, producing (having a comparative advantage in) high-learning goods will lead to higher-than-average real growth *only* if the two goods are good substitutes. Since it is exactly this possibility that the model is designed to capture, the case $\sigma > 1$ seems to me the only one of potential interest. If the terms-of-trade effects of technological change dominated the direct effects on productivity (which would be the case if $\sigma < 1$), those countries with rapid technological change would enjoy the slowest real income growth. There may be instances of such "immiserizing growth," but if so they are surely the exceptions, not the rule. (These are the trade considerations I mentioned earlier.)

This simple model shares with the model of Section 4 the prediction of constant, endogenously determined real growth rates. In addition, it offers the possibility of different growth rates across countries, though such differences would not be systematically related to income levels. In the equilibrium of the model, production patterns are dictated by comparative advantage: Each country produces goods for which its human capital endowment suits it. Given a learning technology like (30), countries accumulate skills by doing what they are already good at doing, intensifying whatever comparative advantage they begin with. This aspect of the theory will tend to lock in place an initial pattern of production, with rates of output growth variable across countries but stable within each country. There is no doubt that we observe forces for stability of this type, but there seem to be offsetting forces in reality that this model does not capture.

One of these has to do with the composition of demand. With homothetic utility the composition of world demand will remain fixed as income grows. In fact, we know that income elasticities for important classes of goods differ significantly from unity (contrary to the assumption of homotheticity). (We know, for example, that demand shifts systematically away from food consumption as income grows.) This force will create comparative advantages in the production of other goods as time passes, altering world production patterns and growth rates as it does.

Another, I would guess more important, force has to do with the continual introduction of new goods and the fall-off of learning rates on old goods. By modeling learning as occurring at fixed rates on a fixed set of goods, I have here abstracted from important sources of change in world trade patterns. Modifying the model to incorporate possibilities of these two types is an entirely practical idea, given current theoretical technology, but the general equilibrium possibilities for such a modified system have not as yet been worked out.[15]

The present model provides a simple context for discussing two popular "strategies" for economic development: "import substitution" and "export promotion." Consider first a country with $q = h_1/h_2$ currently to the right of q^* in Figure 1.2, but with (h_1, h_2) lying above the equilibrium world price line in Figure 1.3. Under free trade, this country will specialize in the production of good 2 forever. Under autarchy (which is just the extreme version of an import substitution policy) this country will specialize in producing good 1. Eventually its expertise in this protected industry will grow to the point where it will have a comparative advantage in good 1 under free trade, and the maintenance of autarchy will no longer serve any purpose; but this need not be so from the beginning.

I hasten to add that this is only one theoretical possibility among many. Another possibility is an initial q value below q^* in Figure 1.2. In this case, autarchy will not provide nurture for the infant industry, but rather will permanently cut off the country from consuming the high-learning good. Within the context of this model, then, there is no substance-free way to deduce useful guides for trade and development policies. One needs to know something about the actual technological possibilities for producing different goods in different places in order to arrive at definite conclusions.

I take an "export promotion" strategy to mean something slightly different: the manipulation through taxes and subsidies of the terms of trade p faced by a country's producers. With this kind of flexibility, one need not simply choose between world price p and autarchy price q, but can rather set any production incentives and hence choose any growth rate between the

15. Again, see Stokey (1988).

two extremes in the free trade equilibrium. Obviously, even with this flexibility it does not follow that "growth-increasing" and "welfare-improving" policies will necessarily coincide, but they certainly might.

My objective in this section has been to offer one example of a theoretical model in which rates of growth differ across countries, and not to offer policy advice. The case for infant industry protection based on external effects that this model formalizes is the classic one, and it does not become either more or less valid, empirically, by being embedded in a slightly new framework. But is it possible, I wonder, to account for the large cross-country differences in growth rates that we observe in a theoretical model that does *not* involve external effects of the sort I have postulated here? I have not seen it done.

6. Cities and Growth

My concern to this point has been almost exclusively with the aggregate mechanics of economic development, and I am afraid the discussion in this chapter will not get much beyond these mechanics. But I believe a successful theory of development (or of anything else) has to involve more than aggregative modeling, and I would like both to explain what I mean by this and to indicate where one might look to extend the analysis to a deeper and more productive level.

The engine of growth in the models of Sections 4 and 5 is *human capital*. Within the context of these two models, human capital is simply an unobservable magnitude or force, with certain assumed properties, that I have postulated in order to account for some observed features of aggregative behavior. If these features of behavior were *all* of the observable consequences of the idea of human capital, then I think it would make little difference if we simply renamed this force, say, the Protestant ethic or the Spirit of History or just "factor X." After all, we can no more directly measure the amount of human capital a society has, or the rate at which it is growing, than we can measure the degree to which a society is imbued with the Protestant ethic.

But this is *not* all we know about human capital. This same force, admittedly unobservable, has also been used to account for a vast number of phenomena involving the way people allocate their time; the way individuals' earnings evolve over their lifetimes; aspects of the formation, maintenance, and dissolution of relationships within families, firms, and other organizations; and so on. The idea of human capital may have seemed ethereal when it was first introduced—at least, it did to me—but after two decades of research applications of human capital theory we have learned to "see" it in a wide variety of phenomena, just as meteorology has taught us to "see" the advent of a warm front in a bank of clouds or "feel" it in the mugginess of the air.

Indeed, for me the development of the theory of human capital has very much altered the way I think about physical capital. We can, after all, no more directly measure a society's holdings of physical capital than we can its human capital. The fiction of "counting machines" is helpful in certain abstract contexts but is not at all operational or useful in actual economies—even primitive ones. If this was the issue in the famous "two Cambridges" controversy, then it has long since been resolved in favor of the English side of the Atlantic. Physical capital, too, is best viewed as a force, not directly observable, that we postulate in order to account in a unified way for certain things we *can* observe: that goods are produced that yield no immediate benefit to consumers, that the production of these goods enhances labor productivity in future periods, and so on.

The fact that the postulates of both human and physical capital theory have many observable implications outside the contexts of aggregate models is important in specific, quantitative ways, in addition to simply giving aggregative theorists a sense of having "microeconomic foundations." For example, in my application of a human capital model to U.S. aggregative figures, I matched the U.S. observations to the predictions of a competitive model (as opposed to an efficient one) in spite of the fact that education, in the United States, involves vast government intervention and is obviously not a competitive industry in any descriptive sense. Why not instead identify the observed paths with the model's efficient trajectories? The aggregative data have *no* ability to discriminate between these two hypotheses, so this choice would have yielded as good a "fit" as the one I made. At this point, I appealed to the observation that most education subsidies are infra-marginal from the individual's point of view. This observation could stand considerable refinement before it could really settle this particular issue, but the point is that aggregate models based on constructs that have implications for data *other* than aggregates—models with "microeconomic foundations," if you like—permit us to bring evidence to bear on questions of aggregative importance that cannot be resolved with aggregate theory and observations alone. Without the ability to do this, we can do little more than extrapolate past trends into the future, and then be caught by surprise every time one of these trends changes.

The particular aggregate models I have set out utilize the idea of human capital quite centrally, but assign a central role as well to what I have been calling the *external effects* of human capital. This latter force is, it seems to me, on a quite different footing from the idea of human capital generally: The twenty years of research I have referred to earlier is almost exclusively concerned with the *internal* effects of human capital, or with investments in human capital the returns to which accrue to the individual (or his immediate family). If it is this research that permits us to "see" human capital, then the external effects of this capital must be viewed as remaining largely invisible, or visible at the aggregative level only. For example, in Section 4 I arrived at an estimate of $\gamma = 0.4$ for the elasticity of U.S. output with respect to the external effects of human capital on production. Does this seem a plausible number? Or, putting the question in a better way: Is $\gamma = 0.4$ consistent with other evidence? But *what* other evidence? I do not know the answer to this question, but it is so central that I want to spend some time thinking about where the answer may be found. In doing so, I will be following very closely the lead of Jane Jacobs, whose remarkable book *The Economy of Cities* (1969) seems to me mainly and convincingly concerned (though she does not use this terminology) with the external effects of human capital.

I have been concerned with modeling the economic growth of *nations*, considered either singly or as linked through trade. In part, this was a response to the form of the observations I cited at the beginning: Most of our data come in the form of national time series, so "fitting the facts" is taken to mean fitting national summary facts. For considering effects of changes in policies the nation is again the natural unit, for the most important fiscal and commercial policies are national and affect national economies in a uniform way. But from the viewpoint of a *technology*—like (11)—through which the average skill level of a group of people is assumed to affect the productivity of each individual within the group, a *national* economy is a completely arbitrary unit to consider. Surely if Puerto Rico were to become the fifty-first state this would not, by itself, alter the productivity of the people now located in Puerto Rico, even though it would sharply increase the average level of human capital of those politically defined as their fellow citizens. The external effects that the term h_a^γ in (11) is intended to capture have to do with the influences people have on the productivity of others, so the *scope* of such effects must have to do with the ways various groups of people interact, which may be affected by political boundaries but are certainly an entirely different matter conceptually.

Once this question of the scope of external effects is raised, it is clear that it cannot have a single correct answer. Many such effects can be internalized within small groups of people—firms or families. By dealing with an infinitely-lived family as a typical agent, I have assumed that such effects are dealt with at the non-market level and so create no gap between private and social returns. At the other extreme, basic discoveries that immediately become common property—the development of a new mathematical result, say—are human capital in the sense that they arise from resources allocated to such discoveries that could instead have been used to produce current consumption, but to most countries as well as to most individual agents they appear "exogenous" and would be better modeled as $A(t)$ in Section 2 than as $h_a(t)$ in Section 4.

If it were easy to classify most external productivity effects either as global in scope or as so localized as to be internalizable at the level of the family or the firm, then I think a model that incorporated internal human capital effects only plus other effects treated as exogenous technical change would be adequate. Such a model would fit time series from advanced countries about as well as any I have advanced, being an intermediate model to those I discussed in Sections 2 and 4, which were in turn not distinguishable on such data alone. Such a model would, I think, have difficulty reconciling observed pressures for immigration with the absence of equivalent capital flows, but perhaps this anomaly could be accounted for in some other way.

But we *know* from ordinary experience that there are group interactions that are central to individual productivity and that involve groups larger than the immediate family and smaller than the human race as a whole. Most of what we know we learn from other people. We pay tuition to a few of these teachers, either directly or indirectly by accepting lower pay so we can hang around them, but most of it we get for free, and often in ways that are mutual—without a distinction between student and teacher. Certainly in my own profession, the benefits of colleagues from whom we hope to learn are tangible enough to lead us to spend a considerable fraction of our time fighting over who they shall be, and another fraction traveling to talk with those we wish we could have as colleagues but cannot. We know this kind of external effect is common to all the arts and sciences—

the "creative professions." All of intellectual history is the history of such effects.

But, as Jacobs has rightly emphasized and illustrated with hundreds of concrete examples, much of economic life is creative in much the same way as is art and science. New York City's garment district, financial district, diamond district, advertising district, and many more are as much intellectual centers as is Columbia or New York University. The specific ideas exchanged in these centers differ, of course, from those exchanged in academic circles, but the process is much the same. To an outsider, it even *looks* the same: a collection of people doing pretty much the same thing, each emphasizing his or her own originality and uniqueness.

Considerations such as these may convince us of the existence of external human capital, and even that it is an important element in the growth of knowledge. But they do not easily lend themselves to quantification. Here again I find Jacobs's work highly suggestive. Her emphasis on the role of cities in economic growth stems from the observation that a city, economically, is like the nucleus of an atom: If we postulate only the usual list of economic forces, cities should fly apart. The theory of production contains nothing to hold a city together. A city is simply a collection of factors of production—capital, people, and land—and land is always far cheaper outside cities than inside. Why don't capital and people move outside, combining themselves with cheaper land and thereby increasing profits? Of course, people like to live near shopping and shops need to be located near their customers, but circular considerations of this kind explain only shopping centers, not cities. Cities are centered on wholesale trade and primary producers, and a theory that accounts for their existence has to explain why these producers are apparently choosing high-cost rather than low-cost modes of operation.

It seems to me that the force we need to postulate to account for the central role of cities in economic life is of exactly the same character as the external human capital I have postulated as a force to account for certain features of aggregative development. If so, then land rents should provide an indirect measure of this force, in much the same way that schooling-induced earnings differentials provide a measure of the productive effects of internal human capital. It would require a much more detailed theory of the external effects of human capital than anything I have provided to make use of the information in urban land rents (just as one needs a more detailed theory of human capital than that in Section 4 to utilize the information in earnings data), but the general logic is the same in the two cases. What can people be paying Manhattan or downtown Chicago rents *for*, if not for being near other people?

7. Conclusions

My aim, as I said at the beginning of this chapter, has been to try to find what I called mechanics suitable for the study of economic development: that is, a system of differential equations the solution to which imitates some of the main features of the economic behavior we observe in the world economy. This enterprise has been taken about as far as I am able to take it, at present, so I will stop and try to sum up what the main features of these mechanics are and the sense in which they conform to what we observe.

The model that I think is central was developed in Section 4. It is a system with a given rate of population growth but which is acted on by no other outside or exogenous forces. There are two kinds of capital, or state variables, in the system: physical capital that is accumulated and utilized in production under a familiar neoclassical technology, and human capital that enhances the productivity of both labor and physical capital, and that is accumulated according to a "law" having the crucial property that a constant level of effort produces a constant growth rate of the stock, independent of the level already attained.

The dynamics of this system, viewed as a single, closed economy, are as follows. Asymptotically, the marginal product of physical capital tends to a constant, given essentially by the rate of time preference. This fact, which with one kind of capital defines the long-run stock of that capital, in the two-capital model of Section 4 defines a curve in the physical capital–human capital plane. The system will converge to this curve from any initial configuration of capital stocks, but the particular point to which it converges will depend on initial conditions. Economies that are initially poor will remain poor, relatively, though their long-run rate of income growth will be the same as that of initially (and permanently) wealthier economies. A world consisting of such economies, then, each operating autarchically, would exhibit uniform rates of growth across countries and would maintain a perfectly stable distribution of income and wealth over time.

If trade in capital goods is introduced into this model world economy, with labor assumed immobile, there will be no tendency to trade, which is to say there will be no systematic tendency for borrowing and lending relationships to emerge between rich and poor countries. Put another way, the long-run relationship between the two kinds of capital that holds in each country implies the same marginal productivity of physical capital, regardless of the level of capital that has been accumulated. The picture I have given for a world of closed economies thus carries over without change to a world with free trade in capital goods.

If labor mobility is introduced, everything hinges on whether the effects of human capital are internal—affecting the productivity of its "owner" only—or whether they have external benefits that spill over from one person to another. In the latter case, and only in the latter case, the wage rate of labor at any given skill level will increase with the wealth of the country in which the worker is employed. Then if labor can move, it will move, flowing in general from poor countries to wealthy ones.

The model I have described fits the evidence of the last century for the U.S. economy as well as the now standard neoclassical model of Solow and Denison, which is to say, remarkably well. This is of course no accident, for the mechanics I have been developing here have been modeled as closely as possible on theirs. It also fits, about as well, what seem to me the main features of the world economy: very wide diversity in income levels across countries, sustained growth in per capita incomes at all income levels (though not, of course, in each country at each income level), and the absence of any marked tendency for growth rates to differ systematically at different levels of income. The model is also consistent with the enormous pressures for immigration that we observe in the world, even with its extreme assumptions that assign no importance to differences in endowments of natural resources and that permit perfectly free trade in capital and consumption goods. As long as people at each skill level are more productive in high-human-capital environments, such pressures are predicted to exist and nothing but the movement of people can relieve them.

Though the model of Section 4 seems capable of accounting for *average* rates of growth, it contains no forces to account for diversity over countries or over time within a country (except for arbitrary shifts in tastes or technology). Section 5 develops a two-commodity elaboration of this model that offers more possibilities. In this setup, human capital accumulation is taken to be specific to the production of particular goods, and is acquired on-the-job or through learning-by-doing. If different goods are taken to have different potentials for human capital growth, then the same considerations of comparative advantage that determine which goods get produced where will also dictate each country's rate of human capital growth. The model thus admits the possibility of wide and sustained differences in growth rates across countries, differences that one would not expect to be systematically linked to each country's initial capital *levels*.

With a fixed set of goods, which was the only case I considered, this account of cross-country differences does not leave room for within-country changes in growth rates. The comparative advantages that dictate a country's initial production mix will simply be intensified over time by human capital accumulation. But I conjecture that a more satisfactory treatment of product-specific learning would involve modeling the continuous introduction of new goods, with learning potentials on any particular good declining with the amount produced. There is no doubt that we observe this kind of effect occurring in reality on particular product lines. If it could be captured in a tractable aggregate model, this would introduce a factor continuously shaking up an existing pattern of comparative advantages, and would offer some interesting possibilities for shifts over time in a country's growth rate, within the same general equilibrium framework used in Section 5.

If such an analysis of trade-related shifts in growth rates should turn out to be possible, this would be interesting, because the dramatic recent development success stories, the "growth miracles" of Korea, Taiwan, Hong Kong, and Singapore (not to mention the ongoing miracle of Japan), have all been associated with increases in exports, and more suggestively still, with exports of goods not formerly produced in these countries. There is surely no strain in thinking that a model stressing the effects of learning-by-doing is likely to shed light on these events.

A successful theory of economic development clearly needs, in the first place, mechanics that are consistent with sustained growth and with sustained diversity in income levels. This was the objective of Section 4. But there is no one pattern of growth to which all economies conform, so a useful theory needs also to capture some forces for change in these patterns, and a mechanics that permits these forces to operate. This is a harder task, certainly not carried out in the analysis I have worked through, but I think the analysis of Section 5 is a promising beginning.

2

WHY DOESN'T CAPITAL FLOW FROM
RICH TO POOR COUNTRIES?

1. Introduction

The egalitarian predictions of the simplest neoclassical models of trade and growth are well known and easy to explain, as they follow from entirely standard assumptions on technology alone. Consider two countries producing the same good with the same constant returns to scale production function, relating output to homogeneous capital and labor inputs. If production per worker differs between these two countries, it must be because they have different levels of capital per worker: I have just ruled everything else out! Then the Law of Diminishing Returns implies that the marginal product of capital is higher in the less productive (that is, the poorer) economy. If so, then if trade in capital goods is free and competitive, new investment will occur only in the poorer economy, and this will continue to be true until capital labor ratios, and hence wages and capital returns, are equalized.

We do, of course, see some investment by wealthy countries in poorer ones, but an example with some rough numbers will help to make clear just how far the capital flows we observe fall short of the flows predicted by the theory I have just sketched. According to Robert Summers and Alan Heston (1988, table 3, pp. 18–21), production per person in the United States is about fifteen times what it is in India. Suppose production in both these countries obeys a Cobb-Douglas-type constant returns technology with a common intercept:

(1) $\quad y = Ax^{\beta}$,

where y is income per worker and x is capital per worker. Then the marginal product of capital is $r = A\beta x^{\beta-1}$, in terms of capital per worker, and thus:

(2) $\quad r = \beta A^{1/\beta} y^{(\beta-1)/\beta}$

in terms of production per worker. Let $\beta = 0.4$ (an average of U.S. and Indian capital shares), again for both countries. Then the formula (2) implies that the marginal product of capital in India must be about $(15)^{1.5} = 58$ times the marginal product of capital in the United States.

If this model were anywhere close to being accurate, and if world capital markets were anywhere close to being free and complete, it is clear that, in the face of return differentials of this magnitude, investment goods would flow rapidly from the United States and other wealthy countries to India and other poor countries. Indeed, one would expect *no* investment to occur in the wealthy countries in the face of return differentials of this magnitude. I worked out the arithmetic for this example to make it clear that there is nothing at all delicate about this standard neoclassical prediction on capital flows. The assumptions on technology and trade conditions that give rise to this example must be drastically wrong, but exactly what is wrong with them, and what assumptions should replace them? This is a central question for economic development. In this chapter I consider four candidate answers to this question.

2. Differences in Human Capital

The sample calculation in the last section treats effective labor input per person as equal in the countries being compared, ignoring differences in labor quality or human capital per worker. The best attempt to correct measured labor inputs for differences in human capital is Anne Krueger's (1968) study. Her estimates are based on data from the 1950s, but the percentage income differentials between very rich and very poor countries have not changed all that much in the last 25 years and, in any case, a rough estimate is better than none at all. Her method is to combine information on each country's mix of workers by level of education, age, and sector with U.S. estimates of the way these factors affect worker productivity, as measured by relative earnings.

Krueger's main results are given in her table III (p. 653), which gives estimates of the per capita income that each of the 28 countries examined could attain, expressed as a fraction of U.S. income, if each country had the same physical capital per worker endowment as did the United States. The estimates range from around .38 (India, Indonesia, Ghana) to unity (Canada) and .84 (Israel). These numbers have the dimension of the relative human capital stocks raised to the power of labor's share, so taking the latter at .6 (as I did in my introductory example), the estimated relative human capital endowments ranged from about .2 to unity. That is, each American or Canadian worker was estimated to be the productive equivalent of about five Indians or Ghanaians. (Compensation per employed civilian in the United States in 1987 was about $24,000, so this estimate implies that a typical worker from India or Ghana could earn about $4,800 in the United States.)

To redo my introductory example with Krueger's estimated human capital differentials, reinterpret y in equations (1) and (2) as income per *effective* worker. Then the ratio of y in the United States to y in India becomes 3 rather than 15, and the predicted rate of return ratio becomes $(3)^{1.5} = 5$ rather than 58. This is a substantial revision, but even so, it leaves the original paradox very much alive: a factor of 5 difference in rates of return is still large enough to lead one to expect capital flows much larger than anything we observe.

If it had turned out that replacing labor with effective labor had *entirely* eliminated the estimated differences in the marginal product of capital, this would have answered the question with which I began this chapter, but only by replacing it with an even harder question. Under constant returns, equal capital returns implies equal wage rates for equally skilled labor, so that if there were no economic motive for capital to flow, there would be no motive for labor flows either. Yet we see immigration at maximal allowable rates and beyond from poor countries to wealthy ones. We do not want to resolve the puzzle of capital flows with a theory that predicts, contrary to the evidence provided by millions of Mexicans, that Mexican workers can earn equal wages in the United States and in Mexico.

3. External Benefits of Human Capital

Obviously, we could resolve the puzzle of the inadequacy of capital flows at any time by *assuming* that marginal products of capital are equalized, and using equation (2) and the estimated income differential to estimate the relative levels of the intercept parameter A (often called the level of technology) in the two countries being compared. This is almost what I will do in this section, but I will do so in a way that has more content, by assuming that an economy's technology level is just the average level of its workers' human capital raised to a power. That is, I assume (as I did in Chapter 1) that the production function takes the form

(3) $y = Ax^\beta h^\gamma$,

where y is income per effective worker, x is capital per effective worker, and h is human capital per worker. I interpret the term h^γ as an external effect (just as in Romer 1986a and b). It multiplies the productivity of a worker at any skill level h, exactly as does the intercept A in (3).

The marginal productivity of capital formula implied by (3) is

(4) $r = \beta A^{1/\beta} y^{(\beta-1)/\beta} h^{\gamma/\beta}$.

I propose to estimate the parameter γ using Edward Denison's (1961) comparison of U.S. productivity in 1909 and 1958, and then to apply this estimate to equation (4) using Krueger's cross-country estimates of relative human capital stocks in 1959 to obtain a new prediction on relative rates of return on capital.

The estimation of γ is as reported in my earlier paper (see Chapter 1, p. 45). Using Denison's estimates for the 1909–1959 period in the United States, output per man-hour grew about one percentage point faster than capital per man-hour. Denison estimates a growth rate of h, attributed entirely to growth in schooling, of .009. With the technology (3), this implies that $(1 - \beta + \gamma)$ times the growth rate .009 of human capital equals .01. With a capital's share $\beta = .25$, these numbers imply $\gamma = .36$. That is to say, a 10 percent increase in the average quality of those with whom I work increases my productivity by 3.6 percent. (This estimate is based on the assumption that the total stock of human capital grows at the same rate, .009, as that part of the stock that is accumulated through formal schooling. I do not have any idea how accurate an assumption this is.)

Now taking the Krueger estimate that five Indians equals one American, the predicted rate of return ratio between India and the United States becomes $(3)^{1.5} 5^{-1} = 1.04$. That is, taking the external effects of human capital into account in the way I have done entirely eliminates the predicted return differential. Notice that this result is in no way built into my estimation procedure. The value of γ estimated from the 1909–1958 U.S. comparison exactly eliminates the return differential in a 1959 India–U.S. comparison.

One might accept this calculation as a resolution of the question I posed in my title. This was the argument in my earlier paper, based on U.S. data only, and I am surprised how well it works in a cross-country comparison. But it is important and troublesome, I think, to note that the cross-country comparison is based on the assumption that the external benefits of a country's stock of human capital accrue *entirely* to producers within that country. Knowledge spillovers across national boundaries are assumed to be zero. Ordinary experience suggests that while some of the external benefits of increases in individual knowledge are local, confined to single cities or even small neighborhoods of cities, others are worldwide in scope. But, without some real evidence on the scope of these external effects, I do not see how to advance this quantitative discussion any further. The argument of this section and the preceding one suggests that correcting for human capital differentials reduces the predicted return ratios between very rich and very poor countries from about 58 at least to about 5, and possibly, if knowledge spillovers are local enough, to unity.

4. Capital Market Imperfections

I have been discussing capital flows in static terms, taking it for granted that differences in marginal products of capital at a point in time imply flows of capital goods through time. In the one-good context I am using, such flows are simply borrowing contracts: the poor country acquires capital from the rich now, in return for promised goods flows in the opposite direction later on.

Suppose countries A and B are engaged in such a transaction, and that the capital stocks in the two countries are growing on paths that will eventually converge to a common value. If we look at goods flows through time between these two countries, we see a phase in which goods flow from advanced A to backward B, followed by a phase (which lasts forever) in which goods flow from B to A in the form of interest payments or repatriated profits. This sort of pattern was implicit in my statement of the capital flow problem. For such a pattern to be a competitive equilibrium, it is evident that there must be an effective mechanism for enforcing international borrowing agreements. Otherwise, country B will gain by terminating its relationship with A at the point where the repayment period begins, and, foreseeing this, country A will never lend in the first place. A capital market imperfection of this type is often summarized by the term "political risk."

A serious difficulty with political risk as an explanation for the inadequacy of capital flows lies in the novelty of the current political arrangements between rich and poor nations. Until around 1945, much of the Third World was subject to European-imposed legal and economic arrangements, and had been so for decades or even centuries. A European lending to a borrower in India or the Dutch East Indies could expect his contract to be enforced with exactly the same effectiveness and by exactly the same means as a contract with a domestic borrower. Even if political risk has been a force limiting capital flows since 1945, why were not ratios of capital to effective labor equalized by capital flows in the two centuries before 1945?

I do not know the answer to this question, but, in seeking one, I see no reason to assume that the role of the colonial powers was simply to enforce a laissez-faire trading regime throughout the world. The following monopoly model, very much in the spirit of Adam Smith's (1776/1976) analysis of an earlier phase of colonialism, seems to me suggestive in several ways.

Consider an imperial power whose investors have access to capital at a (first) world return of r. Assume that the imperialist has exclusive control over trade to and from a colony, but that the labor market in the colony is free. Now suppose, at one extreme, that the colony has *no* capital of its own, and no ability to accumulate any. Then capital per worker, x, in the colony can be chosen by the imperialist, and the entire income repatriated. Under these conditions, what value of x is optimal from the viewpoint of the imperial power, viewed as a monopolist?

Let the production function in the colony be $y = f(x)$. Then the monopolist's problem is to choose x so as to maximize

$$(5) \quad f(x) - [f(x) - xf'(x)] - rx,$$

or total production less wage payments at a competitively determined wage less the opportunity cost of capital. The first-order condition for this problem is

$$(6) \quad f'(x) = r - xf''(x),$$

so that the marginal product of capital in the colony is equated to the world return r plus the derivative of the colony's real wage rate with respect to capital per worker. It is the imperialist's monopsony power over wages in the colony that is crucial. His optimal policy is to retard capital flows so as to maintain real wages at artificially low levels.

With the Cobb-Douglas technology assumed in my earlier examples, the formula (6) implies that $r = \beta^2 x^{\beta-1} = \beta f'(x)$. With a β value of .4, then, the return on capital in the colony should be about 2.5 times the European return. These are quantitatively interesting rents. The possibility that such rents were important is, I think, reinforced by many of the institutional features of the colonial era: the carving up of the Third World by the European powers, and the frequent granting of exclusive trading rights to monopoly companies.[1]

In a country like India or Indonesia, where most of the workforce was (and still is) engaged in traditional agriculture, it is hard to imagine that the ability to control capital inflows from abroad gave the imperialists much monopsony power over the *general* level of wages. Put another way, the value of capital imported from Europe must have been a small fraction of capital in these countries as a whole, most of which was land. If monopoly control over capital imports was an important source of colonial return differentials, it must have been because only a small part of the colonial labor force was skilled enough to work with imported capital in, say, goods manufacturing. But to explore this possibility, we would obviously need a more refined view of the nature of human capital than one in which five day-laborers equal one engineer.[2]

Insofar as monopoly control over trade in capital goods was an important factor in the determination of capital-labor ratios prior to 1945, I do not see any reason to believe that it ceased to be a factor after the political end of the colonial age. Monopoly returns are not of interest to Europeans only. There is much unsystematic evidence of heavy private taxation of capital inflows in Indonesia, in the Philippines, in the Iran of the Shah, and in other poor economies that are otherwise attractive to foreign investors.

---

1. With its emphasis on capital investment, Dobb's (1945) discussion of late nineteenth and early twentieth-century colonialism is closer to the model in this chapter than is Smith's. According to Davis and Huttenback (1989), investment in the late British empire was open to firms from any country on competitive terms, which would obviously be inconsistent with this model. Moreover, they do not find rates of return in the British colonies that exceeded European returns for similar investments.

2. See Nancy Stokey (1988) for a model in which high human capital workers do qualitatively different things than do low human capital workers.

Restrictions on capital flows imposed by the borrowing country are often explained as arising from a mistrust of foreigners or a reluctance to let development proceed "too fast," but I think such explanations warrant a Smithian skepticism.

5. Conclusions

Why does it matter which combination, if any, of the four hypotheses I have advanced is adequate to account for the absence of income-equalizing international capital flows? The central idea of virtually all postwar development policies is to stimulate transfers of capital goods from rich to poor countries. Insofar as either of the human capital–based hypotheses reviewed in Sections 2 and 3 of this chapter is accurate, such transfers will be fully offset by reductions in private foreign investment in the poor country, by increases in that country's investments abroad, or both. Insofar as returns on capital are not equalized, but where return differentials are maintained so as to secure monopoly rents, capital transfers to poor countries will also be fully offset by reductions in private investments. Giving goods to a monopolist does not reduce his interest in exploiting potential rents.

Only insofar as political risk is an important factor in limiting capital flows can we expect transfers of capital to speed the international equalization of factor prices. In a world of largely immobile labor, policies focused on affecting the accumulation of human capital surely have a much larger potential. So too, I think, do policies in which aid of any form is tied to the recipient's openness to foreign investment on competitive terms.

3

MAKING A MIRACLE

1. Introduction

In 1960, the Philippines and South Korea had about the same standard of living, as measured by their per capita GDPs of about 640 U.S. 1975 dollars. The two countries were similar in many other respects. There were 28 million people in the Philippines and 25 million in Korea, with slightly over half of both populations of working age. Twenty-seven percent of Filipinos lived in Manila, 28 percent of South Koreans in Seoul. In both countries, all boys of primary school age were in school, and almost all girls, but only about a quarter of secondary-school-age children were in school. Only 5 percent of Koreans in their early twenties were in college, as compared to 13 percent in the Philippines. Twenty-six percent of Philippine GDP was generated in agriculture, and 28 percent in industry. In Korea, the comparable numbers were 37 and 20 percent. Ninety-six percent of Philippine merchandise exports consisted of primary commodities and 4 percent of manufactured goods. In Korea, primary commodities made up 86 percent of exports, and manufactured goods 14 percent (of which 8 percent were textiles).

From 1960 to 1988, GDP per capita in the Philippines grew at about 1.8 percent per year, about the average for per capita incomes in the world as a whole. In Korea, over the same period, per capita income grew at 6.2 percent per year, a rate consistent with the doubling of living standards every 11 years. Korean incomes are now similar to Mexican, Portuguese, or Yugoslavian, about three times incomes in the Philippines, and about one-third of incomes in the United States.[1]

---

1. The figures in the first paragraph are taken from the 1984 *World Development Report*. The income and population figures in this paragraph and the next are from Summers and Heston (1991).

I do not think it is in any way an exaggeration to refer to this continuing transformation of Korean society as a miracle, or to apply this term to the very similar transformations that are occurring in Taiwan, Hong Kong, and Singapore. Never before have the lives of so many people (63 million in these four areas in 1980) undergone so rapid an improvement over so long a period, nor (with the tragic exception of Hong Kong) is there any sign that this progress is near its end. How did it happen? Why did it happen in Korea and Taiwan, and not in the Philippines?

Questions like these can be addressed at many levels. It is useful to begin simply by listing some of the features of these transformations in addition to their income growth rates. All of the East Asian miracle economies have become large-scale exporters of manufactured goods of increasing sophistication. They have become highly urbanized (no problem for Singapore and Hong Kong!) and increasingly well-educated. They have high savings rates. They have pro-business governments, following differing mixes of laissez-faire and mercantilist commercial policies. These facts—or at least some of them—must figure in any explanation of the growth miracles, but they are additions to the list of events we want to explain, not themselves explanations.

We want to be able to use these events to help in assessing economic policies that may affect growth rates in other countries. But simply advising a society to "follow the Korean model" is a little like advising an aspiring basketball player to "follow the Michael Jordan model." To make use of someone else's successful performance at any task, one needs to be able to break this performance down into its component parts so that one can see what each part contributes to the whole, which aspects of this performance are imitable and, of these, which are worth imitating. One needs, in short, a theory.

There has been a great deal of interesting new theoretical research on growth and development generally in the last few years, some of it explicitly directed at the Asian miracles and much more that seems to me clearly relevant. In this chapter I will examine what recent research offers toward an explanation for these events. My review will be sharply focused on neoclassical theories that view the growth miracles as *productivity* miracles. What happened over the last 30 years that enabled the typical Korean or overseas Chinese worker to produce six times the goods and services he could produce in 1960? Indeed, my viewpoint will be even narrower than the neoclassical theories on which I draw, since I intend to focus on issues of *technology*, with only cursory treatment of consumer preferences and the nature of product market competition. There is no doubt that the issue of who gets the rewards from innovation is a central one, and it is not one that can be resolved on the basis of technological considerations alone, so this narrow focus will necessarily restrict the conclusions I will be able to draw. But there is no point in trying to think through hard questions of industrial organization and general equilibrium without an adequate description of the relevant technology, so this seems to me the right place to start.

I will begin in Section 2 with a brief sketch of some recent theoretical developments and of the image of the world economy these developments offer. This image does not, as I see it, admit of anything one could call a miracle, but it will be useful in motivating my subsequent emphasis on the accumulation of human capital, and in particular human capital accumulation on the job: learning-by-doing. In Section 3 I will review a piece of microeconomic evidence on learning and productivity, just as a reminder of how solid the evidence is and how promising, quantitatively, for the theory of growth. Yet establishing the importance of learning-by-doing for productivity growth on a specific production process is very different from establishing its importance for an entire economy as a whole, or even for an entire sector. This connection is much more problematic than I once believed. But it has been made, in research by Nancy Stokey and Alwyn Young, and I will sketch the main technological implications of their work in Section 4. There is good reason to believe, I will argue, that something like this technology provided the means for the productivity miracles to occur. Section 5 discusses some of the issues involved in developing market equilibrium theories in which differential learning rates account for observed growth rate differences, and offers some speculations about the implications of such a theory for the development prospects of poor countries. Conclusions are presented in Section 6.

2. Theoretical Background

There has been a rebirth of confidence—stimulated in large part by Romer's (1986a) contribution—that explicit neoclassical growth models in the style of Solow (1956) can be adapted to fit the observed behavior of rich and poor economies alike, interacting in a world of international trade. I do not believe we can obtain a theory of economic miracles in a purely aggregative setup in which every country produces the same, single good (and a rich country is just one that produces more of it), but such a framework will be useful in stating the problem and in narrowing the theoretical possibilities.

Consider, to begin with, a single economy that uses physical capital, $k(t)$, and human capital, $h(t)$, to produce a single good, $y(t)$:

$$(2.1) \quad y(t) = Ak(t)^{\alpha}[uh(t)]^{1-\alpha}.$$

Here I multiply the human capital input by u, the fraction of time people spend producing goods.[2] The growth of physical capital depends on the savings rate s:

$$(2.2) \quad \frac{dk(t)}{dt} = sy(t),$$

while the growth of human capital depends on the amount of quality-adjusted time devoted to its production:

$$(2.3) \quad \frac{dh(t)}{dt} = \delta(1-u)h(t).$$

Taking the decision variables s and u as given, which I will do for this exposition, the model (2.1)–(2.3) is just a reinterpretation of Solow's original model of a single, closed economy, with the rate of technological change (the average Solow residual) equal to $\mu = \delta(1-\alpha)(1-u)$ and the initial technology level equal to $Ah(0)^{1-\alpha}$. In this system, the long-run growth rate of both capital and production per worker is $\delta(1-u)$, the rate of human capital growth, and the *ratio* of physical to human capital

---

2. One reader of this chapter found my use of the term "human capital" in this aggregate context idiosyncratic, and I agree that aggregate theorists tend to use terms like "technology" or "knowledge capital" for what I am here calling "human capital." But the cost of having two terminologies for discussing the same thing, one used by microeconomists and another by macroeconomists, is that it makes it too easy for one group to forget that the other can be a source of relevant ideas and evidence.

It was the explicit theme of Schultz (1962) that the theory of human capital, then in its infancy, would prove central to the theory of economic growth, and Schultz included the stock of human capital accumulated on the job in his table 1 (p. S6). His figures were based on estimates provided in Mincer (1962), whose estimation method "treats 'learning from experience' as an investment in the same sense as are the more obvious forms of on-the-job training, such as, say, apprenticeship programs" (p. S51). My usage in this chapter is, I think, consistent with 30 years of practice in labor economics.

converges to a constant. In the long run, the level of income is proportional to the economy's initial stock of human capital.[3]

To analyze a world economy made up of countries like this one, one needs to be specific about the mobility of factors of production. A benchmark case that has the virtues of simplicity and, I think, a decent degree of realism is obtained by assuming that labor is completely immobile, while physical capital is perfectly mobile. That is, if there are n countries indexed by i, assume that the world stock of physical capital, $K = \sum_{i=1}^{n} k_i$, is allocated across countries so as to equate the marginal product in each country to a common world return, r. Then if each country has the technology (2.1) with a common intercept A, this world return is $r = \alpha A(K/H)^{\alpha-1}$, where $H = \sum_i u_i h_i$ is the world supply of effective labor devoted to goods production. Net domestic product in each country is proportional to its effective workforce:

$$(2.4) \quad y_i = A \left(\frac{K}{H}\right)^{\alpha} u_i h_i.$$

If everyone has the same constant savings rate s, the dynamics of this world economy are essentially the same as those of Solow's model. The world capital stock follows $(dK/dt) = sAK^{\alpha}H^{1-\alpha}$, and the time path of H is obtained by summing (2.2) over countries, each multiplied by its own time allocation variable u_i. The long-run growth rate of physical capital and of every country's output is equal to the growth rate of human capital. Each country's income level will be proportional to its initial human capital, not only in the long run but all along the equilibrium path. The theory is thus consistent with the permanent maintenance of any degree of income inequality.

It would be hard to think of another theory as simple as this one that does a better job of fitting the postwar statistics in the back of *World Development Report*. By reinterpreting Solow's technology variable as a

---

3. Of course, essentially the same economics can be obtained from a model in which consumer preferences are taken as given and savings and time allocation behavior are derived rather than assumed. See Uzawa (1965), Lucas (1988), and Caballe and Santos (1993). The particular model sketched in the text is simply one rather arbitrarily selected example from the large number of similarly motivated models that have recently been proposed. See, for example, Jones and Manuelli (1990), King and Rebelo (1990), and Becker, Murphy, and Tamura (1990).

country-specific stock of human capital, a model that predicts rapid convergence to common income levels is converted into one that is consistent with permanent income inequality. But the key assumption on which this prediction is based—that human capital accumulation in any one economy is independent of the level of human capital in other economies—conflicts with the evident fact that ideas developed in one place spread elsewhere, that there is one frontier of human knowledge, not one for each separate economy.

Moreover, as Parente and Prescott (1993) observe, if the model sketched above is realistically modified to permit each economy to be subject to shocks that have some independence across countries, the assumption that each economy undergoes sustained growth due to its own human capital growth *only* would imply ever-growing inequality within any subset of countries. Relative income levels would follow random-walk-like behavior. I do not see how this prediction can be reconciled with the postwar experience of, say, the OECD countries or the EEC. The countries of the world are tied together, economically and technologically, in a way that the model (2.1)–(2.3) does not capture.[4]

One way to introduce some convergence into the model I have sketched is to modify the human capital accumulation technology (2.2) so as to permit any one country's rate of human capital growth to be influenced by the level of human capital elsewhere in the world. For example, let $H(t)$ be the world effective labor variable defined above, and let $Z(t) = H(t)/\Sigma_i u_i$ be the world average human capital level. Replace the human capital accumulation equation (2.3) with:[5]

$$(2.5) \quad \frac{dh(t)}{dt} = \delta(1 - u)h(t)^{1-\theta}Z(t)^{\theta}.$$

With this modification, the dynamics of the world stocks of physical and human capital are essentially unchanged, but now an economy with a human capital stock lower than the world average will grow faster than

---

4. An informative recent debate on income convergence has been stimulated by the exchange between Baumol (1986), De Long (1988), and Baumol and Wolff (1988). My statement in the text simply echoes the shared conclusion of these authors.

5. This external effect might better be captured through the human capital level of the most advanced countries, rather than the world average $Z(t)$. But the use of the latter variable keeps the algebra simple, and I don't think the distinction is critical for any conclusions I wish to draw here.

an above-average economy. For example, if the time allocation is equal across countries, so that $H(t)$ and $Z(t)$ grow at the rate $\delta(1-u)$, a country's *relative* human capital, $z_i = h_i/Z$, follows

(2.6) $\quad \dfrac{d}{dt}z_i(t) = \delta(1-u)z(t)[z(t)^{-\theta} - 1].$

Evidently, $z_i(t)$ converges to one, and from (2.4), this means that relative incomes converge to one at the same rate.

In the world as a whole in the postwar period, income dispersion across all countries appears to be increasing. But, of course, there are many reasons to believe that the assumption of free world trade that leads to (2.6) is a very bad approximation for much of the world, and there are certainly differences across countries in the incentives people have to accumulate both kinds of capital, implying differences in savings rates and the allocation of time. Yet over subsets of countries, or regions of countries, where factor and final goods mobility is high (like the EEC or the 50 U.S. states), convergence can be observed.[6]

Barro and Sala-i-Martin (1992) obtain a regression estimate of an average convergence rate of relative incomes, conditioned on variables that may be interpreted as controlling for a country's adherence to the above assumptions, of slightly less than .02 (table 3, p. 242). As they observe, if one interprets this coefficient as reflecting differential rates of physical capital accumulation in a world in which income differences reflect mainly differences in capital per worker, this rate of convergence is much too low to be consistent with observed capital shares. Alternatively, interpreting this figure as an estimate of $(1/z)(dz/dt)$ in (2.6), their estimate implies $\theta\delta(1-u) = .02$. Since $\delta(1-u)$ is the average rate of human capital growth, also about .02 in reality, this interpretation yields an estimated θ of unity, which from (2.5) would mean that human capital accumulation in any country depends on local effort together with worldwide knowledge, independent of the local human capital level. From this viewpoint, the Barro and Sala-i-Martin estimate seems high.

All of this is by way of a prelude to thinking about growth miracles—about deviations from average behavior. I have described a model of a world economy—reasonably realistic in its description of average behavior of countries at different income levels—in which everyone has the same

---

6. See, for example, Ben-David (1991).

savings rate and allocates time in the same way. What are the prospects for using the same theory to see how variations across economies in the parameters s and u can induce variation in behavior of the magnitude we seek to explain? Here the exercise begins to get hard.

The East Asian economies do indeed have high investment rates. The current ratio of gross domestic investment to GDP in Korea is about .29, as compared to average behavior of around .22. In Taiwan and Hong Kong, the investment ratios are .21 and .24 respectively. In Singapore, it is a remarkable .47. In the Philippines, for comparison, it is .18.[7] In a world with the perfect capital mobility used in my illustration above, these differences in investment rates would have *no* connection with savings rates: any country's higher than average savings would simply be invested abroad. Even with no international capital mobility, to translate a given difference in savings rates into a difference in output growth rates one must multiply by the return on capital (since

$$\frac{\partial}{\partial s}\left(\frac{1}{y}\frac{dy}{dt}\right) = \frac{\partial}{\partial s}\left(\frac{1}{y}\frac{\partial y}{\partial k}\frac{dk}{dt}\right) = \frac{\partial y}{\partial k},$$

from (2.2)). If the return on capital were 10 percent, then, the Korea-Philippines investment rate difference of .11 can account for a difference of .011 in output growth rates, or about one percentage point. Even this effect is only transient, since in the long run differences in savings rates are level effects only.

Now applying the same rough calculation to the Singapore-Philippines investment rate difference of .29, one can account for a difference in output growth rates of nearly three percentage points (and more, if a higher and still defensible return on capital is used), which is close to the differentials I am calling "miraculous." Indeed, Young (1992) demonstrates that output growth in Singapore since the 1960s can be accounted for *entirely* by growth in conventionally measured capital and labor inputs, with nothing left over to be attributed to technological change. But Young's point, underscored by his parallel treatment of Singapore and Hong Kong, is the exceptional character of growth in Singapore, and not that the Asian miracles in general can be attributed to capital accumulation.

---

7. All the figures cited are for 1984. The ratio for Taiwan is from the 1987 Taiwan *National Income*. The others are from the 1986 *World Development Report*.

Growth accounting methods, applied country-by-country as in Young's study, can quantify the role of investment differentials in accounting for growth rate differences. In general, these differentials leave most measured output growth to be explained by other forces. This conclusion, which seems to me so clear, remains controversial. Correlations between investment ratios and growth rates, which tend to be positive, are frequently cited but do not settle anything. If growth is driven by rapid accumulation of human capital, one needs rapid growth in physical capital just to keep up: look at equation (2.4)! It may be that by excluding physical capital from the human capital accumulation equation (2.3) or (2.5) I have ruled out some interesting possibilities: One cannot accumulate skill as a computer programmer without a computer. Perhaps physical capital will assume a more important role when the technology for accumulating human capital is better understood, but if so, it will be at best a supporting part. Let us look elsewhere.

In the framework I am using, the other possible source of growth rate differentials is differential rates of human capital accumulation, stemming from differences in societies' time-allocation decisions. But human capital takes many forms and its accumulation occurs in many ways, so there are decisions in emphasis to be made here as well. The key choice, I think, is whether to stress human capital accumulation at school, or on the job.

If one interprets (2.3) or (2.5) as describing knowledge accumulation through schooling, these equations imply that doubling the fraction in school would double the human capital growth rate, adding only another .02 to the average rate of .02. And, of course, the linearity of (2.3) probably leads to an *overstatement* of the effect of so large a change. As I remarked in the introductory section, the fast-growing Asian economies are not, in general, better schooled than some of their slow-growing neighbors. Emphasis on formal schooling, then, seems to involve the application of a modest multiplier to very slight differences in behavior, leading to the same discouraging conclusion for human capital that I arrived at in the case of physical capital.

This conclusion may seem an inappropriate inference from an oversimplified model, but I think it is in fact reinforced by thinking more seriously about the effects of schooling. Actual schooling decisions take place in a life-cycle context, with school preceding work and each individual deciding on the length of these two career phases. (This is a simplification, too, but a better one than thinking of a representative agent dividing his time in perpetuity.) Now in a steady state or balanced path of an economy in which everyone spends a fraction $1 - u$ of his working life in school, workers with schooling level $1 - u$ are retiring from the labor force at exactly the same rate as new workers with the same education level are entering. No matter what the value of u is in such a steady state, *all* of this investment is replacement investment and there is *no* increase in the average skill level of the workforce. Since (2.3) is a hypothesis about *net* investment, one cannot then identify the variable $1 - u$ with time spent in school. One is left with two choices: first, we can identify *increases* in average schooling levels with net human capital investment. Since schooling levels are increasing in virtually all societies today, this is a possibility worth developing, but it cannot be pursued within a steady state framework. This is an important and neglected respect in which neither advanced nor most backward economies can be viewed as moving along balanced growth paths.

Alternatively, we can think of a balanced path on which time spent in school is constant but the *quality* of schooling is improving as a result of increases in general knowledge. This possibility is analyzed in Stokey (1991b), from which the argument of the last paragraph is taken. In this paper, the rate of expansion of knowledge is taken to be an external effect of the time spent in school, the hypothesis that transforms a level effect into the needed growth effect. But this hypothesis does not salvage the multiplier arguments I applied above, unless one is willing to assume that increases in general knowledge accrue equally from time spent in primary schools and universities. To quantify a model like Stokey's, one would need a much sharper empirical identification of the set of activities that lead to new knowledge—to net investment in a society's human capital—than is provided by any aggregate index of total schooling time. This would be a most interesting avenue to explore but I am not prepared to do so here, so I will end this digression and move on.

Human capital accumulation also occurs at work, as we know from the fact that experienced workers and managers earn more than inexperienced ones. This aspect of human capital accumulation—on-the-job training—could also be (and has been) modeled as a time-allocation decision. Alternatively, in a multiple-good world, one could think of on-the-job accumulation—learning-by-doing—as associated with the type of process one is engaged in. That is, one might think of some activities as carrying with them a high rate of skill acquisition and others, routine or traditional ones, as associated with a low rate. If so, the mix of goods a society produces will affect its overall rate of human capital accumulation and growth.

For understanding diversity, I think this route has promise: The variation across societies, or at least those engaged in international trade, in the mix of goods produced is enormous. In this section, I have tried to motivate a focus on this source of diversity by a process of elimination: Neither physical capital accumulation nor human capital accumulation through schooling seems to have much potential, at least within the framework I have adopted. In the next section, I turn to much more direct, microeconomic evidence on the same point.

3. The Liberty Ship Miracle

In "Mechanics" (Chapter 1 of the present volume) I used a multi-good model, adapted from Krugman (1987), in which different goods were associated with different learning rates to capture the idea that the choice of which goods to produce can be viewed as an implicit choice of a human capital accumulation rate. In a world of open economies, comparative advantage—previously accumulated, good-specific human capital holdings—will determine who produces what, and the mix of goods that this process assigns to a particular economy will determine its rates of human capital growth. This kind of formulation has been taken in interesting directions by Boldrin and Scheinkman (1988) and Matsuyama (1992). It is attractive, for present purposes, because there are such wide differences in product mix across countries and because the fast-growing Asian economies have undergone such dramatic changes in the goods they produce.

But the hypothesis that different goods are associated with *permanently* different learning potentials conflicts sharply with available evidence in two respects. First, examination of growth in total factor productivity (Solow residuals) across both industries and time (as conducted, for example, by Harberger 1990) shows no decade-to-decade stability in the high productivity growth industries. Lumber and wood products can rank fourteenth in the 1950s, first in the 1960s, and disappear from the list of leaders altogether in the 1970s.[8] Second, evidence we have on learning in narrowly defined product lines invariably shows high initial learning rates, declining over time as production cumulates. These two kinds of evidence reinforce each other, and seem decisive against the formulation that Krugman proposed. These observations have led Stokey (1988) and Young (1991) to a

---

8. Harberger (1990), table 3.

very different formulation, one that is much more tightly grounded in microeconomic evidence. I will review this formulation in Section 4, but before doing so I want to reinforce the motivation with a reminder of just how impressive the evidence on the productivity effects of learning-by-doing can be.

The best evidence I know of that bears on on-the-job productivity change in a single, large-scale production process was utilized in studies by Allan D. Searle (1945) and Leonard A. Rapping (1965). Both studies used data on the production of a single type of cargo vessel—the Liberty Ship—in 14 U.S. shipyards during World War II. From December 1941 through December 1944, these yards produced a total of 2,458 Liberty Ships, all to the same standardized design. For several individual yards, Searle plotted man-hours per vessel against number of vessels completed to date in that yard on log-log paper. His results for two yards are reproduced in Figure 3.1. Average results over ten yards are given in Figure 3.2, along

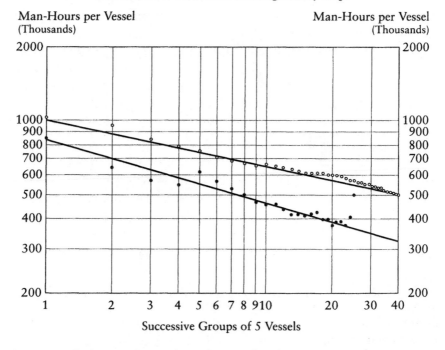

Basic Data for Two Yards Building Liberty Ships

Figure 3.1 Reductions in man-hours per vessel with increasing production, merchant shipyards

Man-Hours per Vessel
(Thousands)

Man-Hours per Vessel
(Thousands)

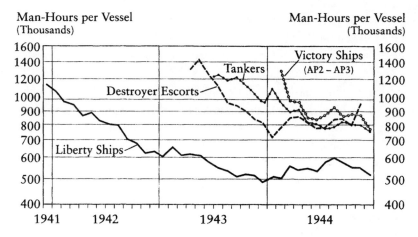

Figure 3.2 Unit man-hour requirements for selected shipbuilding programs, vessels delivered December 1941–December 1944. *Source:* U.S. Department of Labor, Bureau of Labor Statistics

with results for three other vessel types. For Liberty Ships, "the reduction in manhours per ship with each doubling of cumulative output ranged from 12 to 24 percent."[9]

Stimulated in part by Kenneth Arrow's (1962) theoretical suggestion that learning-by-doing might serve as the key factor in growth for an economy as a whole, Rapping incorporated Searle's and other evidence within a neoclassical production framework. He pooled the data for all yards and estimated a Cobb-Douglas production function, controlling for changes in capital per yard, with cumulated yard (not industry) production as an added regressor. He obtained estimates of the learning effect, comparable to Searle's, ranging from 11 to 29 percent. He also showed that the inclusion of calendar time added nothing (the trend came out slightly negative!) to these results.

I do not think there is anything unique to shipbuilding in the findings that Searle and Rapping obtained. The Boston Consulting Group (1968) has obtained fairly clean learning curves, with slopes similar to those estimated by Searle and Rapping, for a variety of industries, and other researchers have done so as well. What *is* unique about the Liberty Ship data is that the ships were built according to exactly the same blueprints over a period of several years and that data were available yard by yard. Figure 3.2, which

---

9. Searle (1945), p. 1144.

gives Searle's learning curve for the industry as a whole, is not nearly as sharp as the curves in Figure 3.1 for individual yards, presumably because industry expansion is a mix of increased production by existing yards and the entry of new, inexperienced yards. Production data even from narrowly defined industries mask continual model and other product mix changes over time, which makes it difficult to use them to identify even strong learning effects. What is exceptional about the Liberty Ship evidence, I think, is the cleanness of the experiment, not the behavior it documents so beautifully.

Quantitatively, these results are interesting to an economist looking for possible sources of miracles. For the three-year period covered by Rapping's study, industry output per man-hour increased at a 40 percent annual rate! There is also considerable ambiguity about what this evidence means. Is it the individual worker who is doing the learning? The managers? The organization as a whole? Are the skills being learned specific to the production process on which the learning takes place, or are they more general? Does learning accrue solely to the individual worker, manager, or organization that does the producing, or is some of it readily appropriable by outside observers? These are questions that the theory of growth needs to address, but I will pass over them here.

A more urgent question, I think, is whether the kind of behavior that Rapping and Searle documented, for one product line for one brief period, can be linked to productivity growth for an entire economy over periods of thirty or forty years. This is the topic of the next section.

4. Learning Models: Technology

In order to examine the possible connection between evidence of learning on individual product lines and productivity growth in an economy as a whole, consider the labor-only technology:

$$(4.1) \quad x(t) = kn(t)z(t)^{\alpha},$$

where $x(t)$ is the rate of production of a good, k is a productivity parameter that depends on the units in which labor input and output are measured, $n(t)$ is employment, and $z(t)$ represents cumulative experience in the production of this good. Cumulative experience is in turn defined by the differential equation:

(4.2) $\quad \dfrac{dz(t)}{dt} = n(t)z(t)^{\alpha},$

and the initial value $z(t_0)$, assumed to be greater than or equal to one, of the experience variable on the date t_0 when production was begun. The general solution to (4.2) is

(4.3) $\quad z(t) = \left[(z(t_0))^{1-\alpha} + (1 - \alpha) \displaystyle\int_{t_0}^{t} n(u)\, du \right]^{1/1-\alpha}.$

The implications of this model for the dynamics of production of a single good are familiar enough. Suppose, to take the simplest case, that employment is constant at $\bar{n}$ over time. Then (4.1) and (4.3) imply that production follows

$$x(t) = k\bar{n} \left[z(t_0)^{1-\alpha} + (1 - \alpha)\bar{n}(t - t_0) \right]^{\alpha/1-\alpha}.$$

Production grows without bound, and the rate of productivity growth declines monotonically from $\alpha\bar{n}(z(t_0))^{\alpha-1}$ to zero. For any initial productivity level $z(t_0) \geq 1$ and any employment level (or path) productivity at date t is an increasing function of the learning rate α.

Notice that the technology (4.2) implies a scale effect: a link between the level of employment and the rate of growth of productivity. This carries the unwelcome implication that a country like India should have an enormous growth advantage over a small country like Singapore. This is a feature of any learning-by-doing theory, but I agree with Matsuyama (1992) that if one is thinking about an entire economy or sizable sector of an economy, it is a nuisance implication that we want to dispose of.[10] Matsuyama proposes thinking of a population as containing a fixed fraction of entrepreneurs, and of a technology that requires that each enterprise be headed by one of them. Then doubling the population means doubling the number of enterprises that are subject to the learning technology, keeping the size of each fixed, and has no growth effects. Insofar as learning effects are partly external to the firm, as I think they are, this device doesn't quite work, and one needs to think of some other limitation on scale—city size, say. I will

---

10. Backus, Kehoe, and Kehoe (1992) is an empirical examination of scale effects on growth rates, formulated in a variety of ways. They find some evidence of such effects in manufacturing, and none for economies as a whole.

simply ignore these scale economies in what follows, assuming that some explanation along the lines of Matsuyama's will be discovered to rationalize this neglect.

With the technology (4.1)–(4.3), one can obviously obtain miraculous rates of productivity growth by shifting a large amount of labor onto a single, new product line. Provided that $\bar{n}(t - t_0)$ is large relative to initial experience (which is the way most people interpret statistical learning curves), the rate of productivity growth t years after production is initiated is approximately $\alpha/((1 - \alpha)t)$. Using the value $\alpha = 0.2$ estimated by Rapping and Searle, productivity growth one year after a product is introduced is $\alpha/(1 - \alpha) = 0.25$. After two years, the growth rate is reduced by half to 0.125, and so on. A growth miracle sustained for a period of decades thus must involve the continual introduction of new goods, not merely continued learning on a fixed set of goods. Even if new goods are introduced, a shift of workers from old goods with low learning rates to new goods with high rates involves an initial drop in productivity: people are better at familiar activities than they are at novel ones. It is not even clear how these factors balance out.

To pursue this question, I follow Stokey (1988) and consider an economy in which a variety of goods, indexed by s, is produced, where a higher index s means a better good. In Stokey (1988), and in different ways in Young (1991) and Grossman and Helpman (1991b), specific assumptions on consumer preferences or the technology give a precise meaning to the sense in which one good is better than another. For my immediate objectives, it will be adequate to consider a small, open economy and to use an assumed schedule $p(s, t) = e^{\mu s}$ of world prices to summarize the quality of goods: a better good means a good with a higher price on world markets. Assume that the economy progresses by introducing better-quality (higher s) goods into production over time, and let $S(t)$ be the index of the good that is first produced at date t. (I will also use $\tau(s)$, where τ is the inverse function of the increasing function S, to denote the date on which good s is first produced.) Then if $x(s, t)$ is production of good s at date t, the value of the economy's total production is

$$(4.4) \quad y(t) = \int_0^{S(t)} e^{\mu s} x(s, t) \, ds.$$

Let $n(s, t)$ be employment on good s at t, and $z(s, t)$ be cumulated experience. Then if learning proceeds independently, good by good, (4.1) and (4.3) imply

$$(4.5) \quad x(s,t) = kn(s,t) \left[(z(s, \tau(s)))^{1-\alpha} + (1-\alpha) \int_{\tau(s)}^{t} n(s,u) \, du \right]^{\alpha/1-\alpha}.$$

Equations (4.4) and (4.5) together describe the implications for total production of a given way of allocating labor across product lines through time.

Consider the following specific labor allocation. Let the rate of new product introduction be a constant λ, so that $S(t) = \lambda t$ and $\tau(s) = s/\lambda$. Let φ be a density function with cdf Φ, and suppose that for all $s \in (0, \lambda t]$, $n(s, t) = \varphi(t - s/\lambda)$ (that $\varphi(t - s/\lambda)$ workers are assigned to produce the goods of age $t - s/\lambda$) and that the remaining $1 - \Phi(t)$ workers produce a good 0 on which no learning occurs. Assume that initial productivity is the same for all goods, at the level $z(s/\lambda, s) = \xi \geq 1$. Under these assumptions, (4.4) and (4.5) imply that the value of total production is

$$(4.6) \quad y(t) = 1 - \Phi(t) + k\lambda e^{\mu\lambda t} \int_{0}^{t} e^{-\mu\lambda u} \varphi(u)[\xi^{1-\alpha}$$

$$+ (1-\alpha)\Phi(u)]^{\alpha/1-\alpha} \, du.$$

The asymptotic growth rate for this economy is evidently $\mu\lambda$. This rate does not depend either on the learning parameter α or on the distribution φ of the workforce over goods of different vintages. Changes in either of these factors are simply level effects. To obtain sustained growth at all in this framework, it is necessary to assume that better goods become producible at some exogenously given rate λ, which then along with the quality gradient μ dictates the long-run growth rate of the system, independent of learning behavior.

Though the production of new goods is continuously initiated in this example, the rate at which this occurs through time is fixed. In Stokey (1988) this rate is made endogenous through the assumption that the experience accumulated in producing good s reduces the cost of producing good $s' > s$. (It may reduce the cost of producing $s' < s$, too, but the spillover effect is assumed to be loaded in the direction of improving productivity on the more advanced good.) As a specific instance of Stokey's hypothesis, very close to that proposed by Young (1991), let us modify the last example by postulating that the initial value $z(s, \tau(s))$ in the learning curve (4.3) depends on the experience that has been accumulated on less advanced goods. Suppose that an economy at some fixed date t has experience summarized by $z(s, t)$ for $s < S(t)$, but has yet to produce any good with index above $S(t)$. Assume that if production of a good $s \geq S(t)$ is initiated at t (if $\tau(s) = t$), then its initial z-value is proportional to an average of the economy's experience on previously produced goods:

$$(4.7) \quad z(s, \tau(s)) = \theta\delta \int_0^s e^{-\delta(s-u)} z(u, \tau(s)) \, du.$$

Equation (4.7) expresses the initial productivity on good s as an average of experience on lower-quality goods. Equivalently, we can express the initial productivity on the good introduced at t, good $S(t)$, as an average of experience on goods introduced earlier:

$$(4.8) \quad z(S(t), t) = \theta\delta \int_0^t e^{-\delta[S(t)-S(t-v)]} z(S(t-v), t) S'(t-v) \, dv,$$

integrating over ages v instead of goods s.

Assume, next, that production on a new good is initiated whenever the expressions (4.7) and (4.8) reach a trigger value $\xi \geq 1$, taken as a given constant. Under this assumption, the left side of (4.8) is replaced with this constant ξ, implying that the function $S(t)$ whose derivative is the rate at which new goods are introduced must satisfy

$$(4.9) \quad \xi = \theta\delta \int_0^t e^{-\delta[S(t)-S(t-v)]} z(S(t-v), t) S'(t-v) \, dv.$$

As in the previous example, we continue to assume that the allocation of employment at any date is described by a density φ and cdf Φ, where $\Phi(u)$ is the fraction of people employed producing goods that were introduced less than u years earlier. In the present case, each good has the initial productivity level ξ, so inserting the solution (4.3) for $z(S(t-v), t)$ with this initial value into (4.9) yields a single equation in the function $S(t)$. For large values of t, the solution $S(t)$ to this equation will behave like $S(t) = \lambda t$, where the constant λ satisfies

$$(4.10) \quad \xi = \theta\delta\lambda \int_0^\infty e^{-\delta\lambda v} [\xi^{1-\alpha} + (1-\alpha)\Phi(v)]^{1/1-\alpha} \, dv.$$

The right side of (4.10) is just an average of the positive, increasing function $\theta[\xi^{1-\alpha} + (1-\alpha)\Phi(v)]^{1/(1-\alpha)}$, taken with respect to an exponential distribution with parameter $\delta\lambda$. Hence it is a positive, decreasing function of $\delta\lambda$, tending toward the value $\theta\xi$ as $\delta\lambda \to \infty$ and toward the value $\theta[\xi^{1-\alpha} + 1 - \alpha]^{1/(1-\alpha)}$ as $\delta\lambda \to 0$. (If the latter expression is less than ξ at $\lambda = 0$, then the economy does not accumulate relevant experience fast enough to introduce new goods in the steady state.) For fixed $\delta\lambda$, the right side of (4.10) is an increasing function of θ, α, and k, and it also increases as the distribution of labor $\varphi(v)$ becomes more concentrated on lower values of v (on newer goods). Hence if a positive solution λ exists, it is inversely proportional to the decay rate of spillover experience, an increasing function of the spillover parameter θ and the learning rate α, and increases as employment is more heavily concentrated on goods that are closer to the economy's production frontier.

The formula (4.6) for the value of total production continues to hold in this second example, and the economy's long-run growth rate is $\lambda\mu$, as before. But under this second, spillover, technology, economies that distribute workers across goods of different ages in different ways will grow at different rates. Of course, this conclusion is not based purely on technological considerations: The value ξ of initial productivity that is assumed to trigger the initiation of production of a new good is of central importance, and needs an economic rationale.

One might view the spillover technologies of Stokey and Young as reconciling the Krugman hypothesis of a manufacturing sector with a constant rate of productivity growth, based on learning, with the fact that learning rates on individual production processes decline over time to zero. For example, one could interpret either of the examples in this section as describing a sector of an economy with a positive asymptotic rate of productivity growth. On this view, the contribution of Stokey and Young is to break down an assumed sectoral learning rate into its components, α, θ, and δ (in my notation), and to relate this rate to the way workers are distributed over goods of different vintages.

This interpretation seems fine to me as long as one is discussing the consequences of a *given* workforce distribution, but if one has in mind applying the theory of comparative advantage to *determining* the way workers in each country are allocated to the production of different goods, it ceases to make sense. In Krugman's theory (as in Section 5 of "Mechanics," Chapter 1) it is a sector *as a whole* that either has or does not have a comparative advantage. In a sectoral interpretation of Stokey and Young's theories, each sector consists of many goods and comparative advantage must be determined good by good. No country can be expected to have a comparative advantage in manufacturing in general, or even in crude aggregates like Chemicals and Allied Products or Printing and Publishing. Comparative advantage will be associated with categories, like acetylene or paperback editions of English poetry, that are invisible even in the finest industrial statistics. As we shall see in the next section, this feature—besides being a step toward greater realism—leads to an entirely different view of trade and growth than is implied by the Krugman technology, the superficial similarity of the two notwithstanding.

The main attraction of a learning spillover technology such as that described in the second example of this section is that it offers the potential of accounting for the great differences in productivity growth rates that are observed among low- and middle-income economies. Of course, little is known about the crucial spillover parameters δ and θ—on which the learning curve evidence described in Section 3 provides no information—but surely an essential first step is to find a formulation that is capable, under *some* parameter values, of generating the behavior we are trying to explain.

5. Learning and Market Equilibrium

The objective of the last section was to set down on paper a *technology* that is consistent with a growth miracle, which is to say, consistent with wide differences in productivity growth among similarly endowed economies. This has been done, following Stokey and Young, in a way that I think is consistent with the main features of the East Asian miracles, all of which have involved sustained movement of the workforce from less to more sophisticated products. A fast-growing economy or sector under this technology is one that succeeds in concentrating its workforce on goods that are near its own quality frontier, and thus in accumulating human capital rapidly through the high learning rates associated with new activities and through the spillover of this experience to the production of still newer goods. These hypotheses are consistent with commonly known facts, and have testable implications for many more. As yet, however, I have said nothing about the *economics* that determine the mix of production activities in which an economy or sector of an economy in fact engages.

The papers of Stokey (1988, 1991a) and Young (1991) develop models of market equilibrium with learning technologies under the assumption that the effects of learning are external—that all human capital is a public good. In this case, labor is simply allocated to the use with the highest current return, independent of learning rates. With the constant returns technology these authors assume, the competitive equilibrium is Ricardian and straightforward to calculate. This is the simplest case, so I will begin with it too.

In such a setting, Stokey (1991a) studies north-south trade, where "north" means relatively well-endowed with human capital. Under specific assumptions about consumer preferences for goods of different qualities, she obtains a unique world equilibrium in which the south produces an interval of low-quality goods, the north produces an interval of high-quality goods, and there is an intermediate range of goods that are produced in neither place. With free trade (as opposed to autarchy) learning-by-doing is depressed in the poor country, which now imports high-quality goods from the rich country rather than attempting to produce them at home. One can see that with dynamics as assumed in Stokey (1988), both countries will enjoy growth but the poor country will remain forever poorer.

A similar equilibrium is characterized in Young (1991), using a parameterization of preferences and the learning technology that permits the explicit calculation of the north-south equilibrium, including a full description of the equilibrium dynamics. There are many possible equilibrium evolutions of his north-south system, depending on the populations of the two regions and on their relative human capital holdings at the time trade is initiated. As in Stokey's (1991a) analysis, the advanced country produces high-quality goods and the poor country produces low-quality goods. Free trade slows learning and growth in the poor country and speeds it in the rich one. In Young's framework, there are equilibria in which the poor catch up to the rich, but only when their larger population lets them enjoy greater scale economies. Young does not emphasize this possibility and, as I have said earlier, I do not wish to either.

The equilibria of Stokey and Young, then, involve sustained growth of both rich and poor, at possibly different rates, and the continuous shifting of production of goods introduced in the north to the lower-wage south. Initial comparative advantage is not permanent, as in Krugman's formulation, since a rich country's experience in producing any given good will eventually be offset by the fact that the good can be produced more cheaply in a less-experienced but lower-wage environment. Yet there are no growth miracles in these theories. Though these equilibria could readily be modified to include cross-country external effects, and hence catching up (for reasons unrelated to economies of scale), as I have done with the Solow model, there would be nothing one would wish to call miraculous about this process.

In the models of Stokey and Young, all human capital benefits are assumed to be external. The learning and growth that occur are always, in a sense, accidental. Other models contain aspects of privately held knowledge, so that individual agents face the capital-theoretic problem of balancing current returns against the future benefits of learning of some kind. Matsuyama (1991) studies a two-sector system in which workers compare the present value of earnings in a traditional sector to the value of earnings in a manufacturing sector in which production is subject to external increasing returns. Young (1993) augments learning with a research activity that yields patentable new products. Grossman and Helpman (1991a and b) postulate two R&D activities—innovation, done only in advanced economies, and imitation, done by poor economies too—with lags that let the discoverer or the successful low-cost imitator enjoy a period of super-normal profits in a Bertrand-type equilibrium. Whether one calls the decision problems that arise in these analyses occupational choice, or research and development, or learning, all involve a decision on the allocation of time-at-work that involves balancing current returns against the benefits of increased future earnings, and all have a similar capital-theoretic structure.

Dropping the assumption that learning has external effects only is certainly a step toward realism, one that raises many interesting theoretical possibilities yet to be explored. It is thus only conjecture, but I would guess that the main features of the equilibria that have been worked out by Stokey and Young will turn out to stand up very well under different assumptions about the ownership, if I can use that term, of human capital. A learning spillover technology gives those who operate near the current goods frontier a definite advantage in moving beyond it. This advantage is decisive when decisions are taken myopically; I do not see why it should disappear when some of the returns from doing so are internalized and workers and firms look to the future in their individual decision problems.

In short, available general equilibrium models of north-south trade do not predict miraculous economic growth for the poor countries taken as a group, nor do I see any reason to expect that the equilibria of more elaborate theories will have this feature. This is a disappointment, perhaps, but it does not seem to me to be a deficiency of these models. These are theories designed to capture the main interactions between the advanced economies taken as a group and the backward economies as a whole, within a two-country world equilibrium framework. Since it is a fact that the poor are either not gaining on the rich or are gaining only very slowly, one wants a theory that does not predict otherwise.

A successful theory of economic miracles should, I think, offer the *possibility* of rapid growth episodes, but should not imply their occurrence as a simple consequence of relative backwardness. It should be as consistent with the Philippine experience as with the Korean. For the purpose of exploring these possibilities, the conventions of small, open-economy trade theory are more suitable (as well as simpler to apply) than those of the theory of a closed, two-country system. If the technology available to individual agents facing world prices has constant returns, then anything is possible. Some allocations will yield high external benefits and growth in production and wages; others will not. There will be a large number of possibilities, with individual agents in equilibrium indifferent between courses of action that have very different aggregative consequences. Theoretically, one can shut off some of these possibilities by introducing diminishing returns in the right places, but I am not sure that these multiplicities should be viewed as theoretical defects, to be patched up. If our objective is to understand a world in which similarly situated economies follow very different paths, these theoretical features are advantageous. A constant returns (at the level of individual producing units) learning spillover technology is equally consistent with fast and slow growth. If our task is to understand diversity, this is an essential feature, not a deficiency.

A second attraction of the learning spillover technology is that it is consistent with the strong connection we observe between rapid productivity growth and trade or openness. Consider two small economies facing the same world prices and similarly endowed, like Korea and the Philippines in 1960. Suppose that Korea somehow shifts its workforce onto the production of goods not formerly produced there, and continues to do so, while the Philippines continues to produce its traditional goods. Then according to the learning spillover theory, Korean production will grow more rapidly. But in 1960, Korean and Philippine incomes were about the same, so the mix of goods their consumers demanded was about the same. For this scenario to be possible, Korea needed to open up a large difference between the mix of goods produced and the mix consumed, a difference that could widen over time. Thus a large volume of trade is essential to a learning-based growth episode.

One can use the same reasoning to see why import-substitution policies fail, despite what can initially appear to be success in stimulating growth. Consider an economy that exports, say, agricultural products and imports most manufactured goods. If this economy shifts toward autarchy through tariff and other barriers, its workforce will shift to formerly imported goods and rapid learning will occur. But this is a one-time stimulus to productivity, and thereafter the mix of goods produced in this closed system can change only slowly, as the consumption mix changes. Note that this argument has to do only with the pace of *change* in an economy's production mix and does not involve scale, though it can obviously be reinforced by scale economies.

I do not intend these conjectures about the implications of a learning spillover technology for small countries facing given world prices to be a substitute for the actual construction of such a theory. To do this, one would need to take a realistic position on these issues touched on in my discussion of Rapping's and Searle's evidence. What is the nature of the human capital accumulation decision problems faced by workers, capitalists, and managers? What are the external consequences of the decisions they make? The papers cited here consider a variety of possible assumptions on these economic issues, but it must be said that little is known, and without such knowledge there is little we can say about the way policies that affect incentives can be expected to influence economic growth.

6. Conclusions

I began by asking what current economic theory has to say about the growth miracles of East Asia. The recent literature on which I have drawn to answer this question is fragmentary, and my survey of it more fragmentary still. Even so, the image of the growth process and the role of these remarkable economies within this process that emerges is, I think, surprisingly sharp, certainly compared to what could have been said on this subject ten years ago. I will conclude by summarizing it.

The main engine of growth is the accumulation of human capital—of knowledge—and the main source of differences in living standards among nations is differences in human capital. Physical capital accumulation plays an essential but decidedly subsidiary role. Human capital accumulation takes place in schools, in research organizations, and in the course of producing goods and engaging in trade. Little is known about the relative importance of these different models of accumulation, but for understanding periods of very rapid growth in a single economy, learning on the job seems to be by far the most central. For such learning to occur on a sustained basis, it is necessary that workers and managers continue to take on tasks that are new to them, that they continue to move up what Grossman and Helpman call the "quality ladder." For this to be done on a large scale, the economy must be a large-scale exporter.

This picture has the virtue of being consistent with the recent experience of both the Philippines and Korea. It would be equally consistent with post-1960 history with the roles of these two economies switched. It is a picture that is consistent with any individual small economy following the East Asian example, producing a very different mix of goods from the mix it consumes. It does not appear to be consistent with the Third World as a whole beginning to grow at East Asian rates: There is a zero-sum aspect, with inevitable mercantilist overtones, to productivity growth fueled by learning-by-doing.

Can these two paragraphs be viewed as a summary of things that are *known* about economic growth? After all, they are simply a sketch of some of the properties of mathematical models, purely fictional worlds, that certain economists have invented. How does one acquire knowledge about reality by working in one's office with pen and paper? There is more to it, of course: Some of the numbers I have cited are products of decades-long research projects, and all of the models I have reviewed have sharp implications that could be, and have not been, compared to observation. Even so, I think this inventive, model-building process we are engaged in is an essential one, and I cannot imagine how we could possibly organize and make use of the mass of data available to us without it. If we understand the process of economic growth—or of anything else—we ought to be capable of demonstrating this knowledge by *creating* it in these pen-and-paper (and computer-equipped) laboratories of ours. If we know what an economic miracle is, we ought to be able to *make* one.

4

SOME MACROECONOMICS
FOR THE TWENTY-FIRST CENTURY

1. Introduction

Economic growth in the second half of the twentieth century was so different from any earlier period in history that anyone educated in the 1950s has
been led to a new view of the world economy simply by watching events
unfold. During the 30-year period 1960–1990, production in the world as
a whole—Communists, former colonies, *everyone*—grew at 4 percent per
year, while world population grew at 2 percent per year. The real income
of an average person has more than doubled since World War II and the
end of the European colonial age.

This remarkable growth in income per person has taken place very un-
evenly: The average figure combines the experiences of economies that have
stagnated at pre-industrial income levels with those of other economies,
equally poor in 1950, that have industrialized at unprecedented rates. The
stakes in understanding the forces that determine which of these paths a
given economy will follow are thus very high, and these high stakes have
attracted a great deal of interesting research in recent years. Theorists have
proposed a variety of explicit models designed to capture aspects of the
diffusion of the industrial revolution that is now taking place, and to see
where we may be headed.

In this chapter I will present a numerical simulation of one such model, a
simplified version of the Tamura (1996) model of world income dynamics,
based on technology diffusion. The model makes predictions for trends in
average world income growth that accord well with observation. It makes
predictions about the evolution of the relative income distribution that
fit the history documented in Pritchett (1997). I will apply the model to
the interpretation of the 1960–1990 period, which has been the subject
of intense econometric examination based on the Penn World Table data
set, described in Summers and Heston (1991). I will also use the model to

forecast the course of world income growth and income inequality over the century to come.

2. A Model of Growth

I consider real production per capita, in a world of many countries evolving through time. For modeling simplicity, take these countries to have equal populations. Think of all of these economies at some initial date, prior to the onset of the industrial revolution. Just to be specific, I will take this date to be 1800. Prior to this date, I assume, no economy has enjoyed any growth in per capita income—in living standards—and all have the same constant income level. I will take this pre-industrial income level to be $600 in 1985 U.S. dollars, which is about the income level in the poorest countries in the world today and is consistent with what we know about living standards around the world prior to the industrial revolution. We begin, then, with an image of the world economy of 1800 as consisting of a number of very poor, stagnant economies, equal in population and in income.

Now imagine all of these economies lined up in a row, each behind the kind of mechanical starting gate used at the race track. In the race to industrialize that I am about to describe, though, the gates do not open all at once, the way they do at the track. Instead, at any date t a few of the gates that have not yet opened are selected by some random device. When the bell rings, these gates open and some of the economies that had been stagnant are released and begin to grow. The rest must wait their chances until the next date, $t + 1$. In any year after 1800, then, the world economy consists of those countries that have not begun to grow, stagnating at the $600 income level, and those countries that began to grow at some date in the past and have been growing ever since.

Figure 4.1 shows the income paths for four of these economies. The exact construction of the figure is based on two assumptions. (The Appendix at the end of this chapter provides an exact statement of the model.) The first assumption is that the first economy to begin to industrialize—think of the United Kingdom, where the industrial revolution began—simply grew at the constant rate α from 1800 on. I chose the value $\alpha = .02$ which, as one can see from the top curve on the figure, implies a per capita income for the United Kingdom of $33,000 (in 1985 U.S. dollars) by the year 2000. There is not much economics in the model, I agree, but we can go back to Solow

(1956) and to the many subsequent contributions to the theory of growth for an understanding of the conditions under which per capita income in a country will grow at a constant rate. In any case, it is an empirically decent description of what actually happened.

So much for the leading economy. The second assumption that underlies Figure 4.1 is that an economy that begins to grow at any date after 1800 grows at a rate equal to $\alpha = .02$, the growth rate of the leader, *plus* a term that is proportional to the percentage income gap between itself and the leader. The later a country starts to grow, the larger is this initial income gap, so a later start implies faster initial growth. But a country growing faster than the leader closes the income gap, which by my assumption reduces its growth rate toward .02. Thus, a late entrant to the industrial revolution will eventually have essentially the same income level as the leader, but will never surpass the leader's level. One can see this catch-up behavior in the other three curves of Figure 4.1, which correspond to economies that began growth in 1850, 1900, and 1950.

To quantify the speed at which this catching up takes place, we need to put a value on the constant of proportionality β that relates the income

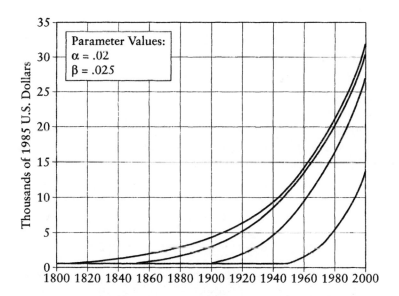

Figure 4.1 Income paths, selected economies

gap between two countries to their relative growth rates. Consider, for example, the country that begins growth in 1850. In 1850, this country has the pre-industrial income of $600, whereas the leader has been growing from this base for 50 years at the constant rate $\alpha = .02$. Thus, the leader's income in 1850 is $e^{(.02)50} = e$ times the pre-industrial level. The *percentage* gap is the natural logarithm of this multiple, ln e, which equals 1. I set the parameter β equal to .025, which amounts to assuming that the new entrant in 1850 grows initially at the rate $\alpha + \beta = .02 + .025 = .045$. Every 50 years, this late-entrant bonus increases by another .025, so that the entrant in 1900 begins growth at $\alpha + (2\beta) = .07$, the 1950 entrant begins at $\alpha + (3\beta) = .095$, and so on. These are the assumptions underlying Figure 4.1: They capture the well-known facts that the late entrants have much higher initial growth rates than the early entrants but do not surpass their income levels.

At any date from 1800 on, the world described by the model that generates Figure 4.1 is made up of economies that began to grow in 1801, those that began in 1802, and so on into the future—for there are still pre-industrial economies in the world today. The world economy is a kind of weighted average of the economies shown in Figure 4.1. To predict the course of the world economy, we need to know these weights, to know how many economies fall into each of these income categories.

Initially I tried a constant hazard rate model of starting times. That is, I assumed that *if* a country has not begun to develop by date t, the probability that it starts to grow at that date—its "hazard rate"—is some value λ that is independent of t. This model failed to fit the facts that the industrial revolution spread very slowly at first, requiring a small value of λ for the nineteenth century, and has diffused rapidly in the postwar period, requiring a high λ for the late twentieth century. For this reason, I assumed a variable hazard rate, beginning at the level $\lambda_m = .001$ in 1800, and gradually evolving upward toward a maximum value of $\lambda_M = .03$.

To describe the transition of λ from .001 to .03, I used the model of the diffusion of the industrial revolution proposed by Tamura (1996). In Tamura's model, an economy departs a stagnant equilibrium and begins to grow when the world stock of knowledge attains a critical level. Assuming that these critical levels differ across the economies that have not yet begun to grow, the model implies a distribution of starting dates. Specifically, I assumed that the hazard rate $\lambda(t)$ applying to an economy that has not yet begun to grow is a weighted average of the two hazard rates λ_m and

λ_M, where the weight that applies to the high hazard rate λ_M is assumed to be an increasing function of the average *level* of income in the world at that date. In 1800, when all economies have an income level of $600, this weight is zero and the hazard rate is .001. As average income in the world grows, the weight on λ_M increases toward one. I gave the formula a little extra flexibility by leaving a parameter δ governing the effect of world income on the hazard rate free to be determined. (Again, see the Appendix for details.)

With this information, I constructed Figure 4.2, a plot of the fraction of economies that have begun to develop against time. This curve describes the *un*conditional probabilities, built up in the usual way from the model of hazard rates—conditional probabilities—described in the last paragraph. Note that Figure 4.2 cannot be drawn without the information obtained from the construction of Figure 4.1. Under the Tamura (1996) model, the probability that a stagnant economy begins to industrialize depends on the level of world income, which in turn depends on the past experience of the growing economies.

The shape of the cumulative distribution function that is plotted in Figure 4.2 captures the idea that the industrial revolution diffused slowly in

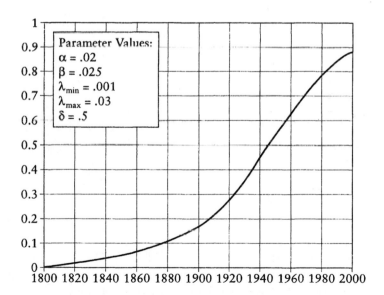

Figure 4.2 Fraction of economies growing, by year

the nineteenth century and then accelerated dramatically through much of the twentieth century. Toward the end of the latter century the diffusion slows, but only because there are so few people left in stagnant, pre-industrial economies. According to the figure, almost 90 percent of the world is now growing.

Everything is now in place to calculate the past, present, and future of this world economy. Figure 4.1 displays the growth of economies that differ by the dates at which they began to industrialize. Figure 4.2 describes the distribution of economies over different dates for the onset of industrialization. Figure 4.3 combines this information to display two time series. One is the rate of growth of average world production. The other is a particular measure of the degree of inequality in the world economy: the standard deviation of the logarithm of income levels at each date. (See equation (6) in the Appendix.) Both series are extended through the present century, to 2100.

According to Figure 4.3, the growth rate of world production per person peaked out around 1970, at something like 3.3 percent, and can be expected to decline thereafter. From the underlying theory, we know that

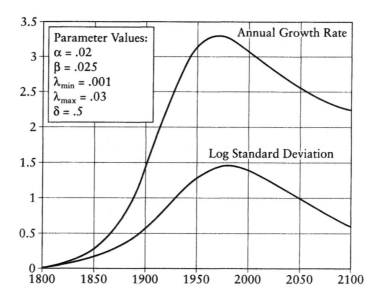

Figure 4.3 World growth rate and income variability

if the figure were extended past 2100, it would approach 2 percent, the assumed growth rate of the leading economies and hence the asymptotic growth rate of all economies. The log standard deviation of incomes, the measure of inequality I am using, begins at zero, reflecting the assumption that all economies were at the common, constant income level of $600 before 1800. This inequality measure rose at an increasing rate until well into the twentieth century, and peaked sometime in the 1970s. It, too, is now declining, and according to the theory it will ultimately return to zero.

This is not the place for a detailed discussion of the evidence that bears on the parameter values I have used in this simulation, but I would like to say a few words about accuracy. The value of $600 in 1985 U.S. dollars is about right (plus or minus $200) for traditional agricultural societies, contemporary and ancient. The growth rate $\alpha = .02$ was chosen to get the per capita income levels of the leading economies about right for 1990, given the $600 level assumed for 1800. But the per capita income growth in the leading economies is more like .015 in the postwar period, and even slower than that since 1970. This leads to an overstatement (.033) of peak world growth, and probably a growing overstatement of growth in the coming century. These deficiencies are surely correctable with four free parameters, but diminishing returns set in quickly in calibrating a model as mechanical as this one.

The model that generates these figures is a model of spillovers, in two ways. The probability that a pre-industrial economy begins to grow is assumed to depend on the level of production in the rest of the world. Once an economy begins to grow, its income growth rate is assumed to depend on its income level *relative to* incomes in the leading economies. Tamura (1996) puts a human capital externality interpretation on these spillovers: the idea that knowledge produced anywhere benefits producers everywhere. Other interpretations have been proposed and are being actively pursued in current research. One approach is to put a political interpretation on spillovers: Governments in the unsuccessful economies can adopt the institutions and policies of the successful ones, removing what Parente and Prescott (1994) call "barriers to growth." A third approach emphasizes diminishing returns and the flow of resources: High wages in the successful economies lead to capital flows to the unsuccessful economies, increasing their income levels.

Gaining a quantitative understanding of all of these forces for diffusion—and, as Parente and Prescott (1994) would stress, the forces that oppose them—is the central question of the theory of economic growth and development. My own emphasis would agree with Tamura's (1996), but there is no reason to pursue this interesting, unresolved debate here. All three sources of diffusion are surely present, important, and complementary. For the purposes of this chapter, there is no need to know their relative strengths.

3. Discussion

The behavior of the model described in the last section is consistent with most of what we know about the behavior of per capita incomes in the last two centuries. Per capita income growth, beginning in one economy, diffuses gradually to other economies. As this occurs, average income growth rises from zero to higher and higher levels. Eventually, the rapid, catch-up growth of the late entrants leads to world average income growth exceeding the growth rate of the leading economies. All of these events have already occurred, though the last emerged only since World War II.[1]

The long phase of increasing income inequality predicted by the model has also occurred. This is the point of Pritchett (1997) and is documented in many other sources. In the model, this phase comes to an end smoothly, so there is a phase in which inequality is neither growing nor shrinking. As I have calibrated the model, the years 1960–1990 make up such a phase. The model is thus consistent as well with the fact that the question of whether inequality is shrinking, or whether convergence is occurring, can be a subtle statistical question if the answer is sought in a data set covering only a few decades.

Some other phenomena that have been remarked on in the empirical literature based on the Penn World Tables also are present in the world of Figures 4.1–4.3. For example, the model fits the fact that in the postwar period growth rates vary much less among the advanced economies than

---

1. In the model, world average annual growth exceeds 2 percent before 1920. In general, the model assigns too much economic development, relative to what actually happened, to the interwar period and too little to the postwar period. Since the model has neither wars nor depressions, perhaps this is not surprising.

among the poor and middle-income economies. It presupposes the existence of an ever-growing "convergence club": a set of rich economies within which income inequality is falling, even in a world in which overall inequality is rising or not changing very much. It can be interpreted as implying a focus on *conditional* convergence, since conditional on both having left the stagnation state, any two economies are getting closer to each other. But of course, the much more interesting implication of the model is that convergence is *unconditional* as well.

An observer of the 1960–1990 time series generated by the model might conclude from the approximate constancy of the log standard deviation of income over this period that he was observing 30 consecutive drawings from an unchanging distribution of relative incomes, even though the position of individuals within the distribution was changing. This is the way Jones (1997b), Quah (1997), and Chari, Kehoe, and McGrattan (1996) viewed observations from the Penn World Table. But we obviously cannot interpret income data over the last century and a half in this way, or we would predict a relative income variance for 1850 that is equal to today's, and thus much higher than the variance in the data reviewed by Pritchett (1997). I think Jones (1997b) makes exactly the same mistake when he runs his Markov model forward and obtains the prediction that no variance reduction can be expected in future decades.

The model underlying Figures 4.1–4.3 is mechanical, without much in the way of explicit economics. It lacks an explicit description of the preferences, technology, and market arrangements that give rise to the implied behavior. Its parameters are not (I hope!) invariant under changes in policy. It entirely omits factors, like capital flows and the demographic transition, that continue to play essential roles in the diffusion of the industrial revolution. It treats important unpredictable forces as though they were deterministic, and other effects that might be predicted as though they were random draws. The model does not address, or attempt to address, many of the central questions of the industrial revolution: why it began in England, why it began in the eighteenth century, why it spread first to other European economies, or why it diffused so slowly for so long.

But for all these deficiencies, it is undeniably an *economic* model: No one but a theoretical economist would have written it down. It is not a theory formed by statistical methods from the Penn World Table or any other single data set. Despite its obvious limitations, the model has nontrivial implications about the behavior of the world economy over the next century. It predicts that sooner or later everyone will join the industrial revolution, that all economies will grow at the rate common to the wealthiest economies, and that percentage differences in income levels will disappear (which is to say, return to their pre-industrial levels).

My conjecture is that these predictions are not simply a consequence of the mechanical character of the model I have developed here, that on the contrary they will hold up as our theories of growth and development are refined, as explicit preferences, technologies, and market structures are introduced, and economic equilibria calculated. The central presumption of the general equilibrium models that are in wide use in macroeconomics today is that people are pretty much alike, that the differences in their behavior are due mainly to differences in the resources that history has placed at their disposal. Of course, there is a vast class of specific theories that are consistent with this presumption, but how can any such theory generate large, permanent differences in incomes across societies that interact in a world economy? Ideas can be imitated and resources can and do flow to places where they earn the highest returns. Until perhaps 200 years ago, these forces sufficed to maintain a rough equality of incomes across societies (not, of course, within societies) around the world.

The industrial revolution overrode these forces for equality for an amazing two centuries: That is why we call it a "revolution." But they have reasserted themselves in the last half of the twentieth century, and I think the restoration of inter-society income equality will be one of the major economic events of the century to come. Of course, this does not entail the undoing of the industrial revolution. In 1800 all societies were equally poor and stagnant. If by 2100 we are all equally rich and growing, this will not mean that we haven't got anywhere!

4. Conclusions

How did the world economy of today, with its vast differences in income levels and growth rates, emerge from the world of two centuries ago, in which the richest and the poorest societies had incomes differing by perhaps a factor of two, and in which no society had ever enjoyed sustained growth in living standards? I have sketched an answer to this question here, an answer that implies some very sharp predictions about the future. If you are reading this in the year 2100, I ask you: Who else told you what the macroeconomics of your century would look like, in advance, with such accuracy and economy?

Appendix

The equations used to generate Figures 4.1–4.3 are as follows. Let $y(s, t)$ denote production per capita in economy s at date t, where each economy is named by the date s at which it switched from stagnation to sustained growth. For the leading economy, $s = 0$, assume that

(1) $\quad y(0, t) = y_0(1 + \alpha)^t$.

For economies $s = 1, 2, \ldots$, assume that

(2) $\quad \dfrac{y(s, t + 1)}{y(s, t)} = (1 + \alpha) \left(\dfrac{y(0, t)}{y(s, t)} \right)^\beta$.

Figure 4.1 plots $y(s, t)$ against t for $s = 0$, 50, 100, and 150, with $y_0 = .6$ (that is, 0.6 thousand) and $\alpha = .02$ and $\beta = .025$.

Let $\pi(t)$ be the probability that an economy begins to grow at date t, and let $\lambda(t)$ be the probability that growth begins at t conditional on stagnation up to t. Then

(3) $\quad \pi(t) = \lambda(t) \left[1 - \sum_{s < t} \pi(s) \right]$.

Let $x(t)$ be average world income at t:

(4) $\quad x(t) - \sum_{s \leq t} \pi(s) y(s, t) + \left[1 - \sum_{s \leq t} \pi(s) \right] y_0$.

I assume that this stock $x(t)$ defined in equation 4 determines the fraction of economies that begin to grow at date t according to the formula:

(5) $\quad \lambda(t) = \lambda_m \exp(-\delta(x(t) - y_0)) + \lambda_M[1 - \exp(-\delta(x(t) - y_0))]$,

where the parameters δ, λ_m, and λ_M are all positive, and $\lambda_m < \lambda_M$. At $t = 0$, before any economy has begun to grow, $x(t) = y_0$ and $\lambda(0) = \lambda_m$. As $t \to \infty$, $x(t) \to \infty$ and $\lambda(t) \to \lambda_M$.

Now suppose the numbers $\{y(s, t)\}$ are calculated using (1) and (2). Then the series $x(t)$, $\pi(t)$, and $\lambda(t)$ are determined recursively using (3)–(5), as follows. For $t = 0$, $x(0) = y_0 = 600$. Then (5) gives $\lambda(0) = \lambda_m$ and then (3) gives $\pi(0) = \lambda_m$. Now for $t > 0$, suppose that $\{x(s), \pi(s), \lambda(s)\}$ have been calculated for $s < t$. Then using $\{y(s, t)\}$ and (4), $x(t)$ is calculated; using this value and (5), $\lambda(t)$ is calculated; using this value and (3), $\pi(t)$ is calculated. This algorithm, with the parameter values indicated, produced Figure 4.2.

The log standard deviation $V(t)$ of income levels is defined as:[2]

$$(6) \quad [V(t)]^2 = \sum_{s \leq t} \pi(s) \left[\ln \left(\frac{y(s, t)}{x(t)} \right) \right]^2$$

$$+ \left[1 - \sum_{s \leq t} \pi(s) \right] \left[\ln \left(\frac{y_0}{x(t)} \right) \right]^2.$$

---

2. Note that I have made the entirely arbitrary choice to use an arithmetic, not a geometric, average to define $x(t)$.

5

THE INDUSTRIAL REVOLUTION:
PAST AND FUTURE

1. Introduction

From the earliest historical times until around the beginning of the nineteenth century, the number of people in the world and the volume of goods and services they produced grew at roughly equal, slowly increasing rates. The living standards of ordinary people in eighteenth-century Europe were about the same as those of people in contemporary China or ancient Rome or, indeed, as those of people in the poorest countries in the world today. Then, during the last 200 years, both production and population growth have accelerated dramatically, and production has begun to grow *much* more rapidly than population. For the first time in history, the living standards of masses of ordinary people have begun to undergo sustained growth. The novelty of the discovery that a human society has this potential for generating sustained improvement in the material aspects of the lives of all of its members, not just of a ruling elite, cannot be overstressed. We have entered an entirely new phase in our economic history.

The progress of the industrial revolution—the somewhat outmoded term for this new phase of sustained growth in living standards—has, of course, differed considerably across societies. It began as a northern European event, and has gradually diffused to other societies, a process that has accelerated dramatically since World War II and that is still very far from completion. The uneven pace of the industrial revolution has given rise to an enormous and unprecedented inequality in average living standards across economies. In 1800, incomes per capita differed by perhaps a factor of two between the richest and poorest countries. It was the problem of explaining differences in income *levels* of this size that Adam Smith undertook in the *Wealth of Nations*. Today, per capita incomes in the United States are about 25 times the average income in India, while per capita incomes in both countries continue to grow at between 1 and 2 percent per year.

Nothing remotely like this economic behavior is mentioned by the classical economists, even as a theoretical possibility. And why should it have been, since nothing like it had yet been observed? The classical economists, or certainly Malthus and Ricardo, took it as a central problem for theory to account for the tendency of per capita incomes in any society to return to a roughly constant, stable level in the face of improvements in technology. Though they did not deny the possibility that this stable income level might differ from one economy to another, they sought a theory that would attribute such differences to differences in preferences or custom, not in technology or available resources. Differences in societies' *abilities* to produce would then induce differences in population only. Ricardo put the Malthusian theory of fertility that produces these consequences at the center of his aggregate theory of production and distribution.

Modern theories of economic growth have also failed to deal adequately with the change in the human condition that the industrial revolution represents. These theories are built around a positive rate of technological change, either simply assumed or generated as an equilibrium outcome by the assumption of constant or increasing returns to the accumulation of knowledge.[1] They are made consistent with the sustained growth of per capita incomes by the even more central assumption of a given, constant rate of population growth. In contrast to the classical prediction that technical change induces *only* changes in population, modern theories typically assume that technical change affects only incomes, with *no* effect on population.

Both classical and modern theories of production thus succeed in accounting for the central features of the contemporary behavior of production and population. The predictions of both theories, however, conflict sharply with the data the other was designed to explain. To understand the industrial revolution, and hence to understand a world in which some economies have joined the industrial revolution and others have not, we

---

1. I will not attempt to list all the descendants of Solow (1956), but recent examples that I have in mind are Romer (1986a), Lucas (1988), Mankiw, Romer, and Weil (1992), and Parente and Prescott (2000).

will need to unify these conflicting theories of production. That is, we need to discover a more general theory of which the two we now have can be seen as special cases, a theory that lets us see the nature of the transition from the situation of stable incomes that has characterized most of history to the sustained growth that has emerged in the last two centuries.

This way of stating the central theoretical problem of growth theory represents a change in my thinking, much influenced by the work of Becker, Murphy, and Tamura (1990) and Tamura (1988, 1994). These papers consider models of equilibrium growth in which a household's choice of the number of children to bear and the amounts of different kinds of capital to accumulate are viewed as simultaneous decisions, thus building on the earlier work of Razin and Ben-Zion (1975) and Becker and Barro (1988). By introducing the fertility decision into growth theory, this research leads one to view the industrial revolution and the associated reduction in fertility levels—generally referred to as the *demographic transition*—as different aspects of a single economic event. In particular, Becker, Murphy, and Tamura (1990) exhibit a combination of production technology and preferences (over children as well as goods consumed) that is consistent with the existence of both a traditional steady state with constant per capita incomes and a modern balanced growth path. A transition from the first kind of behavior to the second can be triggered, in the model, by an increase in the return on investment in human capital.[2]

These ideas are at the center of the sections that follow. Since their appeal, to me, is their close connection to the main facts of the industrial revolution, I will spend some time reviewing the evidence on which these introductory

---

2. Wrigley's (1988) lectures emphasize the inconsistency of classical demography with sustained economic growth. The viewpoint advanced in Nerlove (1974) is also close to that taken here. There is, of course, an enormous literature on the industrial revolution and the associated demographic revolution. Even if one restricts attention to studies that involve explicit theoretical modeling, there are many contributions beyond those cited in the text.

Goodfriend and McDermott (1995) model the onset of the industrial revolution as a population-induced shift of activity between a stagnant household economy and a dynamic market sector. Murphy, Shleifer, and Vishny (1989) also put scale economies at the center of a theory of industrialization. Neither theory associates a reduction in fertility with industrialization.

paragraphs are based. Recent research has filled in our factual knowledge of the economics of the postwar world and also of the more distant past, to the point where it is now possible to set out a fairly comprehensive history of population and production for the entire world. I will do this in Section 2.

Sections 3 and 4 develop a modern—which is to say, mathematically explicit—version of Ricardo's theory of production and distribution for an economy with land and labor as factors of production. Section 5 introduces capital accumulation into this Ricardian economy—an exercise that was beyond the methods at Ricardo's command but well within the capabilities of modern dynamic theory—and reviews the reasons why a theory of the industrial revolution cannot be based on the accumulation of physical capital alone. Section 6 presents models of sustained growth generated by technological change and by human capital accumulation, in which the fertility decision is incorporated. We will see that theories in which sustained growth is generated by exogenous technological change cannot be made consistent with the demographic transition, while otherwise similar models in which growth rates are endogenously determined by human capital investment decisions can do so quite easily. Section 7 outlines a theory of the transition from the Malthusian economy of Sections 3–5 to the growing economy of Section 6. Section 8 presents concluding comments.

2. The Basic Facts of the Industrial Revolution

In the introductory section I proposed using the term *industrial revolution* to refer to the onset of sustained growth in per capita incomes. I want next to provide a quantitative description of this event, and in particular to document the claims that it occurred in the late eighteenth or even early nineteenth century, that it was unprecedented, and that it has proceeded at an accelerating pace up to the present day.[3] Then I will turn to refinements of this description that will be helpful in understanding the origins and the course of the industrial revolution.

---

3. I found Kremer's (1993) presentation of long-term population trends extremely stimulating. So too were similarly motivated overviews of trends in production and living standards provided by Parente and Prescott (1993), Johnson (1997), and Pritchett (1997).

Figure 5.1 plots world population and the total world production of goods and services (GDP) from the year 1000 up to the present. I use a logarithmic scale rather than natural units in this figure so that one can see clearly the *acceleration* in both of these series (which shows up as a deviation from linearity). The scale on the left is millions of persons and billions of 1985 U.S. dollars. Population data for the years since 1500 and production data since 1750 are taken from Tables 5.1 and 5.2 in the Data Appendix at the end of this chapter. Population from earlier years is from McEvedy and Jones (1978), p. 342. Earlier production estimates are extrapolations based on the assumption that *per capita* incomes were equal to their 1750 levels in all earlier years. (Thus prior to 1750 the total population and production series differ by a constant.)

The estimated population for the year 1000 is 265 million, slightly less than the population of the United States today. By 1960, world

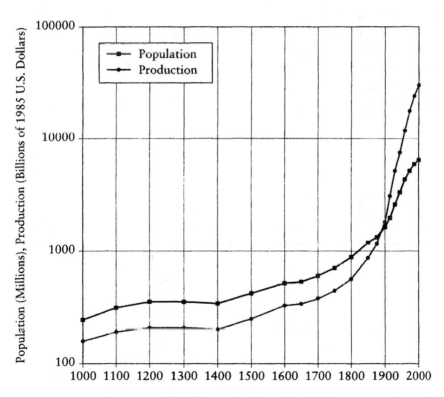

Figure 5.1 World population and production

population had grown to 3 billion; by 1990, it was 5.2 billion. One can see the acceleration of population growth since 1800 on the figure, but as Michael Kremer (1993) has emphasized, there was accelerating growth in earlier years as well.[4] In a world with constant income per capita, population growth is itself a measure of production growth, and hence also of the rate of technological change. Thus whatever it was that was new to economic life in the eighteenth century, it was not simply the fact of technological change, for continued improvement in technology had been needed to support the impressive population growth in all the centuries preceding.

Our knowledge of production and living standards at different places and times has grown enormously in the past few decades. The most recent empirical contribution, one of the very first importance, is the Penn World Table project conducted by Robert Summers and Alan Heston.[5] This readily available, conveniently organized data set contains population and production data on every country in the world, from about 1950 or 1960 (depending on the country) to the present time. Data on real production are converted to common units on the "purchasing power parity" basis that is consistent with index number theory. The availability of this marvelous body of data has given the recent revival of mathematical growth theory an explicitly empirical character that is quite different from the more purely theoretical investigations of the 1960s. It has also encouraged a more universal, ambitious style of theorizing, aimed at providing a unified account of the behavior of rich and poor societies alike.

As a result of the Penn project, we now have for the first time a reliable picture of production in the entire world, for both rich and poor countries. Let us review the main features of this picture, beginning with population

---

4. One can argue about whether the pre-1800 acceleration of population can be seen on my Figure 5.1, but it is clearly visible in the much longer series displayed by Kremer and by McEvedy and Jones and in the curves fit to these data by Kremer.

5. The basic descriptive articles on the Penn World Table are Summers and Heston 1984 and 1991, which contain data for the years 1950–1988. The data themselves are periodically extended and revised, and made available in a numbered series. All data cited in this chapter as "Summers and Heston" or "S&H" are taken from the version PWT5.6, downloaded from the Web site of the National Bureau of Economic Research (*http://www.nber.org*).

estimates. Over the 30-year period from 1960 through 1990, world population grew from about 3 billion to 5.2 billion, or at an annual rate of 1.8 percent. These numbers are often cited with alarm, and obviously the number of people in the world cannot possibly grow at 2 percent per year forever. But the idea that population growth is outstripping available resources, advanced by many recent exponents of what a friend of mine calls "the economics of gloom," is simply nonsense, unrelated to the facts we observe.

There is, certainly, a lot of poverty and starvation in this world, but nothing could be further from the truth than the idea that poverty is increasing. Over the same period during which population has grown from 3 billion to 5.2 billion, total world production grew *much* faster than population, from $6.7 trillion in 1960 to $22.3 trillion in 1990. That is, world production more than tripled over this 30-year period, growing at an annual rate of 4 percent. Production per person—real income—thus grew at 2.2 percent per year, which is to say that the living standard of the average world citizen nearly doubled! It is important to understand that I am not quoting figures only for the advanced economies or for a handful of economic miracles. I am not excluding Africa or the communist countries. These are numbers for the world *as a whole*. The entire human race is getting rich, at historically unprecedented rates.

Average figures like these mask a lot of diversity, of course. Figure 5.2 is one way to use the information in the Penn World Table to summarize the *distribution* of the levels and growth rates of population and per capita incomes in the postwar world. It contains two histograms of per capita incomes, one for 1960 and the other for 1990. The horizontal axis is GDP in thousands of 1985 international dollars (the units used by Summers and Heston, for my purposes indistinguishable from 1985 U.S. dollars) on a logarithmic scale. The vertical axis is population. The volumes on the figures are proportional to the number of people in the world with average incomes in the indicated range, based on the assumption (though of course it is false) that everyone in a country has that country's average income. The total volume over all four income ranges shown is thus total world population in the indicated year, about 3 billion in 1960 and 5.2 billion in 1990. The means of the two distributions are $2200 (1960) and $4300 (1990).

One can see from Figure 5.2 that the *number* of people (not just the fraction) in countries with mean incomes below $1100 has declined between 1960 and 1990. In general, the entire world income distribution has shifted to the right, without much change in the degree of income inequality since 1960. On the other hand, the degree of inequality itself is enormous. The poorest countries in 1990 have per capita incomes of around 600 1985 U.S. dollars, as compared to the U.S. average of $17,000. This is a factor of 17,000/600 = 28! This degree of inequality between the richest and poorest societies is without precedent in human history, just as is the growth in both population and living standards in the postwar period.

A great deal of recent empirical work has focused on the question of whether per capita incomes are converging to a common (growing) level,

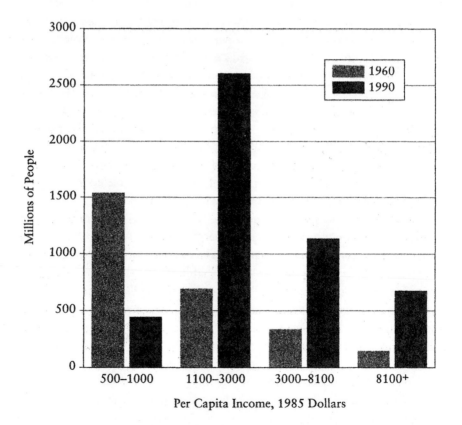

Per Capita Income, 1985 Dollars

Figure 5.2 Income distribution

or possibly diverging.[6] It is evident from Figure 5.2 that this is a fairly subtle question, and one is not surprised that this literature has not converged on a definite conclusion. In any case, it seems obvious that we are not going to learn much about the future of our race by statistical extrapolation of events from 1960 to 1990, however it is carried out. Extrapolating the 2 percent population growth rate backward from 1960, one would conclude that Adam and Eve were expelled from the Garden of Eden in about the year 1000. Extrapolating the 2.2 percent rate of per capita income growth backward, one would infer that people in 1800 subsisted on less than 100 1985 U.S. dollars. Extrapolating forward leads to predictions that the human race will exhaust the earth's water supply (or supply of anything else) in a finite period. Such exercises make it clear that the years since 1960 are part of a period of *transition,* but from what to what?

History can answer half of this question. Well-documented estimates on population, for the world as a whole and for many sub-regions, are available in a variety of sources. Table 5.1, given in the Data Appendix at the end of this chapter, covers population in 21 regions in various years since 1500. It is based almost entirely on McEvedy and Jones's (1978) excellent and readable volume, at least for the years not covered by Summers and Heston. (Where these sources overlap, they generally agree.) Table 5.2 contains per capita real incomes in these same 21 regions for various years since 1750; it is based on Summers and Heston for the post-1950 years. For earlier years, the construction of real GDP series is, of course, rather more complicated.

There is no single source for production data for *all* the world's countries for the years much before 1960, and indeed, most of the world's current nations did not even exist as independent states prior to World War II. But for a few economies—the rich countries that have roughly preserved their boundaries over the years—excellent national product data are available extending well back into the nineteenth century, compiled in historical research projects for individual countries. Many of these estimates are collected in Maddison (1983, 1991), Bairoch (1981), and most recently Maddison (1995). To construct the per capita real GDP estimates given in

---

6. See, for example, Barro and Sala-i-Martin (1992, 1997), Quah (1996), and Jones (1997). For an approach to the issue of convergence that is much closer to the one I take below, see also Baumol (1986) and Pritchett (1997).

Table 5.2 in the Data Appendix, I relied primarily on estimates provided for many relatively rich countries and regions in Bairoch (1981). The details are given in the Appendix.

For poor societies we often have no national product data, or data of very low reliability, even for the postwar years. This lack of data becomes more acute as we go back in time. As discussed in the Data Appendix, the estimates reported in Table 5.2 for Africa and much of Asia for the years before 1960 are in large part extrapolations backward in time of the 1960 estimates provided by Summers and Heston. The idea is that incomes in, say, ancient China cannot have been much lower than incomes in 1960 China and still have sustained stable or growing populations. And if incomes in any part of the world in any time period had been much larger than the levels of the poor countries of today—a factor of two, say—we would have heard about it. Such large percentage differences, had they ever existed, would have made some kind of appearance in the available accounts of the historically curious, from Herodotus to Marco Polo to Adam Smith.

In fact, there are many other sources that provide evidence on production in poor—primarily agricultural—economies. In the front hall of my apartment in Chicago, for example, there is a painting of an agricultural scene, the gift of a Korean student of mine. In the painting, a farmer is plowing his field behind an ox. Fruit trees are in flower, and mountains rise in the background. It is a peaceful scene, probably intended by the artist to inspire nostalgia for an older, simpler time. There is also much information for an economist in this picture. It is not difficult to estimate the income of this farmer, for we know about how much land one farmer and his ox can care for, about how much can be grown on this land, how much fruit the little orchard will yield, and how much the production would be worth at 1985 U.S. dollar prices. This income is about $2000. Moreover, we know that up until recent decades, almost all of the Korean workforce (way over 90 percent) was engaged in traditional agriculture, so this figure of $2000—$500 per capita for the farmer, his wife, and his two children—must be pretty close to the per capita income for the country as a whole. Though we do not have sophisticated national income and product accounts for Korea 100 years ago, we do not need them to arrive at fairly good estimates of the living standards that prevailed back then. Traditional agricultural societies are very like one another, all over the world and over time, and the standard of living they yield is not hard to estimate reliably. Indeed, my Korean farm scene (though perhaps not the style of the painting) could be drawn from any century in this millennium or the last one.

The income detail provided in Table 5.2 makes it possible to illustrate the very uneven course of the industrial revolution in different parts of the world. This is shown in Figure 5.3. To construct this figure, the 21 countries or regions of Table 5.2 were organized into five groups, based on the similarity in income growth histories and ordered by their current income levels. Group I—basically, the English-speaking countries—consists of those in which per capita incomes first exhibited sustained growth. Group III consists of the rest of northwest Europe, the countries that began

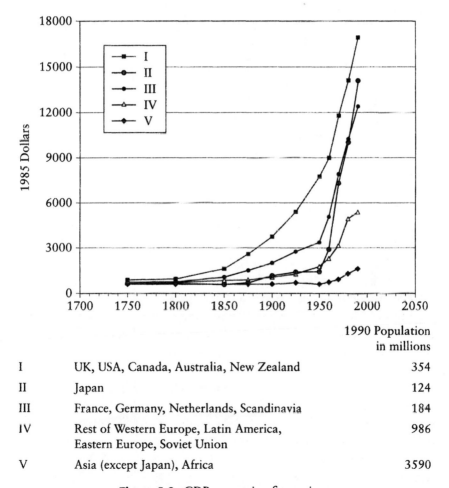

		1990 Population in millions
I	UK, USA, Canada, Australia, New Zealand	354
II	Japan	124
III	France, Germany, Netherlands, Scandinavia	184
IV	Rest of Western Europe, Latin America, Eastern Europe, Soviet Union	986
V	Asia (except Japan), Africa	3590

Figure 5.3 GDP per capita, five regions

sustained growth somewhat later. Group IV is the rest of Europe and the Soviet Union, together with the European-dominated economies of Latin America. Group II is Japan, isolated only because I want to highlight its remarkable economic history. Group V contains the rest of Asia and Africa.

As shown in Figure 5.3, per capita incomes were approximately constant, over space and time, over the period 1750–1800, at a level of something like 600–700 U.S. 1985 dollars. Here and below, income levels must be understood as estimated to an accuracy of perhaps ±200 U.S. 1985 dollars. Following the reasoning I have advanced above, $600 is taken as an estimate of living standards in all societies prior to 1750, so there would be no interest in my extending Figure 5.3 to the left. The inequality among societies that Figure 5.2 displays, then, is a recent event, emerging for the first time in the nineteenth century and reaching current levels only in the twentieth century.

The numbers at the bottom of Figure 5.3 indicate the 1990 populations, in millions of people, for the five groups of countries. One sees in particular that about two-thirds of the world's people live in Group V, which contains all of Africa and Asia except for Japan. Notice that per capita income in this group of countries is constant at 600 1985 U.S. dollars for the entire period up to 1950. The colonial era was a period of impressive population growth, but also one of continued stagnation in the living standards of masses of people. Growth in per capita incomes in Africa and Asia is entirely a postcolonial phenomenon, and this growth is, of course, the main reason that postwar growth rates for the world as a whole have attained such unprecedented levels.

Although I am using sustained growth in per capita incomes as the defining characteristic of the industrial revolution, it is clear enough from Figure 5.1 that it is hopeless to try to account for income growth since 1800 as a purely technological event. Technological change occurred rapidly after 1800, but it occurred at an accelerating rate for centuries prior to 1800 as well. What occurred around 1800 that *is* new—that differentiates the modern age from all previous periods—is not technological change by itself but the fact that fertility increases ceased to translate improvements in technology into increases in population. It is not that the increasing pace of technological change made it impossible for population to keep up, to lift "beyond visible limits the ceiling of Malthus's positive checks."[7] Such

---

7. Landes (1969), p. 41.

a development might be consistent with a Malthusian model, but only if accelerating technology were associated with extremely *high* fertility levels. In fact, the industrial revolution is invariably associated with the *reduction* in fertility known as the demographic transition.

Figure 5.4 provides a rough depiction of the demographic transitions since 1750 that have occurred and are still occurring. The figure exhibits five plotted curves, one for each of the country groups defined in Figure 5.3. Each curve connects 10 points, corresponding to the time periods beginning and ending in the dates indicated at the bottom of Figure 5.3. (Note that the periods are *not* of equal length.) Each point plots the group's average rate of population growth for that period against its per capita income at the beginning of the period. The per capita GDP figures in 1750 can just be read off Figure 5.3; they are about $600 for all five groups. Population growth rates in 1750 average about 0.4 percent and are well below 1 percent for all five groups. For each group, one can see a nearly vertical increase in population growth rates with little increase in GDP per capita, corresponding to the onset of industrialization. This, of course, is precisely the response to technological advance that Malthus and Ricardo told us to expect. Then in groups I–IV a maximum is reached, and as incomes continue to rise,

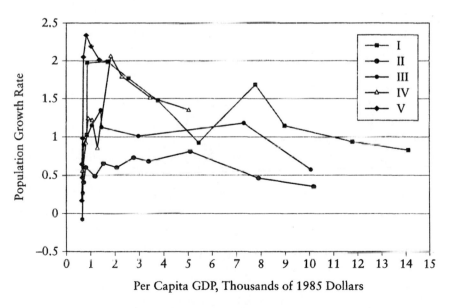

Per Capita GDP, Thousands of 1985 Dollars

Figure 5.4 Demographic transitions

population growth rates decline. In group V—most of Asia and Africa—the curve has only leveled off, but does anyone doubt that these regions will follow the path that the rest of us have already worn? The facts shown in Figure 5.4 can be refined, not only by distinguishing among more than five groups of societies but also by treating changes in birth and death rates and changes in immigration rates separately. I found it striking that the inverted U pattern is so clearly documented even without making such refinements. The demographic transition obviously requires a different view of fertility from that taken by Malthus.

The most striking feature of the data reviewed in this section is the fact that only two types of aggregative behavior are observed, one with per capita income roughly constant at a level in the range of 400 to 800 1985 U.S. dollars, and another with per capita income growing at rates in excess—sometimes far in excess—of 1 percent per year. This observation is the point of departure for Becker, Murphy, and Tamura (1990). It will also be the basis of the theoretical work described in this chapter.

3. The Classical Theory of Production

The methods and results of national income and product accounting were not available to Adam Smith and David Ricardo, but they and the other classical economists had at their disposal and actively debated a vast amount of historical information bearing on levels and rates of growth of living standards. There is no mention of sustained economic growth in the writings of the classical economists, nor would one expect there to be any in view of the facts as displayed, for example, in Figures 5.1 and 5.3 in the last section. For Smith and Ricardo, the wealth of nations meant their income *levels*, not their growth rates, and it was the stability of these levels over time, not growth rates, that called for explanation. When Thomas Malthus (1798) proposed a fertility model that accounted for the observed stability in living standards, his contemporaries quickly accepted it.

Ricardo's *Principles of Political Economy and Taxation* (1817) set out an aggregative theory of income and its distribution, almost explicit enough for a modern economist to call it a *model*. Ricardo put the Malthusian view of fertility at the center of his theory of long-run income determination, and emphasized that a central implication of the theory was the prediction that an improvement in technology would result in an increase in population but no change in real income per person. The theory is *classical:* It makes no use of utility theory. One of the aims of this section is to restate the classical theory in *neoclassical* terms, which is to say in terms that make use of mathematically explicit descriptions of agents' preferences and the technology available to them. Once the classical theory of production and distribution is thus translated into modern terms, it becomes a serviceable empirical model of income determination in economies that predate the industrial revolution, that is, in all economies known to Smith, Ricardo, and their contemporaries.

To begin, consider an animal species, endowed with behavior implying that when food consumption per individual rises above some biologically given subsistence level, numbers increase, while if consumption is below this critical level, numbers decrease. Then if food availability in total is held fixed in the region occupied by this species, the onset of a disease that kills many individuals will induce an increase in consumption per individual, an increase in population growth, and ultimately the restoration of the original consumption level and population. Such a "Malthusian" model has the important virtue of predicting the existence of a stable subsistence level of consumption in the face of shocks to population and technology.

There are other facts about human populations, however, that do not at all resemble the behavior of animal populations. In most human societies, some individuals, or individual families, accumulate vast wealth and engage in consumption far above the consumption level at which most people subsist. In most societies, even prior to the eighteenth century, average consumption is too large to be viewed as a purely biological survival level. Ricardo dealt with this observation crudely, by applying Malthusian assumptions to "workers," referred to as a distinct "race," leaving other "classes," created by systems of property rights, free to reproduce less, consume more, and accumulate the achievements that we call civilizations.

To restate Ricardo's theory in neoclassical terms, and to move beyond it in other respects as well, I will begin by formulating the preferences of a single family or "dynasty" over the number of its children as well as over the quantity of goods it consumes. This will permit the derivation of Malthusian fertility theory as a matter of conscious choice, not merely biology. Later on, I will situate families with these dynastic preferences in a variety of different social arrangements and apply equilibrium reasoning to determine how the interaction of individual and social forces determines fertility, production, and population.

Dynastic Preferences

The Malthusian hypothesis of a desired living standard for children is evidently an assumption about preferences, one that a modern economist naturally formalizes in terms of a utility function. This useful construct was not available to Malthus and Ricardo, but it will not be hard to translate their thinking on demographic questions into neoclassical language. In this subsection I introduce the assumptions about preferences, adapted from those of many earlier, similarly motivated writers, that I will use throughout this chapter.

The typical household whose preferences I will describe can be thought of as a single agent, consuming c units of a single consumption good in its lifetime and producing n children. Thus $n - 1$ is the rate of growth of the population of the household, and a choice of $n = 1$ means that the household is just maintaining its size. Each child then becomes the head of its own household, and so the process continues. The household's preferences are assumed to be described by a utility function $W(c, n, u)$ that depends on its own consumption, the number of children it has, and the lifetime utility u that each child will enjoy. These preferences are about the simplest one can think of that are general enough to accommodate a "quantity-quality trade-off" in the fertility decision. People are assumed to value both the number of children n (quantity) and the lifetime utility u (quality) that each child is expected to enjoy.[8]

Using the subscript t to denote a generation, parent's and child's utilities are linked by the difference equation

(1) $u_t = W(c_t, n_t, u_{t+1})$.

---

8. The particular formulation of dynastic preferences that I am using here was introduced in Razin and Ben-Zion (1975). In my formulation, as in theirs, parents' utility depends on goods consumption, the number of children, and utility per child. See also Becker (1960) (where a quantity-quality trade-off was introduced into the theory of fertility), Willis (1973), Becker and Barro (1988), Barro and Becker (1989), and Alvarez (1995). Recent research has progressed in quantifying the quantity-quality trade-off in the fertility decision. See Ahituv (1995), Doepke (2000), Moe (1998), and Veloso (1999).

Other writers have constructed integrated fertility and growth theories without recourse to the "quantity-quality" trade-off, stressing the value of children as a parental investment. Ehrlich and Lui (1991) and Raut and Srinivasan (1994) are leading examples.

Loury (1981) and Andrade (1998) do not treat the fertility decision, but their analyses of the intergenerational aspects of investment in human capital are evidently complementary to theories that do.

If we solve (1) backward through time by repeated substitution we get an expression

$$u_t = W(c_t, n_t, W(c_{t+1}, n_{t+1}, W(c_{t+2}, n_{t+2}, \ldots)))$$

for the utility u_t of the infinite sequence $\{(c_s, n_s)\}_{s=t}^{\infty}$ of this dynasty's consumption and children per generation at each date from t on. For example, if we assume the familiar additive log utility,

$$W(c, n, u) = (1 - \beta) \ln(c) + \eta \ln(n) + \beta u,$$

where the discount factor β is between 0 and 1, the difference equation (1) has the solution

$$u_t = \sum_{s=0}^{\infty} \beta^t [(1 - \beta) \ln(c_{t+s}) + \eta \ln(n_{t+s})].$$

Barro and Becker (1989) introduced another version of (1),

$$U_t = (1 - \beta)c_t^{\sigma} + \beta n_t^{1-\epsilon} U_{t+1}.$$

The following argument, due to Ivan Werning, shows that the logarithmic example above is a special case of these Barro-Becker preferences. If we transform utilities in this expression by letting $v_t = U_t^{1/\sigma}$, we obtain

$$v_t = \left[(1 - \beta)c_t^{\sigma} + \beta n_t^{1-\epsilon} U_{t+1} \right]^{1/\sigma}$$

$$= \left[(1 - \beta)c_t^{\sigma} + \beta \left(n_t^{(1-\epsilon)/\sigma} v_{t+1} \right)^{\sigma} \right]^{1/\sigma},$$

so current utility (suitably transformed) is a CES function of c_t and the composite argument $n_t^{(1-\epsilon)/\sigma} v_{t+1}$. Now let $\sigma \to 0$, varying ϵ in such a way that the ratio $(1 - \epsilon)/\sigma$ remains constant, at the value η/β, say. Then by the familiar relation of Cobb-Douglas to CES functions,

$$v_t = c_t^{1-\beta} n_t^{\eta} v_{t+1}^{\beta}.$$

Now using a second monotonic transformation $u_t = \ln(v_t)$, we obtain logarithmic preferences.

In general, I will always require of a utility function W that W_u, the derivative of parents' lifetime utility with respect to the lifetime utility of their children, be between 0 and 1 when evaluated along constant sequences of c_t and n_t. That is, I assume that

$$u = W(c, n, u) \quad \text{implies} \quad 0 < W_u(c, n, u) < 1.$$

This is a discounting assumption that is essential to the analysis to follow. Other assumptions that will be maintained below are that W is strictly increasing in both c and n and strictly quasi-concave in (c, n, u), that the "goods" c and n are both non-inferior, and that n and u are complements.[9]

A Hunter-Gatherer Society

In order to get a sense of the implications of these recursive preferences for observed behavior, it will be instructive to situate some of these hypothetical dynasties in a specific setting and see how they behave. I begin with an example of what we might call, today, a hunter-gatherer society. Both Smith and Ricardo make expository use of a similar situation, which they describe as existing "before the appropriation of land." It is not clear whether they intended this as a historical example or, as in my exposition, merely an illustrative one.

Consider, then, a population of N families that supports itself and its progeny on a fixed amount L of land (or territory or resources more generally conceived). Let total production be $Y = F(L, N)$, where F is a constant returns to scale function, so production per household is $y = Y/N = F(L/N, 1) = f(x)$, (say) where $x = L/N$ is the land-population ratio. Maintain the competitive assumption that each household takes this value y as given to it, as beyond its own control and the control of its children, though it may be changing through time in a predictable way. This assumption that there is nothing a parent can do that affects the opportunities available to its children (or, for that matter, of its own future self) is just what we mean by the absence of private property.

In such a setting, consider the decision problem of a single dynasty with preferences $W(c, n, u)$ and the current goods income y_t. There is a cost

9. The last two properties are defined in terms of the problem $\max_{c,n} W(c, n, u)$ s.t. $c + kn \le I$. By non-inferiority of c and n, I mean that the maximizing values of c and n are both increasing functions of I for all values of k. This is true if and only if $W_n W_{cn} - W_c W_{nn} > 0$ and $W_c W_{cn} - W_n W_{cc} > 0$. By the assumption that n and u are complementary, I mean that the optimal value of n in this problem is a non-decreasing function of u. This is true if and only if $W_c W_{nu} - W_n W_{cu} \ge 0$.

(in terms of goods) of k per child. The parents must choose the number of children, n_t, and their own consumption, $c_t = y_t - kn_t$. In the society we have postulated, this household has nothing to leave to its offspring that could affect their utility levels. Nonetheless, expectations about the utility level u_{t+1} that each child will enjoy may affect the parents' attitudes over their own consumption and number of children. Hence the household solves

$$\max_n \ W(y_t - kn, n, u_{t+1}).$$

The first-order condition for this problem is

$$kW_c(y_t - kn, n, u_{t+1}) = W_n(y_t - kn, n, u_{t+1}),$$

which implies one equilibrium condition. Three others are provided by equation (1), by the fact that n_t is a growth rate, and by the technology. The full system that must obtain in equilibrium is thus:

(2) $\quad u_t = W(c_t, n_t, u_{t+1}),$

(3) $\quad kW_c(c_t, n_t, u_{t+1}) = W_n(c_t, n_t, u_{t+1}),$

(4) $\quad x_{t+1} = x_t/n_t,$

(5) $\quad c_t + kn_t = f(x_t).$

Think of (2)–(5) as four equations in the state-like variables x_t and u_t and the flow-like variables c_t and n_t.

At any steady state of this economy, the typical dynasty is just reproducing itself, $n_t = 1$, and parents and children enjoy the same lifetime utility levels, $u_t = u_{t+1}$. The steady state goods consumption and utility levels (c, u) must then be the solutions to the two equations

(6) $\quad u = W(c, 1, u)$

and

(7) $\quad kW_c(c, 1, u) = W_n(c, 1, u)$

that are implied by (2) and (3).

By the discounting assumption $W_u \in (0, 1)$, equation (6) can always be uniquely solved for steady state utility as an increasing function of net consumption: $u = g(c)$, say. Now define the steady state marginal rate of substitution function $m(c)$ by

$$m(c) = \frac{W_n(c, 1, g(c))}{W_c(c, 1, g(c))}.$$

Then (7) implies that steady state consumption levels coincide with solutions to

(8) $m(c) = k.$

Assume that this marginal rate of substitution function satisfies the restrictions $m(0) = 0$ and $m(\infty) = +\infty$, which together ensure that a solution c to (8) exists. At any such solution, the derivative $m'(c)$ of the marginal rate of substitution function has the sign of

$$W_{cn} - kW_{cc} + [W_{nu} - kW_{cu}]g'(c),$$

which is strictly positive from the assumptions that fertility is a normal good, complementary to future utility. Thus as illustrated in Figure 5.5, there exists exactly one steady state consumption level, which I denote c_m (m for Malthus).

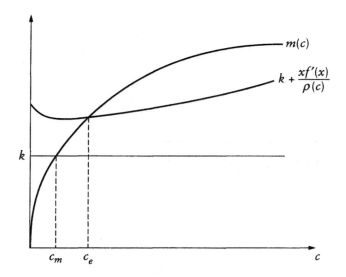

Figure 5.5 Two Ricardian equilibria

In the case of the logarithmic preferences, the function m is given by

$$m(c) = \frac{\eta}{1 - \beta} c,$$

from which it follows that steady state consumption is $c_m = [(1 - \beta)/\eta]k$. Notice that in general as in the logarithmic special case, the steady state level of consumption c_m is determined entirely independently of the goods-producing technology F, or of the levels of population and resources, N and L. It depends only on the goods cost of raising children, k, and on parental attitudes toward children and child raising, as summarized in the function W.

The off-steady-state population dynamics of this economy, given only implicitly in (2)–(5), can be complicated. The logarithmic case offers a simple point of departure. In this case, future utility u_{t+1} does not figure in equation (3), which then specializes to:

$$k\frac{1 - \beta}{c_t} = \frac{\eta}{n_t}.$$

Then eliminating c_t and n_t from (3), (4), and (5) gives:

$$x_{t+1} = k\left(\frac{1 - \beta + \eta}{\eta}\right)[x_t/f(x_t)].$$

If we assume, in addition, that the production function f is Cobb-Douglas, $f(x) = Ax^\alpha$, $\alpha \in (0, 1)$, we have

$$(9) \qquad x_{t+1} = \frac{k}{A}\left(\frac{1 - \beta + \eta}{\eta}\right)x_t^{1-\alpha}.$$

In this case, it is clear that the unique steady state

$$x_m = \left[\left(\frac{1 - \beta + \eta}{\eta}\right)\frac{k}{A}\right]^{1/\alpha}$$

is globally stable.[10]

---

10. To study local stability under more general assumptions on W and f, we need to examine the two roots of the system (2)–(5) at the steady state. Under the assumptions I have imposed (see note 9), these roots are both real, one is between 0 and 1, and one exceeds 1.

An Egalitarian Equilibrium with Private Property

The empirical attraction of the Malthusian dynamics I have just described is that they capture the rough constancy of living standards over many centuries, and reconcile the occurrence of important technological advances with stagnation in per capita incomes and with accelerating population growth. But the assumption that land is held in common obviously does not fit historical societies. In this subsection, I replace this assumption with the assumption of private ownership, including heritability, of land (or of natural resources more generally), under the assumption that land is initially equally distributed over households of equal size. In this case, and given identical preferences, there will be an equilibrium in which land remains equally distributed, and we can characterize this equilibrium by analyzing a society of identical agents.

Consider again, then, the society studied in the last subsection, in which there is a fixed amount of land L and a variable population N. A typical household has the same preferences $W(c, n, u)$ over consumption c, number of children n, and utility per child u that we assumed in the last subsection. If this household's initial land holdings are x and it bears n children, it produces $f(x)$ goods, is obligated to devote kn to child raising, and has $f(x) - kn$ left for parental consumption. We assume that land holdings are bequeathed equally to all children, leaving x/n per child. Denote the lifetime utility of this person by $v(x)$. Then if the number of children is chosen optimally, the function v satisfies the Bellman equation:

$$(10) \quad v(x) = \max_{c,n} W\left(c, n, v(\frac{x}{n})\right),$$

subject to:

$$(11) \quad c + kn \le f(x).$$

The first-order and envelope conditions for this problem are:

$$W_n\left(c, n, v\left(\frac{x}{n}\right)\right) - W_u\left(c, n, v\left(\frac{x}{n}\right)\right) v'\left(\frac{x}{n}\right)\left(\frac{x}{n^2}\right)$$
$$= k W_c\left(c, n, v\left(\frac{x}{n}\right)\right),$$

and

$$v'(x) = W_c\left(c, n, v\left(\frac{x}{n}\right)\right)f'(x) + W_u\left(c, n, v\left(\frac{x}{n}\right)\right)v'\left(\frac{x}{n}\right)\left(\frac{1}{n}\right).$$

Suppose we write $u_t = v(x_t)$, and define $q_t = v'(x_t)$. Then the full dynamic system in this private property equilibrium is:

(12) $\quad u_t = W(c_t, n_t, u_{t+1})$,

(13) $\quad kW_c(c_t, n_t, u_{t+1}) = W_n(c_t, n_t, u_{t+1}) - W_u(c_t, n_t, u_{t+1})q_{t+1}x_{t+1}\left(\frac{1}{n_t^2}\right)$,

(14) $\quad q_t = W_c(c_t, n_t, u_{t+1})f'(x_t) + W_u(c_t, n_t, u_{t+1})q_{t+1}\left(\frac{1}{n_t}\right)$,

(15) $\quad x_{t+1} = x_t/n_t$,

(16) $\quad c_t + kn_t = f(x_t)$.

Think of (12)–(16) as five equations in the three state-like variables u_t, q_t, x_t and the two flow variables c_t and n_t.

Consider possible steady states for such dynasties, in which $n = 1$ and the other four variables are constant. In this situation, the equilibrium conditions (12)–(16) become:

(17) $\quad u = W(c, 1, u)$,

(18) $\quad kW_c(c, 1, u) = W_n(c, 1, u) - W_u(c, 1, u)qx$,

(19) $\quad q = W_c(c, 1, u)f'(x) + W_u(c, 1, u)q$,

(20) $\quad c + k = f(x)$.

We can think of solving (17)–(20) by first using (17) to solve for u as a function $g(c)$ of net consumption c, as we did with equation (6) in the analysis of the hunter-gatherer economy. Then in a steady state the three derivatives of W can be viewed as known functions of c. We use (19) to obtain q in terms of these derivatives:

$$q = (1 - W_u)^{-1}W_c\, f'(x).$$

We then substitute back into (18) to get:

$$f'(x)x = \frac{(W_n - kW_c)(1 - W_u)}{W_c W_u}.$$

Now W_u has the dimensions of a discount factor, so $(1 - W_u)/W_u$ has the dimensions of a discount *rate*. Call this ratio $\rho = \rho(c)$, where c is steady state consumption. Similarly, denote the steady state marginal rate of substitution W_n/W_c by $m(c)$. Then steady state land holdings and consumption levels must satisfy

$$f'(x)x = [m(c) - k]\rho(c)$$

or, rearranging to facilitate comparison to (8),

$$(21) \quad m(c) = k + \frac{f'(x)x}{\rho(c)}.$$

Solutions (c_e, x_e) to (20)–(21) are the possible steady states for the individual land-holding dynasty.

The product $f'(x)x$ has the dimension of a per capita land rent flow; division by the discount rate $\rho(c)$ gives the ratio on the right side of equation (21) the dimension of a present value of land rent. Thus (21) equates the marginal rate of substitution between children and goods consumption to the sum of the direct child-raising cost k, as in (8), and the present value of the income flow that a second child would need to have to be as well off as the first. It is this second term, of course, that is absent when land is not privately owned.

Since the terms $xf'(x)$ obviously depend on the production technology, the solution (c_e, x_e) to (20) and (21) need not have the property that the steady state consumption level is determined by preferences only, as was the case in the last example. But suppose that f is Cobb-Douglas: $f(x) = Ax^\alpha$. Then using (20), $xf'(x) = \alpha f(x) = \alpha(c + k)$, and (21) becomes:

$$(22) \quad m(c) = k + \frac{\alpha(c + k)}{\rho(c)}.$$

Refer again to Figure 5.5. The only feature of the production technology that influences steady state consumption c_e is the share parameter α; the intercept A does not appear in (22).

In the logarithmic utility example, $m(c) = [\eta/(1 - \beta)]c$ and $\rho(c) = (1 - \beta)/\beta$. In this case, with Cobb-Douglas production, (22) can be solved explicitly for

$$c_e = \frac{1 - \beta + \alpha\beta}{\eta - \alpha\beta} k,$$

provided that $\eta > \alpha\beta$. (As an example in the next section will show, only preference parameters satisfying $\eta > \beta$ are consistent with reasonable behavior, so I will impose this assumption in the sequel. Since $\alpha \in (0, 1)$, we must then have $\eta > \alpha\beta$.) The case $\alpha = 0$ corresponds to the equilibrium c_m calculated in the last subsection, so one sees that $c_e > c_m$ for all $\alpha > 0$.

The logarithmic utility, Cobb-Douglas production case is again a convenient context for thinking about the full dynamics of the system (12)–(16). In this case, one can verify that the Bellman equation (10) has a solution of the form

$$v(x) = C + \alpha \frac{1 - \beta + \eta}{1 - \beta + \alpha\beta} \ln(x),$$

and an optimal fertility function given by:

(23) $\quad n(x) = \dfrac{\eta - \alpha\beta}{1 - \beta + \eta} \dfrac{Ax^\alpha}{k}.$

Setting $\alpha\beta = 0$ in the numerator on the right side of (23) amounts to assuming either that people do not value their children's utility ($\beta = 0$) or that they are unable to affect their children's utility ($\alpha = 0$).

Combining (23) and (15), the dynamics of land per household (and hence of population) are described in

(24) $\quad x_{t+1} = \dfrac{k}{\Lambda} \left(\dfrac{1 - \beta + \eta}{\eta - \alpha\beta} \right) x_t^{1-\alpha}.$

The difference equation (24) implies monotonic convergence to the steady state population level

$$N_e = L \left[\left(\frac{\eta - \alpha\beta}{1 - \beta + \eta} \right) \frac{A}{k} \right]^{1/\alpha}$$

and the long run steady state income

$$y_e = \frac{1 - \beta + \eta}{\eta - \alpha\beta} k.$$

These dynamics differ from those for the hunter-gatherer society described in equation (9) by the term $\alpha\beta$ in the denominator on the right side of (24). As one would expect, then, establishing property rights in land gives each family the incentive to reduce fertility. Here is perhaps the most basic instance of the importance of the quality-quantity trade-off in fertility behavior.

The Cobb-Douglas-log-utility example is a borderline case. The general analysis of the effects of changes in technology on equilibrium living standards is complicated. Every dynasty in this economy is both a landowner and a worker. With a Cobb-Douglas technology, factor shares are constant with respect to changes in the production intercept parameter A, and the relative importance of these two roles is unaffected by changes in A. In general, though, increases in A can increase the share of land-rental income in the representative household's total income, strengthening the quality dimension in its quality-quantity trade-off, reducing fertility, and increasing steady state consumption. Or the increase in A could reduce land's share, triggering the opposite reaction. There are a lot of possibilities, but none will be of much quantitative importance unless the elasticity of substitution between land and labor is far from one.

Discussion

There is a historical tradition that the origins of cities and civilized life can be traced to an "agricultural surplus." Certainly it is the case that if not everyone in a society is engaged in producing food, then those who do produce food must provide for those who do not. But if the term *surplus* is taken to mean that it was technical changes in agriculture that generated the surplus, then a fallacy is surely involved. The surplus described in the private property equilibrium of this section, as compared to the equilibrium in the hunter-gatherer society, is generated not by change in the physical methods of production but rather by a change in property rights. A society of hunters that succeeded in establishing and enforcing private property in hunting territories would generate a "hunting surplus" without any changes in hunting technology. (Indeed, the privatization of hunting rights or gathering rights must have preceded or at least paralleled the development of agriculture. Who would undertake to domesticate an animal if everyone else had the right to kill and eat it?)

In the two examples discussed in this section, the reason the private property equilibrium has a higher per capita income than the equilibrium that arises when resources are held in common has nothing to do with differences in technology. The income difference arises solely out of the concern people have for the well-being of their descendants, combined with a change in property rights that permits people to pass productive resources on to these descendants. The interaction of these forces produces an income "surplus" in the egalitarian society of independent farmers studied in this section. In the next section, we will see that this continues to be the case when we consider a society organized along class lines.

4. The Role of Class in the Classical Theory

The egalitarian economies of hunter-gatherers and small farmers described in the last section are possible ways for a society to be organized, and one can think of examples of economies that are reasonably well approximated by such models. Such representative agent systems are very much in the spirit of modern macroeconomics, in which questions of distribution are typically kept to one side in order to focus on questions of production and investment. But they are very far from the spirit of classical economics, in which the idea of *class* plays a central role, certainly in exposition and, I believe, in substance as well.

In the analysis of an economy with privately held land in the last section, I began with a collection of households in identical positions, sought a symmetric evolution of the system, and found one. In this section, I ask whether asymmetric steady state equilibria, in which land is unequally distributed and remains so, may also exist for exactly the agricultural economy set out in Section 3. I begin with the analysis of equilibrium possibilities in a system, much closer to Ricardo's, in which an asymmetric equilibrium is simply *imposed* by the assumption of a particular kind of class structure. I then turn to the question of whether the same kind of inequality might also arise in a competitive equilibrium.

An Equilibrium with Two Classes

Consider, then, an economy with the technology and preferences of Section 3, but with a class structure *imposed* on the equilibrium by the assumptions that workers do not (or cannot) acquire land and that landowners do not work. In such an equilibrium, landowners simply live off rental income, and their fertility behavior will determine the number of families $N_{\ell t}$ (say) over which society's total land rents will be distributed. Production will depend on the quantity of land L and the number of workers N_{wt} (say) and not at all on $N_{\ell t}$. In these circumstances, a worker household is in exactly the same propertyless position as were all the households in the hunter-gatherer economy studied in Section 3. The equilibrium conditions are given by the system (2)–(3) in Section 3, except that the state variable x_t must be interpreted as the ratio $z_t = L/N_{wt}$ of land to the number of workers only (not total population), and income per worker $f(x_t)$ must be replaced by wage income per worker, $f(z_t) - z_t f'(z_t)$.

In a steady state, worker consumption will be c_m, the unique solution to

(1) $m(c) = k,$

where $m(c)$ is the steady state marginal rate of substitution function defined in the last section. The equilibrium wage rate w_m (say) must equal $c_m + k$, so that

(2) $w_m = c_m + k = f(z) - zf'(z).$

Since c_m is given by (1), equation (2) determines the steady state land-labor ratio, $z = L/N_w$. This ratio in turn determines the steady state land rent, $r = f'(z)$. The population of landowners, their preferences, and the nature of their decision problem all play no role in determining any of these quantities and prices, either in a steady state or along a transition path to the steady state. This implication is, I think, the essence of the labor theory of value.

In a steady state, the Bellman equation for a landowning, non-working dynasty is

(3) $\varphi(x) = \max_{c,n} W(c, n, \varphi(x/n))$

subject to

(4) $c + kn \leq rx,$

where the state variable x is the dynasty's land holding and where the land rental rate r is a parametrically given price. We specialize the first-order and envelope conditions for the problem (3) to the case $n = 1$. With the discount rate function $\rho(c)$ defined as in the last section, these conditions imply that a landowner's steady state consumption must satisfy

$$m(c) = k + \frac{rx}{\rho(c)}.$$

Using the budget constraint (4) to eliminate rx, this implies

$$(5) \quad m(c) = k + \frac{c+k}{\rho(c)}.$$

We solve (5) for landowner consumption, $c_\ell > c_m$ (see Figure 5.6 on p. 141). Now go back to the budget constraint (4) to find the equilibrium land holding per landowning dynasty, x:

$$c_\ell + k = f'(z)x.$$

Given z, there are $N_\ell = L/x$ landowning families in equilibrium.

Note the recursive structure of this two-class system. We get the real wage by Malthusian reasoning, which sets the land-labor ratio via marginal productivity, which sets the rental rate on land, which determines landowner fertility, which determines the number of landowners. It is a Ricardian round robin, in which no simultaneous equations need to be solved. Our first general equilibrium theorist needed no help from Brouwer![11]

In the log-utility-Cobb-Douglas production case, worker consumption is

$$c_m = \frac{1-\beta}{\eta} k,$$

as in the hunter-gatherer example, and landowner consumption is

$$c_\ell = \frac{k}{\eta - \beta}$$

provided that $\eta > \beta$. (If $\beta > \eta$, the number of children is a "bad," and a landowning parent would choose to have an arbitrarily small number of children, each endowed with arbitrarily high wealth! This is why the assumption $\eta > \beta$ was imposed above, and why I think it should be maintained.)

The population of workers is determined by $z = L/N_w$ and equation (2):

$$c_m + k = (1 - \alpha)Az^\alpha.$$

---

11. The assumption used here that workers and landowners have the same utility function, which comes naturally to a modern economist, would not have occurred to Ricardo. It plays no role in the argument of this section and can obviously be dropped.

The population of landowners is then given by the equality of total land rents and total landowner consumption (including child-raising expenses):

$$N_w \alpha A z^\alpha = N_\ell(c_\ell + k).$$

Thus

$$N_\ell/N_w = \frac{\alpha}{1-\alpha} \frac{\eta - \beta}{\eta}.$$

Oddly, *average* consumption in the steady state is

$$\frac{N_w}{N_w + N_\ell} c_m + \frac{N_\ell}{N_w + N_\ell} c_\ell = \frac{1 - \beta + \alpha\beta}{\eta - \alpha\beta} k,$$

which is exactly average consumption in the representative agent economy of Section 3. (This finding must be peculiar to the parametric example.)

Modern economists are, rightly I think, skeptical of theories that depend on large numbers of people acting in concert in ways that may serve their joint, "class" interests but not their interests as individuals. For this reason, the assumptions that workers do not save and that landowners do not work are not particularly appealing as positive economics. One might prefer to think of the equilibrium calculated here as an allocation engineered through state-enforced taxation of land rents. For example, if we think of imposing taxation of land rents on the egalitarian equilbrium of Section 3, the agents in that model will rely increasingly on wage income, and as land tax rates increase to maximum levels, their fertility and consumption behavior will approach Malthusian levels. The state, in effect, becomes a single, large landowner. Equivalently, I suppose, we could say that a landowner class becomes the state.

Inequality in Competitive Equilibrium

It is worth repeating that the equilibrium characterized in the last subsection is *not* a competitive equilibrium in the usual sense. At the prices I have calculated, workers were not permitted to save and acquire land and landowners were not allowed to earn wage income. Might there be assumptions on preferences under which there could exist a competitive-equilibrium steady state in which families with large land holdings and high consumption coexist with other families with less land and lower consumption? In such an equilibrium, the wealthier families would devote more resources to children than poor families do, but these additional resources would take the form of higher "quality" per child, brought about by granting each child more inherited land. This possibility is explored in this subsection.

In a steady state equilibrium in which each household takes as given a constant wage rate w, land rental r, and land price q, the Bellman equation for each household is:

$$(6) \qquad \psi(x) = \max_{c,n,y} W(c, n, \psi(y/n))$$

subject to

$$(7) \qquad c + kn + q(y - x) = w + rx.$$

Here the dynasty begins with one unit of labor and x units of land. The labor yields w units of goods in wage income; the land yields rx of goods in rental income. The household can then add to, or subtract from, its disposable income $w + rx$ by selling $x - y$ units of land at the market price q. The unsold land y is bequeathed to children at y/n units per child. The egalitarian allocation of the last section, the solution (c, u, x, q) to (17)–(20), is one such equilibrium with the associated prices $w = f(x) - xf'(x)$ and $r = f'(x)$.

Now we ask whether there may also be equilibria with constant prices (w, r, q), not necessarily equal to those associated with the symmetric equilibrium, at which different, price-taking households maintain different long-run land holdings. To characterize any such steady state equilibrium, obtain the first-order and envelope conditions for the problem (6), specialize to the situation in which $n = 1$ and $y = x$, and define the functions $m(c)$ and $\rho(c)$ as in the last section. Then the equilibrium conditions include

$$(8) \qquad m(c) = k + \frac{rx}{\rho(c)},$$

$$(9) \qquad \rho(c) \geq \frac{r}{q} \quad \text{with equality if} \quad x > 0,$$

and

$$(10) \qquad c + k = w + rx.$$

In the log utility case, to begin with a familiar example, the left side of (9) is constant at the value $\rho = \beta^{-1} - 1$, and (9) fixes the ratio r/q. Eliminating rx between (8) and (10) gives

$$\left(1 - \frac{\eta}{\beta}\right) c = w - \frac{k}{\beta}.$$

Under the assumption, imposed above, that $\eta > \beta$, there is a unique consumption level for any wage w, and since everyone faces the same wage in equilibrium, this implies that the egalitarian solution is the only possible steady state. Of course, if land were initially unequally distributed, inequality would persist in a transition to a steady state but, if the system were stable, it would disappear in the long run. In short, under log utility the two-class equilibrium calculated in the last subsection does not have a competitive market interpretation.

More generally, if the function ρ satisfies $\rho'(c) > 0$—the condition that Lucas and Stokey (1984) call *increasing marginal impatience*—then (4) implies a unique steady state consumption level at any given prices, and (5) implies unique equilibrium land holdings x. Again, any steady state must be egalitarian.[12] I turn, then, to an examination of the possibilities when increasing marginal impatience does not obtain. Again, we focus on a two-class situation, in which one class consists of landless workers.

Consider steady states for such a two-class economy, restricting attention to equilibria in which behavior *within* each class is identical. Our task is to determine equilibrium prices (w, r, q), the populations of the two classes, N_w and N_ℓ, the consumption levels of each class, and the average land holdings x of dynasties that do hold land. If we proceed in the right order, this is no harder to carry out than was the Ricardian analysis of the last subsection.

In a steady state, the consumption of anyone without rental income—a "worker"—will be c_m, the unique solution to (1). The equilibrium wage rate is again equal to $c_m + k$, so the economy-wide land-labor ratio

$$(11) \quad z = \frac{L}{N_w + N_\ell}$$

---

12. The case $\rho'(c) < 0$ is not symmetrically interesting, because the steady state at which (9) holds with equality would not be stable. See Lucas and Stokey (1984).

is determined by (2). This ratio in turn determines the steady state land rent, $r = f'(z)$. So far, then, we have determined both equilibrium prices without any reference to the resources in the system, L, to the population of landowners, or to their preferences and the nature of their decision problem.

Given the prices w and r, the behavior of landowner families is determined by (8)–(10). Eliminating rx between (8) and (10) yields

$$(12) \quad m(c) = k + \frac{c + k - w}{\rho(c)}.$$

From (1) and (2), one solution to (12) is c_m, but this cannot correspond to an equilibrium in which someone earns positive land rents. Suppose, then, that preferences W, and hence the functions $m(c)$ and $\rho(c)$, are consistent with Figure 5.6. Interpret the larger solution on the figure, c_ℓ say, as landowner consumption. Then average land holdings per landowning dynasty x can be obtained from the budget constraint (10), and the number of landowning families is $N_\ell = L/x$. Finally, (11) determines the number of landless families, N_w. Given z, there are $N_\ell = L/z$ landowning families in equilibrium.

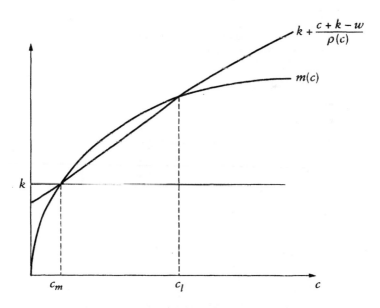

$$k + \frac{c + k - w}{\rho(c)}$$

$$m(c)$$

Figure 5.6 Ricardian equilibrium with two classes

The equilibrium condition (9) has not been used in this construction. Since (9) must hold with equality for the wealthy class, the interest rate and hence the price of land are determined by

$$\rho(c_\ell) = \frac{r}{q} = \frac{f'(z)}{q}.$$

Then if the construction just described is in fact an equilibrium, one in which landless families can acquire land at the price q but choose not to do so, (9) implies that

$$\rho(c_m) \geq \rho(c_\ell).$$

In summary, a two-class competitive-equilibrium steady state would require decreasing marginal impatience at low incomes and, for reasons given in Lucas and Stokey (1984), increasing marginal impatience at higher incomes.

Discussion
The central feature of all of the models developed in this section and the last is a steady state income of a worker, $c_m + k$, that is determined independently of the technology or of the levels of population and resources. It depends only on the goods cost of raising children, k, and on parental attitudes toward children and child raising. Ricardo credits Malthus with this population theory, but it is worth stressing that what he takes from Malthus is the sensible idea of a dynamically stable steady state income level, not the famous nonsense about geometric versus arithmetic growth rates. As Ricardo documents, this same idea is present in Smith, although there with the important qualification that the income level that is determined by fertility behavior alone is "the wages of the inferior classes of workmen" (Ricardo 1817, p. 215). In short, all of the classical economists were "Malthusians," and none of them saw the potential for reductions in fertility to make possible sustained growth in living standards.

Ricardo (p. 93) calls the income level $c_m + k$ "the natural price of labour," defining it, as I just have, as a steady state: "that price which is necessary to enable the labourers . . . to subsist and to perpetuate their race, without either increase or diminution." What I have done here is to deduce this level and its stability using utility theory, unknown to the classical economists but entirely consistent with their discussion of the determinants of this "natural price." In my formulation, it is unclear whether the parameter k and perhaps the function W should be viewed as describing tastes or technology. The question-begging "necessary" in Ricardo's definition reflects the same ambiguity. He later refers to "those comforts which custom renders absolute necessaries," but then still later adds (p. 96): "It is not to be understood that the natural price of labour, estimated even in food and necessaries, is absolutely fixed and constant. It varies at different times in the same country, and very materially differs in different countries. It essentially depends on the habits and customs of the people."

The idea that tastes determine living standards has both possibilities and dangers. In the first edition of *Principles*, Ricardo proposed: "Give to the Irish labourer a taste for the comforts and enjoyments which habit has made essential to the English labourer, and he would be then content to devote a further portion of his time to industry, that he might be enabled to obtain them." To this George Ensor asked, reasonably enough, "But how are these tastes to be excited in the Irish labourers? Is it supposed that they are not like other human creatures? but that they make choice of privations?" In later editions, Ricardo dropped the suggestion that taste differences could be used to account for English-Irish income differentials.[13] Since Ricardo retreated from his attempt at a cultural account of income differences, innumerable other cultural explanations have been proposed, only to be forced into retreat by historical fact.

Classical arguments over differences among countries' living standards and what the causes of such differences might be were certainly of legitimate interest. The same issues continue to engage economic historians today. In a world in which Malthusian dynamics dictate that any society have an average income of, say, 600 ± 200 1985 U.S. dollars, it is obviously of considerable interest whether a given economy is at $800 or $400. But even if differences of this magnitude between eighteenth-century incomes in Europe and Asia can be defended, it certainly does not follow that such differences were in any sense a key to the origins of the industrial revolution. What kinds of economic forces transform small initial differences in income levels into sustained differences in rates of growth?

---

13. This exchange is described by Sraffa in Ricardo (1817), p. 100.

5. Capital Accumulation and Fertility

Despite their awareness of the importance of both physical and human capital accumulation, the classical economists lacked a method that could let them see how its possibility would affect equilibrium values. An operational theory of capital is entirely a development of the twentieth century. An advantage of restating the classical theory of production in explicit, neoclassical terms is that it becomes straightforward to incorporate reproducible capital into the theory. It will be useful to carry out this modification explicitly, to see how it is related both to classical theory and to modern growth theory, to see how a theory of fertility can be added to modern growth theory, and to verify once again Solow's (1956) conclusion that physical capital accumulation alone does not suffice to transform a static economy into a perpetually growing one.[14] With these conclusions established, we will be in a position to consider the preconditions for sustained income growth.

We could think of introducing reproducible capital with a class structure—introducing a capitalist class to go along with the workers and landowners in the model of Section 4. Such an approach would be in the Ricardian spirit, but its maintenance would entail strictures that neither workers nor landowners could own capital, analogous to the requirement in the last section that workers cannot acquire land. In view of the way capitalist economies have evolved in the last 200 years, however, assumptions designed to maintain rigid class lines have become increasingly dubious empirically as well as hard to reconcile with individual rationality. I will deal here with models of classless societies only.[15]

We also need to decide whether to introduce reproducible capital in place of or in addition to the land input. So as not to stray too far from the Ricardian setups of Sections 3 and 4, let us begin by retaining the land input and consider the representative agent economy of Section 3 with reproducible capital added as a third factor of production. Let x be land

---

14. The models discussed in this section descend directly from Razin and Ben-Zion (1975). Intellectual debts are also acknowledged to Ahituv (1995), Benhabib and Nishimura (1993), Ehrlich and Lui (1997), Galor and Weil (1996), Nerlove, Razin, and Sadka (1987), and Razin and Sadka (1995).

15. Of course, a "classless" society is not the same thing as an equal-income society.

per household, as in Section 3, and let z be the stock of reproducible capital per household. Then a pair (x, z) of the two kinds of assets is a complete description of a household's situation, and we seek to formulate a Bellman equation for its value function $v(x, z)$.

As the accumulation of capital of various kinds receives greater emphasis, it becomes more critical whether one thinks of the costs of children as taking the form of *time* or of *goods*. For now, we continue with the assumption of Sections 3 and 4 that each child entails an outlay of k units of goods. Assume that goods production per household is a constant returns to scale function of the capital, labor, and land inputs, and with the labor input fixed at unity, write $f(x, z)$ for the production of a one-person household. Let end-of-period capital per child be y (so that total capital is yn) and assume, purely for simplicity, that there is no physical depreciation of capital. We adopt a one-sector approach: There is a single produced good, which may be used either as consumption or as capital. Then a household's resource constraint is

$$(1) \qquad c + (k + y)n \le f(x, z) + z.$$

Its Bellman equation is

$$(2) \qquad v(x, z) = \max_{c,n,y} W\left(c, n, v(x/n, y)\right),$$

subject to (1). Equation (2) reflects the distinction between reproducible capital, accumulated by investment out of goods production, and non-reproducible land, where the stock x is simply divided equally among the n children, each receiving x/n.

The first-order and envelope conditions for the problem (2) are:

$$W_n(c, n, u') = (k + y) W_c(c, n, u') + W_u(c, n, u')v_x(x/n, y)x/n^2,$$

$$W_u(c, n, u')v_z(x/n, y) = nW_c(c, n, u'),$$

$$v_z(x, z) = W_c(c, n, u')(f_z(x, z) + 1),$$

$$v_x(x, z) = W_c(c, n, u')f_x(x, z) + W_u(c, n, u')v_x(x/n, y)\frac{1}{n},$$

where

$$u' = v(x/n, y).$$

In a steady state, in which $n = 1$, $z = y$, and $u = u' = v(x, z)$, this system reduces to

(3) $\quad u = W(c, 1, u)$,

(4) $\quad c + k = f(x, z)$,

(5) $\quad W_n(c, 1, u) = (k + z)W_c(c, 1, u) + W_u(c, 1, u)v_x(x, z)x$,

(6) $\quad W_u(c, 1, u)v_z(x, z) = W_c(c, 1, u)$,

(7) $\quad v_z(x, z) = W_c(c, 1, u)(f_z(x, z) + 1)$,

(8) $\quad v_x(x, z) = W_c(c, 1, u)f_x(x, z) + W_u(c, 1, u)v_x(x, z)$.

Use the envelope conditions (7) and (8) to eliminate the two derivatives of the value function. Then the first-order conditions (5) and (6) can be restated as

(9) $\quad \dfrac{W_n(c, 1, u)}{W_c(c, 1, u)} = k + z + \dfrac{W_u(c, 1, u)}{1 - W_u(c, 1, u)}f_x(x, z)x$,

(10) $\quad W_u(c, 1, u)(f_z(x, z) + 1) = 1$.

View (3), (4), (9), and (10) as four equations in the steady state values of u, c, x, and z.

Following the procedure used in Section 3, solve (3) for $u = g(c)$ and define the marginal rate of substitution function $m(c)$ and the discount rate function $\rho(c)$ as in Section 3. In terms of these functions, (9) and (10) can be restated as

(11) $\quad m(c) = k + z + \dfrac{f_x(x, z)x}{\rho(c)}$,

(12) $\quad f_z(x, z) = \rho(c)$.

Now we solve (4), (11), and (12) for the steady state values of c, x, and z. Given the equilibrium amount of land per person, z, the given quantity of land determines the equilibrium population.

With the per capita values c and x constant, these equations obviously do not describe an economy undergoing sustained growth. But is this system Malthusian, in the sense that steady state consumption and welfare are independent of the technology? The case of Cobb-Douglas production is again helpful, though not conclusive. Let $f(x, z) = Ax^\alpha z^\nu$, $\alpha + \nu < 1$, so that (4), (11), and (12) become

(13) $c + k = Ax^\alpha z^\nu$,

(14) $m(c) = k + z + \dfrac{\alpha Ax^\alpha z^\nu}{\rho(c)}$,

and

(15) $\nu Ax^\alpha z^{\nu-1} = \rho(c)$.

Use (15) to eliminate x and substitute into (13) and (14) to obtain

(16) $c + k = z\dfrac{\rho(c)}{\nu}$

and

(17) $m(c) = k + \left(\dfrac{\alpha + \nu}{\nu}\right) z$.

Eliminating z between these equations gives

(18) $m(c) = k + (\alpha + \nu)\dfrac{c + k}{\rho(c)}$,

which replicates (8) in Section 3 for the land-only economy.

In a steady state with no capital depreciation, then, land and reproducible capital enter fully symmetrically. The system can again be solved recursively, one-variable-at-a-time. Equation (18) yields steady state consumption, given child-raising costs k and the production function parameters α and ν. The production function intercept A does not affect this level. Given c, the equilibrium discount rate $\rho(c)$ is determined, and the level of reproducible capital z can be obtained from (16): It, too, is independent of A. Finally, land per household x can be obtained from (15). With total land quantity given, this amounts to determining the equilibrium population. Increases in A induce increases in population only, exactly as in the economies of Sections 3 and 4.[16]

---

16. As in Sections 3 and 4, the sharp distinction between the effects of changes in the production function intercept A and of changes in the share parameters α and ν is very much specific to the Cobb-Douglas assumption. Away from this borderline case, other possibilities emerge.

Two Variations

The equilibrium just developed is fragile, in the sense that some of its most essential features depend critically on specific assumptions. One of these is the presence of land as an input, alongside capital. If we were to introduce capital *in place of* land as an input, so that the value function depends on the single state variable z, the system of first-order and envelope conditions is replaced by the three conditions

$$W_n(c, n, u') = (k + y) W_c(c, n, u'),$$

$$W_u(c, n, u')v'(y) = n W_c(c, n, u'),$$

$$v'(z) = W_c(c, n, u')(f'(z) + 1).$$

The steady state equation system, analogous to (3), (4), (9), and (10), becomes

(19) $u = W(c, 1, u)$,

(20) $c + k = f(z)$,

(21) $\dfrac{W_n(c, 1, u)}{W_c(c, 1, u)} = k + z$,

(22) $W_u(c, 1, u)(f'(z) + 1) = 1$.

But (19)–(22) are four equations in the three unknowns c, u, and z: the system is over-determined!

In the absence of land as an essential input, the analogue to a steady state equilibrium is found by leaving the fertility level n free and solving the system

(23) $u = W(c, n, u)$,

(24) $c + (k + z)n = f(z) + z$,

(25) $\dfrac{W_n(c, n, u)}{W_c(c, n, u)} = k + z$,

(26) $W_u(c, n, u)(f'(z) + 1) = n$.

A solution (c, u, n, z) to the system (23)–(26) corresponds to a kind of balanced growth path, on which population is growing (or declining!) at the constant rate $n - 1$, and per capita capital and consumption are constant. We can think of such an equilibrium path as the counterpart to the original growth models of Solow (1956) and Cass (1965), without exogenous technical change, but with the non-zero population growth rate determined by the model rather than simply assumed. As in Razin and Ben-Zion (1975), we obtain a theory of sustained growth in total production, but not in living standards.

It is also essential to the existence of a steady state population *level* in the basic model of this section that the cost of bearing children take the form of an amount of goods rather than simply of *time*. To see this, we pursue a second variation. We reintroduce land as a factor of production, but assume that raising n children requires using kn units of the household's unit *time* endowment and no goods. That is, we reformulate the resource constraint as

$$(27) \quad c + yn \le f(x, 1 - kn, z) + z,$$

where $f(x, \ell, z)$ is a constant returns function of the three inputs: land, x, labor, ℓ, and reproducible capital, z. The household's Bellman equation in this case is

$$(28) \quad v(x, z) = \max_{c,n,y} W\left(c, n, v(x/n, y)\right),$$

subject to (27).

We will study this problem under the assumptions that W is homogeneous of degree one in the pair (c, u), for any fixed n, and that production is Cobb-Douglas: $f(x, \ell, z) = Ax^\alpha \ell^{1-\alpha-\nu} z^\nu$. Under these conditions, the change of variable

$$w = x^\alpha z^{\nu-1}$$

(similar to that used by Caballe and Santos 1993) is useful in reducing the dimension of the state space from two to one. In terms of the pair (x, w) the production function is

$$f(w, \ell, z) = A\ell^{1-\alpha-\nu} zw,$$

and the resource constraint (27) becomes

$$(29) \quad c + yn \le A(1 - kn)^{1-\alpha-\nu} zw + z.$$

With the state variables (z, w), the household's Bellman equation is:

$$(30) \quad \psi(z, w) = \max_{c,n,y} W\left(c, n, \psi\left(y, wn^{-\alpha}\left(\frac{y}{z}\right)^{\nu-1}\right)\right),$$

subject to (29).

Let $\omega = c/z$ and $\gamma = y/z$. Then it is a reasonable conjecture that (30) has a solution of the form $\psi(z, w) = z\varphi(w)$, where the function φ satisfies

$$(31) \quad \varphi(w) = \max_{\omega,n,\gamma} W[\omega, n, \gamma\varphi(wn^{-\alpha}\gamma^{\nu-1})]$$

subject to

$$(32) \quad \omega + n\gamma \le A(1 - kn)^{1-\alpha-\nu}w + 1 - \delta.$$

We formalize this idea as follows:

Lemma. If $\varphi(w)$ solves (31), then $\psi(x, w) \equiv x\varphi(w)$ solves (30).

Proof. Suppose φ satisfies (31). Fix w and let (ω, n, γ) attain (31). Then (32) is satisfied and the triple $(c, n, y) = (\omega z, n, \gamma z)$ satisfies (29). Then if $(z\hat{\omega}, \hat{n}, z\hat{\gamma})$ is any triple that satisfies (29), $(\hat{\omega}, \hat{n}, \hat{\gamma})$ also satisfies (32) and we have

$$\psi(z, w) = z\varphi(w) = zW[\omega, n, \gamma\varphi(wn^{-\alpha}\gamma^{\nu-1})]$$

$$\ge zW[\hat{\omega}, \hat{n}, \hat{\gamma}\varphi(w\hat{n}^{-\alpha}\hat{\gamma}^{\nu-1})]$$

$$= W\left[z\hat{\omega}, \hat{n}, z\hat{\gamma}\varphi\left(w\hat{n}^{-\alpha}\left(\frac{z\hat{\gamma}}{z}\right)^{\nu-1}\right)\right]$$

$$= W\left[z\hat{\omega}, \hat{n}, \psi\left(z\hat{\gamma}, w\hat{n}^{-\alpha}\left(\frac{z\hat{\gamma}}{z}\right)^{\nu-1}\right)\right].$$

Note that the next-to-last step uses the homogeneity of W. ∎

Steady states and balanced growth paths of this system, solutions that have the property that the state variable w is constant, will satisfy

$$w = wn^{-\alpha}\gamma^{\nu-1},$$

or

$$(33) \quad n = \gamma^{(\nu-1)/\alpha}.$$

Thus a steady state with constant population, $n = 1$, will have a constant level of physical capital as well, $\gamma = 1$. But the existence of such a steady state would be purely coincidental. In general n will differ from one, and equation (33) requires that capital grows at the rate that will maintain constancy of the marginal product of capital (proportional, in this Cobb-Douglas case, to the output-capital ratio). Suppose, for example, that $n > 1$, so that population is increasing forever. Then since the total quantity of land is constant, land per household is decreasing forever, and since land and capital are complements, this in itself would imply that the marginal product of capital is decreasing forever. To maintain constancy, and hence to keep (33) satisfied, capital per household and goods consumption per household have to be decreasing forever too. Imagine a world in which ever more numerous but smaller people cultivate ever-smaller plots of land with ever-decreasing quantities of capital!

The problem with these variations on the basic model of this section is that both of them, in different ways, break the link between resources and human physiology. In the first variation, neither land nor any other fixed resource is used in production, so the economics of the situation can determine no more than the ratio of people to reproducible capital. In the second variation, only adult *time* is used to produce a new adult. Land is needed to produce goods, but the consumption of goods per person can either grow or decline indefinitely. Later on, when we want to approximate a modern economy in which limits on land have become less and less important, something like this second variation will serve as an interesting and helpful approximation. But in the present context, where we are seeking theoretical possibilities for capital accumulation that have the potential to help a society to free itself from Malthusian demography, neither of the variations explored in this subsection is of much interest.

Discussion
None of the classical economists would have viewed the failure of the models of this section to produce sustained growth in per capita income as either a surprise or a deficiency. To see the aggregate behavior they were attempting to understand, cover up Figure 5.3 from 1817 (when Ricardo's *Principles* was first published) on. Indeed, what is truly remarkable is the

lack of interest on the part of Smith's and Ricardo's nineteenth-century successors to the industrial revolution that was occurring around them. As George Stigler (1960, p. 37) remarked,

At the height of the industrial revolution, when great technological advances were crowding hard upon one another, the main tradition of classical economics treated the state of the arts as a datum. The arts were held to be subject to sporadic improvements, but not of a magnitude comparable to the force of diminishing returns in agriculture. Here, then, the most overwhelming characteristic of economic life was excluded from economic theory.

So strong was the force of Ricardo's theory that his successors were blind to the onset of sustained economic growth!

But by the middle of the nineteenth century, it was evident to Karl Marx and Friedrich Engels (at least) that something had happened in the wealthiest nations that was entirely new in human history. Remember their paragraph on the economic achievements of capitalism in *The Communist Manifesto:*[17]

The bourgeoisie, during its rule of scarce one hundred years, has created more massive and more colossal productive forces than have all preceding generations together. Subjection of Nature's forces to man, machinery, application of chemistry to industry and agriculture, steam navigation, railways, electric telegraphs, clearing of whole continents for cultivation, canalization of rivers, whole populations conjured out of the ground—what earlier century had even a presentiment that such productive forces slumbered in the lap of social labor?

Marx believed that the industrial revolution described in this paragraph was a transition from one steady state to a new one, following a shift in technology—the "factory system"—that made capital-intensive production more profitable. He viewed it as an event that would be completed without permanently altering the living standards of the poor, not as the onset of sustained growth in living standards. Surely this was a defensible position in 1848: see again Figure 5.3. We now scorn Marx for this unsuccessful

---

17. Marx and Engels (1848), p. 209.

forecast, though as Stigler observes, his classical contemporaries shared it. We should rather credit him for his empirical judgment in distinguishing the genuinely new from the familiar.

One can see from equation (18) that without a class structure an increase in the elasticity v of capital will induce an increase in steady state consumption (and welfare). The same is true for an increase in the land elasticity α. Either change in the productivity of a kind of inheritable capital alters the terms of the quantity-quality trade-off in favor of reduced fertility. Some modern observers attempt to reconcile the fact of sustained income growth with the idea of the industrial revolution as a transition from one steady state to another by thinking of a succession of technology shocks of this type. One reads of the first industrial revolution, the second, and so on, in stages that are either simply numbered or given more colorful labels. There must be something to this—we do not get sustained growth by making the same invention over and over—but no one has had any empirical success with models based on a succession of discrete, widely separated, big shocks. I am inclined to take such popular usage as a reflection of lack of analytical technique rather than a substantive insight into the process of technical change and growth.

6. Fertility and Sustained Growth

We know that in a model in which population growth is taken as given, the accumulation of physical capital is not sufficient, by itself, to generate sustained growth in per capita incomes. Since adding a fertility decision to the theory does not provide an engine of growth, it is hardly surprising that this modification does not yield a theory of growth. In this section, I consider two modifications that have been used to generate sustained growth in models without a fertility decision: the introduction of exogenously given technological change, and the introduction of endogenous human capital accumulation under a constant returns technology. We will see that these two potential engines of growth interact with the theory of fertility in very different ways.

A Model with Exogenous Human Capital Growth
Looking ahead to the construction of balanced-growth equilibrium paths, it will be essential to maintain the assumption that the dynastic preference

function W is homogeneous of degree one in the pair (c, u), for any fertility level n. This property holds for the example

(1) $W(c, n, u) = c^{1-\beta} n^{\eta} u^{\beta}$

used repeatedly (in log version) in earlier discussion.

On the technology side, it will be simplest to begin with a constant-returns, labor-only technology for producing goods. Specifically, goods production per household is assumed to be $h_t u_t$, where u_t is the fraction of the household's unit time endowment that is devoted to goods production, and h_t is the human capital of the household head. In this example, I assume that h_t simply grows at the given, constant rate $\gamma - 1$,

$$h_{t+1} = \gamma h_t.$$

The only other use of time is assumed to be child raising. The technology for this activity involves a fixed amount k of time (not goods) per child, so that a parent with n children spends $1 - kn$ units of time producing goods. The resource constraint of a typical household is then

(2) $c \leq h(1 - kn).$

The household's Bellman equation is:

(3) $v(h) = \max_{c,n} W\left(c, n, v(\gamma h)\right),$

subject to (2).

Equation (3) will have a solution of the form $v(h) = Bh$, where the constant B satisfies

$$Bh = \max_n W\left(h(1 - kn), n, B\gamma h\right) = \max_n hW\left(1 - kn, n, B\gamma\right)$$

by the first-degree homogeneity property of W. Canceling gives:

(4) $B = \max_n W\left(1 - kn, n, B\gamma\right).$

The first-order condition for the problem (4) is:

(5) $W_n(1 - kn, n, B\gamma) = kW_c(1 - kn, n, B\gamma).$

We can think of (5) and

$$B = W\left(1 - kn, n, B\gamma\right)$$

as two equations to be solved for n and B, independent of the technology level h.

For the example (1), the solution for n is given by

$$(6) \quad kn = \frac{\eta}{1 - \beta + \eta},$$

analogous to the solution for the hunter-gatherer example of Section 3.[18] In this case, note that the rate of technological change γ does not affect fertility at all: The parameter B is an increasing function of γ (provided $\beta\gamma < 1$, as I assume), but neither B nor γ affects the solution for n.

More generally, as long as we retain the complementarity assumption (see note 9) that an increase in future utility per child increases the marginal utility of children to the parent—that parents would rather bear happy children than unhappy ones—this theory implies a fertility level that is non-decreasing in the rate of technological change. I do not see how one can get a demographic transition out of such a theory. On the other hand, if we reverse the complementarity assumption we lose the stability of the Mathusian equilibrium in the models of pre-industrial societies.

A Model with Endogenous Human Capital Growth

Restating this labor-only model as a model of endogenous technical change completely resolves this impasse, as I will next show. Replace the exogenously given growth rate γ for human capital with the equation

$$(7) \quad h_{t+1} = h_t\varphi(r_t),$$

where r_t is the fraction of the household's unit time endowment that is devoted to investment in the human capital of one's children. I continue to assume that there is a minimum amount k of time (not goods, in this case) per child, so that the resource constraint of a typical household is

$$(8) \quad c \leq h(1 - (r + k)n).$$

---

18. The analogy is natural, since that example and this one involve labor-only technologies; it is inexact because in the present example child-raising costs take the form of time rather than goods.

The household's Bellman equation is now written:

$$(9) \qquad v(h) = \max_{c,n,r} W\left(c, n, v(h\varphi(r))\right),$$

subject to (8).

Once again, we can see that the homogeneity property of W implies that a solution to (9) will take the form $v(h) = Bh$, and that the constant of proportionality B must satisfy

$$(10) \qquad B = \max_{n,r} W\left(1 - (r+k)n, n, B\varphi(r)\right).$$

The two first-order conditions are

$$(11) \qquad W_n\left(1 - (r+k)n, n, B\varphi(r)\right) = (r+k)W_c\left(1 - (r+k)n, n, B\varphi(r)\right),$$

$$(12) \qquad W_u\left(1 - (r+k)n, n, B\varphi(r)\right)B\varphi'(r) = nW_c\left(1 - (r+k)n, n, B\varphi(r)\right).$$

Specializing to the example (1), equation (11) becomes:

$$\frac{\eta}{n} = (r+k)\frac{1-\beta}{1-(r+k)n},$$

which can be rearranged to give the expression

$$(13) \qquad (r+k)n = \frac{\eta}{1-\beta+\eta}$$

for the *total* time expenditure on children. Compare (13) to the solution (6) for the exogenous technical change case, but in contrast to (6), equation (13) determines neither fertility n nor human capital investment r separately.

In this parametric example, the first-order condition (12) becomes

$$\beta\frac{\varphi'(r)}{\varphi(r)} = n\frac{1-\beta}{1-(r+k)n}.$$

Assuming the form

$$\varphi(r) = (Cr)^\varepsilon$$

for the human capital accumulation technology, we have

$$(14) \qquad \beta\varepsilon = rn\frac{1-\beta}{1-(r+k)n}.$$

Now use (13) and (14) to solve for r and n separately:

$$n = \frac{1}{k} \frac{\eta - \beta\varepsilon}{1 + \eta - \beta}$$

and

$$r = \frac{\beta\varepsilon}{\eta - \beta\varepsilon} k.$$

In this particular, exponential example, then, a change in the parameter C of the human capital accumulation function does not affect behavior, but an increase in the exponent ε induces both an increase in the time r devoted to acquiring human capital and a decrease in fertility.[19] This is certainly not the first example I have discussed in which the quantity-quality trade-off plays a role in determining fertility, but it is the first in which an improvement in technology—which an increase in ε represents—leads to a permanent reduction in fertility. This is the central idea in the Becker, Murphy, and Tamura (1990) account of the demographic transition.

Some recent research on economic growth has assigned great importance to the assumption that the engine of growth—technological change—is *exogenous*. (Some writers even take this feature as the defining characteristic of a *neoclassical* model!) This emphasis seems to me badly misplaced: Surely technological change must arise from some time-consuming activity. The present example shows that to explain the observed behavior of fertility during a demographic transition, one needs to assign an important role to endogenous human capital accumulation, motivated by the private rate of return to this activity. Of course, one need not assume equality of the private and social returns to investment in human capital. It may well be that new knowledge accrues to some who do not invest at all, in which case they might perceive it as "exogenous."

---

19. The functional form $\varphi(r) = (Cr)^\varepsilon$ facilitates the explicit solution in this example, but it does not make a lot of sense at all values of r: think of the case $r = 0$. I think of the parameter C as chosen so that equilibrium growth is positive, which requires $Cr > 1$. In this case, an increase in ε increases the growth rate of human capital for each level of r, and so unambiguously represents an improvement in technology.

Elaborations with Physical Capital

When physical capital is added to this model, one obtains essentially the theory of "Mechanics" (Chapter 1) and Caballe and Santos (1993), modified to include the fertility decision. Assume, to be specific, that goods production per household is a constant returns function of physical capital z and the labor input h. (This entails the assumption that one person with human capital h is the productive equivalent of two people with $h/2$ each.) Let physical capital depreciate at the rate δ, so a household in state (z, h) that produces $f(z, h)$ has $f(z, h) + (1 - \delta)z$ units of goods at its disposal, to be divided between consumption c, capital left over for its children, yn, and child raising costs $(r + k)hn$. Finally, assume the human capital technology (7). The resource constraint of a typical household is then

$$(15) \quad c + [y + (r + k)h]n \le f(z, h) + (1 - \delta)z,$$

and the household's Bellman equation is:

$$(16) \quad v(z, h) = \max_{c,n,r,y} W\left(c, n, v(y, h\varphi(r))\right),$$

subject to (15).

The change of variable similar to that used in the last example of Section 5 can reduce this problem to one with a single state variable. Let $w = z/h$ be the *ratio* of physical to human capital, let $\theta = c/h$ be the ratio of consumption to human capital, and let $\gamma = y/x$, so that $\gamma - 1$ is the growth rate of physical capital per capita. The resource constraint (15), restated in terms of the pair (w, h), is then:

$$(17) \quad \theta + (\gamma w + r + k)n \le f(w, 1) + (1 - \delta)w.$$

It is a reasonable conjecture that if the function $\phi(w)$ solves

$$(18) \quad \phi(w) = \max_{\theta,n,r,\gamma} W\left(\theta, n, \varphi(r)\phi\left(\frac{\gamma w}{\varphi(r)}\right)\right),$$

subject to (17), then $h\phi(z/h)$ will solve (16). We formalize this as a

Lemma. If $\phi(w)$ satisfies (18), then $h\phi(x/h)$ satisfies (16).

The proof, an application of the fact that $W(c, n, u)$ is homogeneous of degree one in the pair (c, u), is essentially the same as that of the Lemma in Section 5.

Without working out all the details, we can see that the system of first-order and envelope conditions for the problem (18) can be made consistent with a balanced equilibrium path, on which consumption and the two stocks of capital z and h all grow at the constant, common rate $\gamma = \varphi(r)$, and the ratio $w = z/h$ is constant: this is essentially the model of Section 4 of "Mechanics" (Chapter 1). On such a balanced path, the fertility level n and the level of human capital investment in each child, r, are both constant.

Conclusions

Models of sustained per capita income growth can be based on exogenous improvements in technology, or knowledge, or human capital, or they can be based on economic decisions to invest in activities that produce such improvements. With the population growth rate taken as fixed, such models can be hard to distinguish on the basis of aggregative time series. Once fertility is viewed as an economic decision, however, these two classes of models have sharply different predictions. Theories of exogenously given technological change imply that higher growth should be associated with higher fertility: People prefer to bring more children, not fewer, into a world that offers them a more prosperous life. Theories in which higher growth is viewed as a response to increases in the return to investment in human capital, in contrast, can imply that increases in growth are associated with reductions in fertility. This is the case in the second example of this subsection. Under the technology of this example, a family that wants to take advantage of an increase in the return to investment in knowledge does so, in part, by reducing the number of children so as to devote more time and resources to each child. Only this second class of theories, those based on endogenous human capital growth, is consistent with the demographic transition.

Human capital is a broad term, encompassing cognitive achievements that range from basic scientific discoveries to a child's learning how to read or how to plow behind a horse. Which particular activities are we thinking of if we center our view of economic growth and the industrial revolution on human capital accumulation? When Paul Romer stresses "knowledge capital" as "blueprints," he is thinking of human capital at the most abstract and ethereal end of the spectrum: important additions to a society's human capital that are, for almost all of us, events that happen to us without our doing anything to bring them about. When another economist stresses improvements in literacy, he is thinking of human capital at the other end of the spectrum, far from Science with a capital S, capital that is accumulated only if many people devote their time and energy to doing so. In any actual society, the accumulation of knowledge takes both of these extreme forms, as well as the range of possibilities in between, but it is *only* the second kind that can simultaneously also help us to explain the reduction in fertility that is essential to defeat the logic of Malthusian theory.

The demographic transition necessarily involves more than the accumulation of knowledge by a privileged class or subset of people. Such accumulation has taken place for centuries, inducing technical change, improved living standards, and increases in population, but ultimately leading to a return to the living standards of earlier ages. The new element that must have been involved in the demographic transition was an increase in the return to human capital accumulation that affected *everyone,* and hence every family's fertility choices. The industrial revolution required a change in the way people viewed the possibilities for the lives of their children that was widespread enough to reduce fertility across economic classes, affecting propertied and propertyless people alike.

The fact that the colonial system failed to bring sustained income growth to the colonized societies of Asia and Africa seems to me consistent with such an economically democratic view of the industrial revolution. Certainly the flow of European ideas brought increases in productivity and (hence) in population to British India and the Dutch East Indies. What colonialism did *not* bring to these societies were increases in the return to investment in children of ordinary familes, increases with the potential to change the quantity-quality trade-off faced by these families and to induce a demographic transition. Independence (I conjecture) brought about the removal of the limits on upward mobility imposed by the colonial system, altering the terms of this trade-off and opening the way for growth in per capita as well as total production.

7. A Demographic and Industrial Transition

The model of growth with endogenous human capital accumulation in Section 6 is essentially the "Ak" model used in Becker, Murphy, and Tamura (1990). By modifying the technology for human capital accumulation ($h_{t+1} = h_t \varphi(r_t)$ in my notation) at low levels of human capital, these authors obtain a locally stable steady state value h^*, which they call Malthusian. Because of the quantity-quality trade-off built into their model, fertility is higher at h^* than it is on the path of sustained growth that is also a solution to their model. In that sense, moving from the low-level steady state to the sustained growth path represents a demographic transition. But there is really nothing Malthusian about the low-level steady state in the Becker, Murphy, and Tamura model: Land is not a factor of production, and the pressure of increasing population on a fixed supply of land plays no role in their population dynamics.

Hansen and Prescott (1998) provide an alternative description of a transition from a Malthusian economy to a perpetually growing one that is also suggestive. In their model, goods can be produced with a land-and-labor-using technology that lacks any engine of growth. There is also a fertility relationship that links population to the level of production per capita. As long as the land-using technology is the only one that operates, the economy goes to and remains at a steady state that can reasonably be called Malthusian.

Hansen and Prescott postulate a second technology that uses labor but not land, and that improves at an exogenously given rate, as in Solow (1956). As long as the level of this second technology is low enough it is irrelevant, but sooner or later it becomes economic to operate both technologies side by side. Over time, more and more labor moves to the growth technology, though an Inada condition on the land-using technology keeps it from ever being abandoned. Asymptotically, this model is an "Ak" economy too.

What is happening to population growth as this transition occurs? The fertility–income level relationship is simply postulated to have an inverted-U shape. As income increases from its Malthusian steady state level, population growth first increases, then decreases. The role played by demography in this model is entirely passive. There is no quantity-quality trade-off, no choice between population growth and per capita income growth.

Both sets of authors address central issues of the industrial revolution, but both are trying to get by with a single endogenous state variable: human capital per person in the case of Becker, Murphy, and Tamura, and land per person in the case of Hansen and Prescott. (Physical capital can be added to either model without changing essentials.) Their models are useful in thinking about the onset of industrialization, but what is needed, I think, is a merger of the two approaches. In this section I develop this idea.

My point of departure will be to assume the existence of two production technologies, both taken essentially from Hansen and Prescott. We consider a household with h units of human capital and x units of land that devotes

ℓ units of time to producing a single consumption good. This good can be produced with two different technologies, one using labor and land that produces $Ax^\alpha \ell^{1-\alpha}$ units of goods, and the other using skilled labor only that produces $Bh\ell$ units of goods. Note that the skill level h contributes nothing in the land-using technology. The household can use $\theta \in [0, \ell]$ units of labor on the land-using technology and the remaining $\ell - \theta$ units on the growth technology. If this allocation is carried out optimally, total goods production will be

(1) $F(x, h, \ell) = \max_{\theta}[Ax^\alpha \theta^{1-\alpha} + Bh(\ell - \theta)].$

The first-order condition for the problem (1) is

$(1 - \alpha)Ax^\alpha \theta^{-\alpha} \geq Bh,$ with equality if $\theta < \ell.$

The problem is solved by the labor allocation

$$\theta = \min\left[\left(\frac{(1-\alpha)A}{Bh}\right)^{1/\alpha} x, \ell\right].$$

There is thus an indirect production function given by

$$F(x, h, \ell) = Bh\ell + \alpha(1 - \alpha)^{1/\alpha - 1}A^{1/\alpha}(Bh)^{1-1/\alpha}x$$

$$\text{if}\quad \left(\frac{(1-\alpha)A}{Bh}\right)^{1/\alpha} x < \ell,$$

and

$$F(x, h, \ell) = Ax^\alpha \ell^{1-\alpha}\quad \text{if}\quad \left(\frac{(1-\alpha)A}{Bh}\right)^{1/\alpha} x \geq \ell.$$

To examine the implications of this technology, we assume once again that household preferences take the Cobb-Douglas form:

$$W(c, n, u) = c^{1-\beta}n^\eta u^\beta.$$

The household has one unit of labor, of which rn units are allocated to child raising and $\ell = 1 - rn$ units are used in the production of goods. It produces $c + kn = F(x, h, \ell)$ units of goods, c of which are consumed by adults and kn by children. A time investment of r per child when parents' human capital is h endows each child with $h\varphi(r)$ units of human capital.

With these assumptions on preferences and technology, one can see that the stage is set for a transition from the classical economy studied in

Section 3 and the model with endogenous human capital growth introduced in Section 6. If only the land-using technology is used, the model reduces to the Ricardian model of Section 3. This equilibrium can occur and be maintained indefinitely, as we shall see. If only the growth technology is used, the model almost reduces to the endogenous human capital model of this section. ("Almost" because here the fixed cost k per child takes the form of goods rather than time, as assumed in Section 6.) With the Cobb-Douglas land-labor technology I have assumed, this will never occur exactly—some labor will always be combined with available land—but the fraction of labor used with the growth technology can approach one under appropriate conditions.

To formalize these ideas, begin with the household's Bellman equation:

$$v(x, h) = \max_{c,n,r} W(c, n, v(x/n, h\varphi(r))),$$

subject to

(2) $c + kn \leq F(x, h, 1 - rn)$.

Eliminating the variable c,

(3) $v(x, h) = \max_{n,r} W(F(x, h, 1 - rn) - kn, n, v(x/n, h\varphi(r)))$.

Let the policy functions for the dynamic program (3) be $c(x, h)$, $n(x, h)$, and $r(x, h)$. Then the state variables (x_t, h_t) evolve according to the autonomous difference equations

$$x_{t+1} = \frac{x_t}{n(x_t, h_t)}$$

and

$$h_{t+1} = h_t \varphi(r(x_t, h_t)).$$

Our aim is to characterize these solution paths.

To do so, we study the first-order and envelope conditions for the problem (3), specialized to the case of Cobb-Douglas preferences. These are

(4) $n(1 - \beta)[F_\ell(x, h, 1 - rn)r + k] = \eta c - \beta \frac{c}{u'} v_x[x/n, h\varphi(r)] \left(\frac{x}{n}\right)$,

(5) $n(1 - \beta)F_\ell(x, h, 1 - rn) \geq \beta \dfrac{c}{u'} v_h[x/n, h\varphi(r)]h\varphi'(r),$

with equality if $r > 0,$

(6) $v_x(x, h) = (1 - \beta) \dfrac{W}{c} F_x(x, h, 1 - rn) + \beta \dfrac{W}{u'} v_x[x/n, h\varphi(r)] \left(\dfrac{1}{n}\right),$

(7) $v_h(x, h) = (1 - \beta) \dfrac{W}{c} F_h(x, h, 1 - rn) + \beta \dfrac{W}{u'} v_h[x/n, h\varphi(r)] \varphi(r),$

where u' is shorthand for $v[x/n, h\varphi(r)]$.

Next, consider steady states (x, h) with $h = 0$. Under the functional forms I am assuming, an economy that is initially without human capital can never accumulate human capital, so $r = 0$ and equations (5) and (7) can be set aside. The marginal products of labor and land in this case are $F_\ell(x, h, 1) = (1 - \alpha)Ax^\alpha$ and $F_x(x, h, 1) = \alpha Ax^{\alpha-1}$. In a steady state, $n = 1$ and $c = W = u'$. Conditions (4) and (6), specialized to this case, become

$$(1 - \beta)k = \eta c - \beta v_x(x, 0)x,$$

and

$$v_x(x, 0) = (1 - \beta)\alpha Ax^{\alpha-1} + \beta v_x(x, 0).$$

We can eliminate the marginal value of land, $v_x(x, 0)$, between these two equations and apply the fact that $Ax^\alpha = c + k$ to obtain

$$c = \frac{1 - \beta + \alpha\beta}{\eta - \alpha\beta}k.$$

This is exactly the formula for steady state consumption obtained for the classical economy of Section 3. There is a corresponding steady state land holding per person, x_e. As shown in Section 3, this steady state is stable for all (x, h) with $h = 0$.

We now go to the opposite extreme, to examine the behavior of the system (4)–(7) for large values of h. This case is interesting because once the growth technology comes into use, if it ever does, h will grow without limit and the relative importance of land will fade. I will seek a solution on which n and r are constant at values that satisfy $n \geq 1$ and $\varphi(r) > 1$. On such a solution path, x remains bounded, tending to zero if $n > 1$, and h grows at the rate $\varphi(r) > 1$. The following limits, based on the production technology, will be useful in this analysis.

$$\lim_{b \to \infty} \frac{c}{b} = \lim_{b \to \infty} \frac{c+k}{b}$$

$$= \lim_{b \to \infty} \frac{1}{b} \left[Bb(1 - rn) + \alpha(1 - \alpha)^{1/\alpha - 1} A^{1/\alpha} (Bb)^{1 - 1/\alpha} x \right]$$

$$= B(1 - rn).$$

Similarly,

$$\lim_{b \to \infty} \frac{1}{b} F_\ell(x, b, \ell) = B,$$

$$\lim_{b \to \infty} F_b(x, b, 1 - rn) = B(1 - rn),$$

$$\lim_{b \to \infty} F_x(x, b, \ell) = \lim_{b \to \infty} [\alpha(1 - \alpha)^{1/\alpha - 1} A^{1/\alpha} (Bb)^{1 - 1/\alpha}] = 0.$$

Using these facts, the large-b version of (4)–(7) is:

(8) $n(1 - \beta)r = \eta(1 - rn),$

(9) $n(1 - \beta)B = \beta \dfrac{c}{u'} v_b[x, b\varphi(r)]\varphi'(r),$

(10) $v_x(x, b) = \beta \dfrac{W}{u'} v_x[x, b\varphi(r)] \dbinom{1}{n},$

(11) $v_b(x, b) = (1 - \beta) \dfrac{W}{c} B(1 - rn) + \beta \dfrac{W}{u'} v_b[x, b\varphi(r)]\varphi(r),$

where either $n = 1$ or $x = 0$ must hold.

I will seek a solution path with the marginal values v_b and v_x both constant, and with n and c/b constant. On such a path, $W/b = u'/(b\varphi(r))$ will be constant, and we have

$$\frac{W}{b} = \left(\frac{c}{b}\right)^{1-\beta} n^\eta \left(\frac{u'}{b}\right)^\beta = \left(\frac{c}{b}\right)^{1-\beta} \left(\frac{W}{b}\right)^\beta n^\eta (\varphi(r))^\beta$$

which implies that

$$\frac{W}{b} = \left(\frac{c}{b}\right) n^\eta \varphi(r)^{\beta/(1-\beta)} = B(1 - rn)n^\eta \varphi(r)^{\beta/(1-\beta)}.$$

Then $W/c = \varphi(r)^{\beta/(1-\beta)}$, $W/u' = 1/\varphi(r)$, and $c/u' = (W/u')/(W/c) = (1/\varphi(r))/(\varphi(r)^{\beta/(1-\beta)}) = \varphi(r)^{-1/(1-\beta)}$, and (9)–(11) can be simplified to

(12) $n(1 - \beta)B = \beta\varphi(r)^{-1/(1-\beta)}v_b\varphi'(r),$

(13) $\quad v_x = \beta \dfrac{1}{\varphi(r)} v_x \left(\dfrac{1}{n} \right),$

(14) $\quad v_h = (1 - \beta)\varphi(r)^{\beta/(1-\beta)} B(1 - rn) + \beta v_h.$

Since $\beta < 1$, $n \geq 1$, and $\varphi(r) > 1$, (13) implies that $v_x = 0$. We can use (14) to eliminate v_h and substitute into (12) and simplify to get

(15) $\quad n(1 - \beta) = \beta(1 - rn)\dfrac{\varphi'(r)}{\varphi(r)}.$

Equation (8) implies

(16) $\quad rn = \dfrac{\eta}{1 - \beta + \eta},$

which is the same as equation (13) of Section 6 when k is set equal to 0. Equations (15) and (16) together can then be used to solve for r and n separately, exactly as in Section 6.

These are the long-run possibilities for this two-state-variable system: a Malthusian steady state with a constant income level, and an "Ak"-like system in which income is perpetually growing, driven by the accumulation of human capital. Little is known about the possibilities for this model away from these two steady states, and since the intended subject of this section is the transition from one to the other, this is a serious limitation. Nevertheless, Figures 5.7 and 5.8 illustrate some possible kinds of behavior.

Think of the curve

(17) $\quad h = \dfrac{(1 - \alpha)A}{B} x^\alpha$

on which it is a matter of indifference whether to use the growth technology or to shut it down. If the state (x, h) is on this curve, one possibility is to set $r = 0$ and let h decrease. If that decision is optimal, then it will be optimal to let h decay to 0, and since h is never used, $v_h(x, h) = 0$. For (x, h) on or below the curve (17), we can just project down to the x-axis to get $v(x, h) = v(x, 0)$ and $n(x, h) = n(x, 0)$. In this case, there will be a curve above (17) at which r moves to a positive value. On this second curve, r must jump to a value that will lead h to increase; otherwise the positive r would just be wasted. Figure 5.7 exhibits a phase diagram with the features just described.

Figure 5.8 provides a phase diagram based on the opposite possibility that $r > 0$ along the curve (17). In this case, there will be a curve—dashed

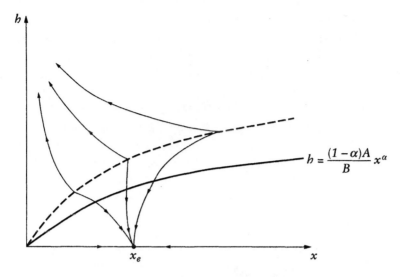

Figure 5.7 Possible transition dynamics: 1

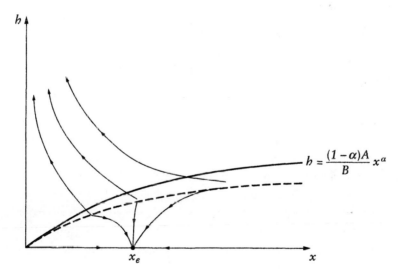

Figure 5.8 Possible transition dynamics: 2

on the figure—below (17) at which *h* begins to increase even though it is not yet economic to use it in production. Here agents must foresee the economic value of human capital before it is ever used in production!

To see which, if either, of these dynamic possibilities might actually materialize would require a much more extensive analysis of the system (4)–(7) than I have provided here.[20] The behavior shown in Figure 5.8 seems to me to place too great a burden on the assumption of perfect foresight: People are assumed to foresee that an industrial revolution will soon occur—even though nothing like it has ever occurred before—and to begin to accumulate the skills that this revolution will make useful.

The way to use Figure 5.7 to think about the beginnings of industrialization is to begin with a society in the position (*x*, *h*) with *h* > 0 and ask what shocks might move this society into the sustained growth region, the region above the dashed curve, in the figure. How did this society obtain a positive *h* position in the first place? Some skills are useful in the pre-industrial economy (though the model has no place for this). Some skills are accumulated for non-economic reasons: arts and science supported by patronage, say. Now suppose some factor shifts down the curve (17) and with it the dashed curve above (17) that describes the critical *h*-levels for initiating growth. An increase in *B*—the efficiency of the growth technology—could have this effect. So too could a loss of land or a decrease in the agricultural production function, *A*. So could a decrease in $1 - \alpha$, the labor intensity of the agricultural technology—freeing labor for other uses.

One could theorize about economic factors that might bring about such shifts, and it could be very useful to do so. My aim in this section has been the more modest one of trying to imagine an economic environment, consistent with the facts that both classical and modern economic theories were designed to explain, in which once-and-for-all shifts have the potential to initiate a transition from Malthusian stagnation to sustained growth.

Is the behavior just discussed, induced on Figure 5.7 by a jump of the initial coordinates (*x*, *h*) to a position above the dashed curve, fairly described as a *demographic transition*? Instead of returning to the steady state $(x_e, 0)$, at which population and income per person are both constant, a system that crosses the dashed line—somehow—will follow a path of growing income *and* growing population forever. Perhaps population growth will be faster

---

20. It would be particularly interesting to simulate a realistically calibrated version of the model, as Moe (1998) and Veloso (1999) have done in related contexts.

at first and then slow down; it might even slow to zero or some negative level. Whether parameters could be chosen so that the population growth jumps initially to the very high levels observed in some newly industrializing economies today, and then decreases in a generation or two to much lower rates, is very much an open question.

8. Conclusions

Defined as the onset of sustained income growth, the industrial revolution was not exclusively, or even primarily, a technological event. Important changes in technology have occurred throughout history, yet the sustained growth in living standards is an event of the last 200 years. The invention of agriculture, the domestication of animals, the invention of language, writing, mathematics, and printing, the utilization of the power of fire, wind, and water, all led to major improvements in the ability to produce goods and services, and these and many other inventions made possible enormous growth in population. Depending on where such inventions occurred, some of them induced important shifts in the relative power of different societies. By the seventeenth century, indeed, their ability to generate new technology had enabled the Europeans to conquer much of the world. Yet none of these inventions led to *any* substantial increase in the living standards of ordinary people, Europeans or others. All of this is precisely as the theory of Malthus and Ricardo explicitly predicted, or more likely, as it was designed to explain.

Of course this is not to say that prior to the last two centuries everyone lived at a level of subsistence, even where subsistence is given an economic as opposed to a biological definition, as I have done. Wherever property rights in land and other resources have been established, property owners have enjoyed incomes in excess of, often far in excess of, subsistence.[21]

---

21. According to Johnson (1948), the share of farm income accruing to land in the United States, 1910–1946, was between 0.30 and 0.35 (table IV, p. 734). This fraction is apparently fairly stable across different levels of income. McEvedy and Jones (1978) estimate that Egypt's population at the time of the conquest by Rome was 4m. At a per capita income of 600 1985 U.S. dollars, this corresponds to a GDP of $2.4b., almost all of which was farm income. Multiplying by 0.3 gives an estimate of land rental income of $720m. Some of this annual income flow must have gone to those who enforced and administered Roman rule, but even so it is not hard to see how some very comfortable life-styles and impressive monuments were financed.

Virtually everything we think of as civilization has been sustained by land's share in production, and most of political and military history is the history of conflicts over how this share shall be disposed. The existence and indeed the persistence over centuries of wealthy landowning families need not conflict with the Malthusian or Ricardian fertility theory, for parents with any kind of inheritable property are faced with a Beckerian trade-off between the quantity of children and the "quality" (that is, utility) of each child.

Our common sense tells us that the kind of quantity-quality trade-off entailed in the heritability of land cannot generate sustained income growth. A redistribution of land can reduce the fertility of some families and increase the fertility of others, but as in the example worked out in Section 4, such a redistribution need not even affect the long-run *level* of average income, and surely it cannot affect the long-term growth rate under any reasonable assumptions. The accumulation of reproducible capital adds new possibilities, but for the reasons familiar from Solow's (1956) original paper, diminishing returns prevent physical capital from serving as an engine of growth. This leaves human capital.

That the accumulation of human capital can serve as an engine of sustained growth is by now well known, and this idea has been embedded in a wide variety of tractable models. But human capital is a very broad term, so broad indeed that human-capital-based growth theories can be little more than older theories with key terms relabeled. I have argued in the last section that incorporating a fertility decision into theories of growth can help to sharpen our thinking considerably on the kind of human capital growth that is essential to income growth. What is needed are opportunities for human capital investment that face the mass of households in a society with a quantity-quality trade-off. A small group of leisured aristocrats can produce Greek philosophy or Portuguese navigation, but this is not the way the industrial revolution came about.

Transition

The model of an economy's transition from a traditional, stagnant-income steady state to one of perpetual growth offered in Becker, Murphy, and Tamura (1990) has stimulated much of this chapter. Their model exhibits two possibilities for long-run behavior, one with high fertility and low growth and another with low fertility and high growth. But their low-growth equilibrium is not really Malthusian or classical in any sense: Land plays no role, and the population *level* is not determined by the theory. Laitner (1994) has modeled the changing role of land as a factor of production over the course of the industrial revolution in a way that is technically promising and closely grounded in evidence. Hansen and Prescott (1998) have proposed an even simpler model of a transition, in which a stationary, land-using technology is gradually supplanted by a technology that is subject to ongoing, exogenously given improvements.

In this concluding section, I have tried to synthesize the ideas in these papers in a model in which both land per person and the level of human capital (or technology) serve as state variables. The analysis provided here is far from complete and is entirely qualitative, but it leads in a direction that I find promising. By focusing on forces that raise the return to human capital accumulation, the model isolates dynamics that can simultaneously influence production growth, fertility, and investment in human capital in the directions we have observed in economy after economy.

Diffusion

An understanding of the onset of the industrial revolution would presumably also yield an improved understanding of its gradual *diffusion* to country after country. Tamura (1991, 1996) proposes a mechanism for the diffusion of the industrial revolution, based on the idea that the return to accumulating human capital in any economy is an increasing function of the level of human capital in the world economy as a whole. According to this model, once any economy has entered into a phase of sustained human capital growth, the world stock is destined to grow without bound, and this growth eventually leads, via an external effect, to an increase in the return on human capital investment sufficient to trigger a demographic transition in every other economy. The model fits our sense of the diffusion of knowledge, and also our sense that the industrial revolution is a single event, not many independent events. The fact that human-capital-based models of growth lend themselves, with external effects, to such diffusion is, I think, yet another point in their favor.

How do these external effects occur? What is the process by which knowledge in one society affects its rate of accumulation in another? Geography is obviously part of the answer: One can see industrialization diffusing in space in the historical data. But physical proximity cannot be the key element: Albania did not share in Italy's postwar miracle, nor North Korea in Japan's. Geographic proximity must matter because it increases *economic* proximity, through trade and the interchange of ideas that trade stimulates. Stokey (1988, 1991a) and Young (1991) have formalized a connection between trade and human capital growth. Chuang (1993) and Irwin and Klenow (1994) have demonstrated the empirical importance of learning spillovers. In "Making a Miracle" (Chapter 3) I argue for their central importance, and I interpret Parente and Prescott (1994) as a complementary view.

Prediction

Modern theories of sustained growth, such as those of Section 6 in this chapter, abstract from considerations of land supply and limited resources generally. Such theories can, and do, fit long stretches of economic time series fairly well, but obviously they cannot fit forever. At some point, population will attain an upper bound and either stay there or begin to decline. Popular discussion has emphasized limits imposed by finite supplies of fuel, but predictions of fuel exhaustion—especially exhaustion that catches everyone by surprise—have not received much support from economic analysis. Limited land supply may ultimately show up in rising relative prices of food, though there is certainly no sign of this yet, or in prices of residential land. Residential space has a high income elasticity, so it may be that if per capita incomes continue to grow without bound, population growth will ultimately turn negative. We may become an ever less numerous race, with ever more palatial estates! Obviously none of the models I have explored here would be of much help in thinking about these questions concerning the very distant future, but this does not mean that economic reasoning could not usefully be applied to them.[22]

If it is clear that population must eventually be bounded, no analogous reasoning applies to per capita incomes. There are a number of theoretical models that relate population growth rates to the growth rate of knowledge, with the property that zero population growth implies zero growth in productivity, but this feature seems accidental, readily modified, and not

---

22. Cohen (1995) contains a stimulating, but entirely non-economic, discussion of the estimation of very long term population.

supported by evidence.[23] Economies with rapidly growing populations do not have systematically higher rates of productivity growth than other economies (Backus, Kehoe, and Kehoe 1992). On the other hand, there is enough mystery surrounding the discovery of new knowledge that it is hard to be sure that twentieth-century rates of growth will continue into the indefinite future. All one can say is that no tendency for scientists and others to run out of unsolved problems has yet been observed. The nineteenth-century idea that Science would get to the bottom of things has not fared well in the twentieth.

Even if it is impossible to tell whether productivity growth in the wealthiest economies will accelerate or diminish, the evolution of *relative* productivities has a clear and theoretically intelligible pattern. The industrial revolution began when a few economies entered into a phase of sustained growth, leaving the rest of the world in a Malthusian equilibrium. By the mid-nineteenth century, this process of sustained growth in some countries and stagnation in others had led to perhaps a factor of 1.7 difference in living standards between Europe and mainly European-occupied countries and the rest of the world; by the beginning of the twentieth century, this difference had grown to something like a factor of 3.2.[24] Throughout the first half of the twentieth century this gap continued to grow, leading to a factor of 5.7 difference between European and non-European societies by 1950, and to a factor of 15 to 25 differences in income between the richest and poorest societies.

In the period since World War II and the end of the colonial age, measures of income inequality across countries have stayed fairly stable. During this period, many societies have joined the industrial revolution, which has tended to reduce measured inequality, but others have continued to stagnate, increasing inequality. It is hard to read the future in data from 1960 to 1990, but I think it is becoming increasingly clear that the enormous inequality of the postwar period is at its all-time peak, and will decline in the future until something like the relative incomes of 1800 are restored. Within Europe, and between Europe and America, there has been a dramatic equalization since 1950. One non-European nation after another has followed Japan into rapid income growth, and no one can see anything but

---

23. The earliest is Arrow (1962).

24. By "European and mainly European-occupied countries" I mean Regions I, III, and IV as defined in Figure 5.3.

unstable domestic politics and mercantilist trade policies that keep the rest from doing so.

At the beginning of the twentieth century, many sophisticated observers were persuaded that northern Europeans must have racial or cultural advantages that accounted for the income differentials that had emerged during the nineteenth century. Now, at the beginning of a new century, it is abundantly clear that full participation in the economic benefits of the industrial revolution is open to countries of all races and cultural backgrounds. Figure 5.9 plots the share of the total world population in European-dominated economies, and also the European share in total product, from 1750 to the present. These shares were roughly equal, at about .24, in 1750, reflecting approximate equality in per capita production at that date. The share of world population in countries of mainly European populations peaked in the 1920s, at about .37. It was just under .30 in 1850 and has returned to that level today. The share of production in the European economies reached a peak of .76 in 1950, and is now .65. Does anyone doubt where these two time series are headed? The legacy of economic growth that we have inherited from the industrial revolution is an irreversible gain to humanity, of a magnitude that is still unknown.

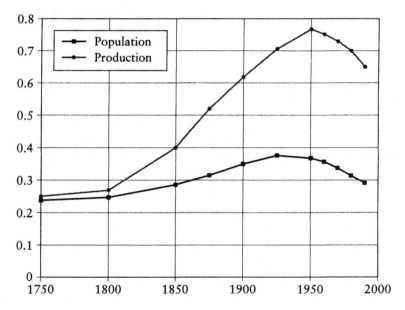

Figure 5.9 European shares of world production and population

It is becoming increasingly clear, I think, that the legacy of inequality, the concomitant of this gain, is a historical transient.

Data Appendix
This appendix describes the sources and procedures used to construct Figures 5.1–5.5 in the text. All of these figures are based on the population and per capita GDP data provided in Tables 5.1 and 5.2. Table 5.1 gives population estimates for 21 regions of the world, for the 15 indicated years from 1500 to 1990. Table 5.2 provides estimates of per capita GDP in 1985 U.S. dollars for the 11 indicated years from 1750 to 1990. I will first describe the sources and general procedures used for obtaining the population estimates, then the sources and procedures for the production estimates, and finally, I will define the 21 regions and discuss any special problems that arise with them.

Unless otherwise noted, the population estimates in Table 5.1 from 1960 on are from version PWT5.6 of the Penn World Tables described in Summers and Heston (1991). I abbreviate this source as S&H. Population figures from 1950 and earlier for all regions are from McEvedy and Jones (1978), which I abbreviate M&J. Postwar population figures for countries not found in either of these sources are usually taken from the U.N. Statistical Yearbooks, abbreviated U.N. Other sources are cited as pertinent. All these secondary sources use primary census data and official estimates, wherever available, so differences among them are minor. Comparison of population data for 1950 from M&J and S&H shows very close agreement for most regions.

Per capita production data are presented in Table 5.2, for these same 21 regions. Where both GDP and GNP are available, GDP is used. Otherwise, GNP is used. In all cases, I refer to the measure as GDP. Unless otherwise noted, all GDP estimates from 1960 on (from 1950 on, where available) are from S&H. The entries in boldface in Table 5.2 are the earliest figures taken from S&H. I use Variable 2 (RGDPCH) from S&H as the per capita GDP estimate. As described in the source, RGDPCH is a chain index series that values a country's real gross product in international prices of a base year. The listed figures are in 1985 international prices.

For the years 1950 and earlier, I used Bairoch (1981), which I abbreviate B, as the source of per capita GDP. (Maddison 1983, 1991, and 1995 also provides per capita GDP estimates for various countries and parts of the world.) These estimates are in 1960 U.S. dollars. I converted to 1985 dollars

Table 5.1 World population (in millions), 1500–1990

	1500	1600	1650	1700	1750	1800	1850	1875	1900	1925	1950	1960	1970	1980	1990
1 Africa	38	44	48	52	56	60	68	76	88	111	162	235	301	381	510
2 North Africa & Middle East	28	35	34	33	34	36	44	52	63	77	111	143	188	242	303
3 United States	1	1	1	1	2	6	24	44	76	115	150	181	205	228	250
4 Canada	0.2	0.2	0.2	0.2	0.3	0.5	2	4	5	10	14	18	21	24	27
5 Mexico	5	4	4	4	5	6	8	9	14	15	27	38	53	67	82
6 Southern Cone	1	1	1	1	1	1	3	5	9	16	25	31	36	42	49
7 Rest of Latin America	7	6	6	7	8	11	22	29	43	67	111	149	197	250	307
8 Japan	17	22	25	29	29	28	32	36	45	60	84	94	104	117	124
9 China	110	160	140	160	225	329	433	413	472	527	582	668	820	983	1136
10 East Asia	4	5	5	7	8	10	12	13	15	23	39	47	64	79	91
11 Southeast Asia	20	22	24	26	29	33	44	57	85	122	180	219	283	362	442

12 Indian subcontinent	105	135	150	165	175	190	230	255	290	330	445	553	700	887	1108
13 United Kingdom	5	5	6	7	8	11	21	29	38	45	50	53	56	56	57
14 France	15	18	21	22	24	29	36	38	41	40	42	46	51	54	57
15 Germany	9	12	11	13	15	18	27	33	43	55	70	72	78	78	79
16 Low countries	2	3	4	4	4	5	8	9	12	16	19	21	23	24	25
17 Scandinavia	2	2	3	3	4	5	8	10	12	16	18	20	21	22	23
18 Rest of Western Europe	22	29	27	31	37	46	60	67	77	88	108	116	125	134	139
19 Former Soviet Union	17	21	23	27	34	45	74	93	124	168	181	214	243	266	289
20 Eastern Europe	13	17	17	18	23	31	43	53	68	82	87	98	106	115	120
21 Australia & New Zealand	0.2	0.3	0.3	0.3	0.4	0.4	1	2	4	8	10	13	15	18	20

Table 5.2 Per capita GDP in 1985 U.S. dollars, 1750–1990

	1750	1800	1850	1875	1900	1925	1950	1960	1970	1980	1990
1 Africa	455	455	455	466	489	525	636	763	961	1116	966
2 North Africa & Middle East	542	542	542	571	634	742	1129	1647	2574	3583	3494
3 United States	837	870	1519	2581	3943	6034	8772	9895	12963	15295	18054
4 Canada	821	854	1279	1923	3095	4254	6380	7258	10124	14133	17173
5 Mexico	826	858	922	1105	1373	1646	2198	2836	3987	6054	5827
6 Southern Cone	826	858	958	1262	1756	2313	3594	4028	4987	5720	4600
7 Rest of Latin America	817	858	907	1041	1228	1409	1757	1983	2664	3853	3598
8 Japan	636	636	625	681	1025	1401	1430	2954	7307	10072	14331
9 China	630	630	630	630	630	630	500	568	697	973	1325
10 East Asia	630	630	630	630	630	630	630	1004	1812	3458	6807
11 Southeast Asia	630	630	630	630	630	630	630	696	915	1403	1954

12 Indian subcontinent	630	630	630	630	630	630	630	779	873	935	1296
13 United Kingdom	805	840	1864	2633	3527	4362	**5395**	6823	8537	10167	13217
14 France	665	752	1207	1612	2152	3110	**4045**	5823	9200	11756	13904
15 Germany	652	738	1048	1488	2179	2974	3122	**5843**	8415	11005	13543
16 Low countries	665	752	1274	1795	2464	3564	**4518**	5851	8844	11222	13158
17 Scandinavia	692	783	979	1373	2044	2879	**4930**	6541	9450	11798	14444
18 Rest of Western Europe	665	753	1126	1408	1840	2301	2813	**3951**	6622	8694	10729
19 Former Soviet Union	578	620	697	815	991	1114	1713	**2397**	4088	6119	7741
20 Eastern Europe	578	620	709	797	911	1078	1340	**1823**	2621	3986	3970
21 Australia & New Zealand	837	870	1862	2650	3672	3984	**6676**	7815	10505	12143	13962

Note: Boldface indicates earliest estimate from Summers and Heston.

using the ratio of deflators for 1960 and 1985 from S&H, which entails simply multiplying all Bairoch estimates by 3.5.

Where overlapping estimates exist, generally for 1960, there are differences between S&H and Bairoch estimates. When the difference was 4 percent or less, I simply multiplied all Bairoch estimates again by the ratio of the S&H to Bairoch estimate for the overlapping year. These multiplicative factors are listed in the region-specific sections below, for all regions where this procedure was applied.

When the difference between overlapping year estimates exceeded 4 percent, I used a different procedure. For these cases, I used Bairoch's estimates of income *levels* for 1800, and used his estimates for later years to estimate rates of growth from this base. I then multiplied all these growth rates by a constant chosen to make the adjusted Bairoch estimates and the S&H estimates agree for 1960 (1950, when available in S&H). The details differ from region to region, and are provided below in the region-specific sections.

I next define the 21 regions, and provide data sources for each.

1. *Africa.* Includes all of Africa except for the northern tier of countries: Morocco, Algeria, Tunisia, Libya, and Egypt.

Population: The populations of the Maghreb (M&J, p. 221), Libya (p. 225), and Egypt (p. 227) were subtracted from Africa as a whole (p. 206). Some interpolations were used for 1650, 1750, 1875, and 1925. Livi-Bacci (1992), table 1.3, also provides population data for the entire continent of Africa. These estimates are consistently higher than the M&J estimates for Africa as a whole, substantially so for the earlier years. (For example, the 1500 estimates from these two sources are 46 and 87 million respectively.)

GDP: Estimates from 1960 on are from S&H. Estimates for 1950 and earlier are based on the Bairoch, table 1.7, estimates for Africa as a whole, provided for the years 1800, 1860, 1913, 1938, 1950, and 1960. The 1800 estimate, $455 = 130 \times 3.5$, was applied to 1750 as well. Estimates for later years were interpolated and used to estimate the annual growth rates given for Region 1 in Table 5.3. As indicated in Row 1 of Table 5.3, these growth rates were then multiplied by the constant .957, chosen so that the 1960 per capita income estimate agrees with the S&H estimate, and then used to interpolate per capita GDP for the indicated years from 1850 to 1950.

2. *North Africa and the Middle East.* Includes Morocco, Algeria, Tunisia, Libya, and Egypt; and Turkey, Syria, Lebanon, Palestine (Israel, Jordan),

Table 5.3 Relative growth rates by region

Region	1800–50	1860–75	1875–1900	1900–25	1925–50	1950–60	Source	Constant
1	0	0.001	0.002	0.003	0.008	0.019	Table 1.7	0.957
2	0	0.001	0.002	0.003	0.008	0.019	Table 1.7	2.1
5	0.001	0.005	0.006	0.005	0.008	0.011	Table 1.7	1.45
6	0.001	0.005	0.006	0.005	0.008	0.011	Table 1.7	2.2
7	0.001	0.005	0.006	0.005	0.008	0.011	Table 1.7	1.1
13	0.015	0.013	0.011	0.008	0.008	—	Table 1.4	1.06
14	0.009	0.011	0.011	0.014	0.01	—	Table 1.4	1.052
16	0.01	0.013	0.012	0.014	0.009	—	Table 1.4	1.055
18	0.009	0.01	0.012	0.01	0.009	0.038	Table 1.6	0.89
19	0.003	0.008	0.01	0.006	0.022	0.043	Table 1.4	0.78
20	0.004	0.007	0.008	0.01	0.013	0.046	Table 1.6	0.67
21	0.014	0.013	0.012	0.003	0.019	—	Table 1.4	1.087

"Source" column indicates table in Bairoch (1981) on which most growth rates are based.

Arabia (Kuwait, Bahrain, the U.A.E., Saudi Arabia, Oman, Yemen, Qatar), Iran, Iraq, and Afghanistan.

Population: To the populations of the Maghreb, Libya, and Egypt (above, 1) were added the populations of Turkey-in-Europe (M&J, p. 113), Turkey-in-Asia (p. 134), Syria and Lebanon (p. 138), Palestine and Jordan (p. 143), Arabia (p. 144), Iraq (p. 150), Iran (p. 152), and Afghanistan (p. 154). Some interpolations are used for 1650, 1750, 1850, 1875, and 1925. For comparison, M&J report 112m. for 1950, while S&H (supplemented by the U.N. yearbooks) report 118m.

GDP: Data from 1960 on are from S&H, with minor extrapolations. Data before 1960 are from B, table 1.7. The average of the Asia and Africa estimates is used for 1800: 542 1985 U.S. dollars. This figure is applied to 1750 as well. The years between 1800 and 1960 are interpolated, using the assumption that the growth rates were proportional to those given for Africa in Table 5.3. The necessary constant of proportionality in this case is 2.1.

3. *U.S.A.*

Population: M&J, pp. 287 and 290. Hawaiian population is given separately, pp. 334–336.

GDP: B, table 1.4, has per capita figures for the U.S. and Canada separately from 1830. North American figures from table 1.6 are used for 1750 and 1800, for both the U.S. and Canada. S&H data are used from 1950 on. Estimates before 1960 are multiplied by 1.04, the ratio of the S&H to Bairoch estimates for 1950.

4. *Canada.*

Population: M&J, p. 285.

GDP: B, table 1.4, is used after 1830. North American figures from table 1.6 are used for 1750 and 1800. S&H data are used from 1950 on. Estimates before 1960 are multiplied by 1.02, the ratio of the S&H to Bairoch estimates for 1950.

5. *Mexico.*

Population: M&J, p. 293. M&J note that the population figure for 1500 is controversial, with estimates as different as 5 million and 30 million. M&J choose the lower. Interpolation is needed for 1650.

GDP: Estimates from 1950 on are from S&H. Estimates for 1925 and earlier are based on the Bairoch, table 1.7, estimates for "Third World America" as a whole, provided for the years 1800, 1860, 1913, 1928, 1938, and 1950. The 1800 estimate is 858. This figure was extrapolated to 1750 as well, keeping the ratio to the U.S. fixed: This gave (858/870) × 837 = 825. Estimates for later years were based on interpolations of the estimates in Bairoch, table 1.7, which imply the annual growth rates given in Row 5 of my Table 5.3. My estimated growth rates are proportional to these, with the constant of proportionality 1.45.

6. *South American Cone.* Argentina, Chile, and Uruguay.

Population: M&J, pp. 315–317.

GDP: Data for 1950 and later years are from S&H. The estimate for 1800 is from Bairoch, table 1.7, for all of Latin America. It was extrapolated back to 1750 with the same procedure (and the same resulting number) as with Mexico. Incomes for the indicated years from 1850–1950 were interpolated, assuming that Southern Cone growth rates were proportional to those in Row 6 of Table 1.3, with the constant of proportionality 2.2.

7. *Rest of Latin America and the Caribbean.* Includes the Caribbean Islands, Central America (Guatemala, Belize, El Salvador, Honduras, Nicaragua, Costa Rica, and Panama), Colombia, Venezuela, the Guyanas, Suriname, Brazil, Ecuador, Peru, Bolivia, and Paraguay.

Population: M&J, pp. 295–311. Interpolations are used for 1650, 1750, 1875, and 1925. From 1950 on the population figures for individual countries from S&H are used, where available, and where not, data are from the U.N. yearbooks.

GDP: From 1960 on, S&H data are used, with minor exceptions. Before 1960, data from B, table 1.7, are used, with exactly the same procedures applied in 5 and 6. These implied the growth rates given in Row 7 of Table 5.3. My estimated growth rates are proportional to these, with the constant of proportionality 1.1.

8. *Japan.*

Population: M&J, p. 181.

GDP: Estimates before 1950 are from B, table 1.6. S&H is used for the remaining years. Estimates from Bairoch are multiplied by 1.01, the ratio of the S&H to Bairoch estimates for 1950.

9. *China.* Includes Mongolia and Tibet, but excludes Taiwan and Hong Kong.

Population: Starting with the estimate given in M&J, p. 167, the populations of Taiwan (p. 175) and Hong Kong are subtracted, and the population of Mongolia (p. 164) is added. The Hong Kong population was negligible until 1900. The figures of 0.37m. in 1901, 0.71m. in 1925, and 1.93m. in 1950 (the last two are interpolated) from the U.N. demographic report on Hong Kong are subtracted for the later years. S&H provide no data on China for 1950, so the M&J estimate is used. The 1975 S&H estimate, 916m., is considerably higher than the M&J figure of 815m.

GDP: Estimates from 1960 on are from S&H. B, table 1.7, contains estimates for earlier years, but the Bairoch estimate for 1960 is 1.41 times the S&H estimate for that year, and even the Bairoch estimate for 1800 is 1.29 times the S&H estimate for 1960! Rather than working from these numbers, I used 500 for 1950 (reflecting some of the 1950 to 1960 growth recorded in B, table 1.7) and then 630 for *all* earlier years. See the discussion in 10, 11, and 12 below.

10. *East Asia.* Includes Taiwan, South and North Korea, and Hong Kong.

Population: M&J, pp. 174–178, for Taiwan and Korea. Interpolations are used for 1650, 1750, and 1875. As mentioned in section 9, Hong Kong's population for 1900 to 1950 is taken from the (1974) U.N. demographic report on Hong Kong; population before 1900 is taken to be negligible. S&H are used from 1960 on. North Korean figures from 1960 onward are from the U.N. yearbooks.

GDP: Estimates for before 1950 are based on the B, table 1.7, estimates for all of Asia. These estimates indicate no growth between 1800 and 1950. The 1800 estimate of 630 = 180 × 3.5 was used for 1750 and for all years through 1950. Data from 1960 on are from S&H. Extrapolation was used for North Korea.

11. *Southeast Asia.* Includes Burma, Thailand, Indo-China (Laos, Vietnam, Khmer Republic/Cambodia), Malaysia, Singapore, Indonesia, and the Philippines. Oceania is also included: Melanesia (Papua New Guinea, Bismarcks, Solomon Islands, New Hebrides, Fiji) and Polynesia (Tonga, Samoa, Tahiti, Cook Islands).

Population: M&J, pp. 190–203 and 330–336. Interpolations are used for 1650 and 1750.

GDP: As discussed in section 10, the B, table 1.7, estimate of 630 is used for all of the years 1750–1950. Data from 1960 on are from S&H, with the following amendments. Appendix B of S&H estimates Vietnamese per capita GDP to be 3.1 percent of that of the U.S. in 1985. I use this ratio for all of Indo-China from 1960 to 1990.

12. *Indian Subcontinent.* Includes Pakistan, India, Bangladesh, Sri Lanka, Nepal, Sikkim (now part of India), and Bhutan.

Population: M&J, p. 183. Interpolations are used for 1650 and 1750.

GDP: As discussed in section 10, the B, table 1.7, estimate of 630 is used for all of the years 1750–1950. Data from 1960 on are from S&H. I assume that the per capita GDP of Bhutan is the same as that of Bangladesh.

13. *United Kingdom.*

Population: M&J, pp. 43, 47.

GDP: Estimates from 1950 on are from S&H. Estimates for 1750 and 1800 are taken from the "most developed" column in B, table 1.3, multiplied by 3.5. Growth rates from 1800 to 1950 were estimated using interpolations of the estimates for the U.K. in B, table 1.4, which imply the annual growth rates given in Row 13 of my Table 5.3. My estimated growth rates are proportional to these, with the constant of proportionality 1.06.

14. *France.*

Population: M&J, pp. 57–59.

GDP: Estimates from 1950 on are from S&H. Estimates for 1750 and 1800 are taken from the "Western Europe" column in B, table 1.6, multiplied by 3.5. Growth rates from 1800 to 1950 were estimated using interpolations of the estimates for France in B, table 1.4, which imply the annual growth rates given in Row 14 of my Table 5.3. My estimated growth rates are proportional to these, with the constant of proportionality 1.052.

15. *Germany.* Includes West and East Germany when they were separate states.

Population: M&J, p. 69. East Germany (including East Berlin) figures for 1950, 1960, and 1990 are taken from the U.N. yearbooks.

GDP: Estimates from 1970 on are from S&H. For 1960, the estimate for West Germany is from S&H and the estimate for East Germany is interpolated using the assumption that the 1960 ratio of West to East German GDP per capita equals the 1970 ratio (from S&H). Estimates for 1750 and 1800 are taken from the "Western Europe" column in B, table 1.6, multiplied by 3.5. Income levels from 1800 to 1960 were estimated using interpolations of the estimates for Germany in B, table 1.4. For 1950 I used .72 times Bairoch's estimate for West Germany plus .28 times his East Germany estimate. For 1960 I used .77 times Bairoch's estimate for West Germany plus

.23 times his East Germany estimate. These are population weights from S&H. All estimates from Bairoch are multiplied by .98, the ratio of the 1960 S&H estimates to those from Bairoch.

16. The Low Countries. Includes Belgium, Luxembourg, and the Netherlands.

Population: M&J, pp. 62–64.

GDP: Estimates from 1950 on are from S&H. Estimates for 1750 and 1800 are taken from the "Western Europe" column in B, table 1.6, multiplied by 3.5. Estimates for Belgium and the Netherlands in B, table 1.4, are aggregated, using the population weights .46 and .54 from S&H for 1950. Growth rates from 1800 to 1950 were estimated using interpolations of these estimates, which imply the annual growth rates given in Row 16 of my Table 5.3. My estimated growth rates are proportional to these, with the constant of proportionality 1.055.

17. Scandinavia. Includes Denmark, Sweden, Norway, and Finland.

Population: M&J, p. 51.

GDP: Estimates from 1950 on are from S&H. Estimates for 1750 and 1800 are taken from the "Western Europe" column in B, table 1.6, multiplied by 3.5. Estimates for Denmark, Finland, Norway, and Sweden in B, table 1.4, are aggregated, using the population weights .23, .22, .18, and .37 from S&H for 1950. Income levels from 1800 to 1950 were estimated using interpolations of these estimates. All estimates from Bairoch are multiplied by 1.04, the ratio of the 1950 S&H estimates to those from Bairoch.

18. Rest of Western Europe. Includes Ireland, Switzerland, Austria, Spain, Portugal, Italy, Albania, Greece, Cyprus, Malta, Iceland, Greenland, and the islands that are now part of Spain and Portugal.

Population: M&J, pp. 47, 87, 89, 105, 107, 113, and 119. Interpolations are used for 1650, 1750, and 1875. Data from 1950 on are from S&H, except for Albania (all years) and Malta (1950 and 1990), whose population figures are from the U.N. yearbooks.

GDP: Estimates from 1960 on are from S&H. GDP per capita in Albania was estimated at .26 times the level in Yugoslavia for the years 1960, 1970, 1980, and 1990, based on the 1990 figures given in the World Almanac and Book of Facts. Estimates for 1750 and 1800 are taken from the "Western Europe" column in B, table 1.6, multiplied by 3.5. Growth rates from 1800 to 1960 were estimated using interpolations of the estimates for Western Europe in B, table 1.6, which imply the annual growth rates given in Row 18 of my Table 5.3. My estimated growth rates are proportional to these, with the constant of proportionality .89.

19. *Former Soviet Union.*

Population: M&J estimates for Russia-in-Europe (p. 79), Caucasia (p. 158), Siberia (p. 161), and Russian Turkestan (p. 163) were added. Interpolations were used for 1650, 1750, and 1875. S&H is used for 1960, 1970, and 1980. The U.N. yearbooks were used for 1950 and 1990. There is a sizable discrepancy between the 1950 estimates of M&J (181m.) and the 1951 U.N. yearbook (193m.). Livi-Bacci (table E.1) reports 180m. I use the M&J figure.

GDP: Estimates from 1960 on are from S&H. Estimates for 1750 and 1800 are taken from the "Eastern Europe" column in B, table 1.6, multiplied by 3.5. The growth rates from 1800 to 1830 were taken from the estimates for Eastern Europe in B, table 1.6. Growth rates from 1830 to 1960 were estimated using interpolations of the estimates for the Soviet Union in B, table 1.4. These sources imply the annual growth rates given in Row 19 of my Table 5.3. My estimated growth rates are proportional to these, with the constant of proportionality .78.

20. *Eastern Europe.* Includes Poland, Czechoslovakia, Hungary, Romania, the former Yugoslavia, and Bulgaria.

Population: M&J estimates for "present day Poland" (p. 75), Czechoslovakia (p. 85), Hungary (p. 92), Romania (p. 97), Yugoslavia (p. 113), and Bulgaria (p. 113) were added. Interpolations were used for Yugoslavia and Bulgaria for 1750. For 1950 and later, estimates from S&H were used, with the exceptions of Czechoslovakia (1950), Romania (1950 and 1990), Bulgaria (1950, 1960, and 1970), and Poland (1950 and 1960), which came from the U.N. yearbooks.

GDP: Estimates from 1960 on are from S&H, with the following exceptions. Bulgaria per capita GDP for 1960 was interpolated using the assumption that the ratio to U.S. income for these years equaled the 1980 ratio. Hungary and Poland for 1960 were interpolated using the assumption that the ratios to U.S. income for that year equaled the 1970 ratios. Estimates for 1750 and 1800 are taken from the "Eastern Europe" column in B, table 1.6, multiplied by 3.5. Growth rates from 1800 to 1960 were estimated using interpolations of the estimates for Eastern Europe in B, table 1.6, which imply the annual growth rates given in Row 20 of my Table 5.3. My estimated growth rates are proportional to these, with the constant of proportionality .67.

21. *Australia and New Zealand.*

Population: M&J, pp. 329 and 339. Interpolations are used for 1650, 1700, 1750, and 1875.

GDP: Estimates from 1950 on are from S&H. Estimates for 1750 and 1800 are taken as equal to the U.S. (Population is neglible for these years.) Income levels from 1800 to 1950 were estimated using interpolations of the estimates for Australia in B, table 1.4, supplemented by U.S. income for years before 1860. These imply the annual growth rates given in Row 21 of my Table 5.3. My estimated growth rates are proportional to these, with the constant of proportionality 1.087.

Aghion, Philippe, and Peter Howitt. 1992. "A Model of Growth Through Creative Destruction." *Econometrica*, 60: 323–351.

Ahituv, Avner. 1995. "Fertility Choices and Optimum Growth: A Theoretical and Empirical Investigation." University of Chicago doctoral dissertation.

Alvarez, Fernando. 1995. "Social Mobility: The Barro-Becker Children Meet the Loury-Laitner Dynasties." University of Pennsylvania working paper.

Andrade, Eduardo De Carvalho. 1998. "Growth, Distribution, and School Policy." University of Chicago doctoral dissertation.

Arrow, Kenneth J. 1962. "The Economic Implications of Learning by Doing." *Review of Economic Studies*, 29: 155–173.

Backus, David K., Patrick J. Kehoe, and Timothy J. Kehoe. 1992. "In Search of Scale Effects in Trade and Growth." *Journal of Economic Theory*, 58: 377–409.

Bairoch, Paul. 1981. "The Main Trends in National Economic Disparities Since the Industrial Revolution." Chapter 1 in Paul Bairoch and Maurice Levy-Leboyer, eds., *Disparities in Economic Development Since the Industrial Revolution*. New York: St. Martin's Press.

Barro, Robert J., and Gary S. Becker. 1989. "Fertility Choice in a Model of Economic Growth." *Econometrica*, 57: 481–501.

Barro, Robert J., and Xavier Sala-i-Martin. 1992. "Technological Diffusion, Convergence, and Growth." *Journal of Economic Growth*, 2: 1–26.

——— 1997. "Convergence." *Journal of Political Economy*, 100: 223–251.

Baumol, William. 1986. "Productivity Growth, Convergence and Welfare: What the Long-Run Data Show." *American Economic Review*, 76: 1072–1085.

Baumol, William, and Edward N. Wolff. 1988. "Productivity Growth, Convergence and Welfare: Reply." *American Economic Review*, 78: 1155–1159.

Becker, Gary S. 1960. "An Economic Analysis of Fertility." In Richard Easterlin, ed., *Demographic and Economic Change in Developed Countries.* Universities-National Bureau Conference Series, no. 11. Princeton: Princeton University Press.

———— 1964. *Human Capital.* New York: Columbia University Press, for the National Bureau of Economic Research.

Becker, Gary S., and Robert J. Barro. 1988. "A Reformulation of the Economic Theory of Fertility." *Quarterly Journal of Economics,* 103: 1–25.

Becker, Gary S., Kevin M. Murphy, and Robert Tamura. 1990. "Human Capital, Fertility, and Economic Growth." *Journal of Political Economy,* 98: S12–S37.

Ben-David, Dan. 1991. "Equalizing Exchange: A Study of the Effects of Trade Liberalization." National Bureau of Economic Research Working Paper No. 3706.

Benhabib, Jess, and Kazuo Nishimura. 1993. "Endogenous Fertility and Growth." In Robert Becker et al., eds., *General Equilibrium, Growth, and Trade, Volume 2: The Legacy of Lionel McKenzie.* San Diego, London, Sydney, Toronto: Harcourt Brace, Academic Press.

Boldrin, Michele, and Jose A. Scheinkman. 1988. "Learning-by-Doing, International Trade, and Growth." In Santa Fe Institute Studies in the Sciences of Complexity, *The Economy as an Evolving Complex System,* 285–300.

Boston Consulting Group. 1968. *Perspectives on Experience.* Boston: Boston Consulting Group.

Boxall, Peter J. 1986. "Labor and Population in a Growth Model." University of Chicago doctoral dissertation.

Burmeister, Edwin, and A. Rodney Dobell. 1970. *Mathematical Theories of Economic Growth.* New York: Macmillan.

Caballe, Jordi, and Manuel S. Santos. 1993. "On Endogenous Growth with Physical and Human Capital." *Journal of Political Economy,* 101: 1042–1067.

Cass, David. 1965. "Optimum Growth in an Aggregative Model of Capital Accumulation." *Review of Economic Studies,* 32: 233–240.

Chari, V. V., Patrick J. Kehoe, and Ellen R. McGrattan. 1996. "The Poverty of Nations: A Quantitative Exploration." National Bureau of Economic Research Working Paper No. 5414.

Chuang, Yih-Chyi. 1993. "Learning by Doing, the Technology Gap, and Growth." University of Chicago doctoral dissertation.

Cohen, Joel. 1995. *How Many People Can the Earth Support?* New York: W. W. Norton.

Davis, Lance E., and Robert A. Huttenback. 1989. "Businessmen, the Raj, and the Pattern of Government Expenditures: The British Empire, 1860–1912." In David W. Galenson, ed., *Markets in History*. Cambridge: Cambridge University Press.

De Long, Bradford J. 1988. "Productivity Growth, Convergence, and Welfare: Comment." *American Economic Review*, 78: 1138–1154.

Denison, Edward F. 1961. *The Sources of Economic Growth in the United States*. New York: Committee for Economic Development.

Directorate-General of Budget, Accounting, and Statistics, executive Yuan. 1987. *National Income in Taiwan Area, The Republic of China*.

Dixit, Avinash K., and Joseph E. Stiglitz. 1977. "Monopolistic Competition and Optimum Product Diversity." *American Economic Review*, 67: 297–308.

Dobb, Maurice. 1945. *Political Economy and Capitalism*. Westport: Greenwood.

Doepke, Mathias. 2000. "Fertility, Income Distribution, and Growth." University of Chicago doctoral dissertation.

Ehrlich, Isaac, and Francis T. Lui. 1991. "Intergenerational Trade, Longevity, and Economic Growth." *Journal of Political Economy*, 99: 1029–1059.

——— 1997. "The Problem of Population and Growth: A Review of the Literature from Malthus to Contemporary Models of Endogenous Population and Endogenous Growth." *Journal of Economic Dynamics and Control*, 21: 205–242.

Galor, Oded, and David N. Weil. 1996. "The Gender Gap, Fertility, and Growth." *American Economic Review*, 86: 374–387.

Goodfriend, Marvin, and John McDermott. 1995. "Early Development." *American Economic Review*, 85: 116–133.

Gordon, Robert J. 1971. "Measurement Bias in Price Indexes for Capital Goods." *Review of Income and Wealth*, Series 17.

Griliches, Zvi, and Dale W. Jorgenson. 1967. "The Explanation of Productivity Change." *Review of Economic Studies*, 34: 249–282.

Grossman, Gene M., and Elhanan Helpman. 1991a. "Quality Ladders and Product Cycles." *Quarterly Journal of Economics*, 106: 557–586.

——— 1991b. *Innovation and Growth in the World Economy*. Cambridge, Mass.: MIT Press.

Hansen, Gary, and Edward C. Prescott. 1998. "From Malthus to Solow." University of Chicago working paper.

Harberger, Arnold C., ed. 1984. *World Economic Growth*. San Franscisco: ICS Press.

Harberger, Arnold C. 1990. "Reflections on the Growth Process." Working paper.

Irwin, Douglas A., and Peter J. Klenow. 1994. "Learning-by-Doing Spillovers in the Semiconductor Industry." *Journal of Political Economy*, 102: 1200–1227.

Jacobs, Jane. 1969. *The Economy of Cities*. New York: Random House.

———— 1984. *Cities and the Wealth of Nations*. New York: Random House.

Johnson, D. Gale. 1948. "Allocation of Agricultural Income." *Journal of Farm Economics*, 30: 724–749.

———— 1997. "Agriculture and the Wealth of Nations." *American Economic Review*, 87: 1–12.

Jones, Charles I. 1997a. "Convergence Revisited." *Journal of Economic Growth*, 2: 131–154.

———— 1997b. "On the Evolution of the World Income Distribution." *Journal of Economic Perspectives*, 11: 19–36.

Jones, Larry E., and Rodolfo E. Manuelli. 1990. "A Convex Model of Equilibrium Growth: Theory and Policy Implications." *Journal of Political Economy*, 98: 1008–1038.

Kamien, Morton I., and Nancy L. Schwartz. 1982. *Market Structure and Innovation*. Cambridge: Cambridge University Press.

King, Robert G., and Sergio Rebelo. 1990. "Public Policy and Economic Growth: Developing Neoclassical Implications." *Journal of Political Economy*, 98: S126–S150.

Kremer, Michael. 1993. "Population Growth and Technological Change: One Million B.C. to 1990." *Quarterly Journal of Economics*, 107: 681–716.

Krueger, Anne O. 1968. "Factor Endowments and Per Capita Income Differences Among Countries." *Economic Journal*, 78: 641–659.

———— 1983. "The Developing Countries' Role in the World Economy." Working paper.

Krugman, Paul R. 1987. "The Narrow Moving Band, the Dutch Disease, and the Competitive Consequences of Mrs. Thatcher: Notes on Trade in the Presence of Dynamic Scale Economies." *Journal of Development Economics*, 27: 41–55.

Kuznets, Simon. 1959. *Six Lectures on Economic Growth*. Glencoe: The Free Press.

Laitner, John. 1994. "Structural Change and Economic Growth." University of Michigan working paper.

Landes, David S. 1969. *The Unbound Prometheus*. Cambridge: Cambridge University Press.

Livi-Bacci, Massimo. 1992. *A Concise History of World Population*. Cambridge, Mass., and Oxford: Blackwell.

Loury, Glenn C. 1981. "Intergenerational Transfers and the Distribution of Earnings." *Econometrica*, 49: 843–867.

Lucas, Robert E., Jr. 1967. "Tests of a Capital-Theoretic Model of Technological Change." *Review of Economic Studies*, 34: 175–189.

——— 1971. "Optimal Management of a Research and Development Project." *Management Science*, 17: 679–697.

——— 1988. "On the Mechanics of Economic Development." *Journal of Monetary Economics*, 22: 3–42. (Chapter 1 of the present volume.)

——— 1993. "Making a Miracle." *Econometrica*, 61: 251–272. (Chapter 3 of the present volume.)

Lucas, Robert E., Jr., and Nancy L. Stokey. 1984. "Optimal Growth with Many Consumers." *Journal of Economic Theory*, 32: 139–171.

Maddison, Angus. 1982. *Phases of Capitalist Development*. Oxford: Oxford University Press.

——— 1983. "A Comparison of Levels of GDP Per Capita in Developed and Developing Countries, 1700–1980." *Journal of Economic History*, 43.

——— 1991. *Dynamic Forces in Capitalist Development*. Oxford: Oxford University Press.

——— 1995. *Monitoring the World Economy, 1820–1992*. Paris and Washington, D.C.: Development Centre Studies, OECD.

Malthus, Thomas R. 1798. "First Essay on Population." *Reprints of Economic Classics*. New York: Augustus Kelley, 1965.

Mankiw, N. Gregory, David Romer, and David Weil. 1992. "A Contribution to the Empirics of Economic Growth." *Quarterly Journal of Economics*, 107: 407–438.

Marx, Karl, and Friedrich Engels. 1848. *The Communist Manifesto*. In Eugene Kamenka, ed., *The Portable Karl Marx*. Viking Penguin, 1983.

Matsuyama, Kiminori. 1991. "Increasing Returns, Industrialization, and the Indeterminacy of Equilibrium." *Quarterly Journal of Economics*, 106: 617–650.

—— 1992. "Agricultural Productivity, Comparative Advantage, and Economic Growth."*Journal of Economic Theory*, 58: 317–334.

McEvedy, Colin, and Richard Jones. 1978. *Atlas of World Population History*. London: Allen Lane and Penguin.

Mincer, Jacob. 1962. "On-the-Job Training: Costs, Returns, and Some Implications." *Journal of Political Economy*, 70: S50–S79.

Moe, Karine S. 1998. "Fertility, Time Use, and Economic Development." *Review of Economic Dynamics*, 1: 699–718.

Murphy, Kevin M., Andrei Shleifer, and Robert W. Vishny. 1989. "Industrialization and the Big Push." *Journal of Political Economy*, 97: 1003–1026.

Nakajima, Tomoyuki. 1999. "Essays on Macroeconomic Theory." University of Chicago doctoral dissertation.

Nerlove, Marc. 1974. "Household and Economy: Toward a New Theory of Population and Economic Growth." *Journal of Political Economy*, 82: S200–S233.

Nerlove, Marc, Assaf Razin, and Efraim Sadka. 1987. *Household and Economy: Welfare Economics and Endogenous Fertility*. Boston: Academic Press.

Parente, Stephen L., and Edward C. Prescott. 1993. "Changes in the Wealth of Nations." *Federal Reserve Bank of Minneapolis Quarterly Review*, 17: 3–16.

—— 1994. "Barriers to Technology Adoption and Development." *Journal of Political Economy*, 102: 298–321.

—— 2000. *Barriers to Riches*. Cambridge, Mass.: MIT Press.

Pritchett, Lant. 1997. "Divergence, Big Time." *Journal of Economic Perspectives*, 11.3: 3–18.

Quah, Danny T. 1996. "Convergence Empirics Across Economies with (Some) Capital Mobility." *Journal of Economic Growth*, 1: 95–124.

—— 1997. "Empirics for Growth and Distribution: Stratification, Polarization, and Convergence Clubs." *Journal of Economic Growth*, 2: 27–60.

Rapping, Leonard A. 1965. "Learning and World War II Production Functions." *Review of Economics and Statistics*, 47: 81–86.

Raut, L. K., and T. N. Srinivasan. 1994. "Dynamics of Endogenous Growth." *Economic Theory*, 4: 777–790.

Razin, Assaf. 1972. "Optimum Investment in Human Capital." *Review of Economic Studies*, 39: 455–460.

Razin, Assaf, and Uri Ben-Zion. 1975. "An Intergenerational Model of Population Growth." *American Economic Review*, 65: 923–933.

Razin, Assaf, and Efraim Sadka. 1995. *Population Economics*. Cambridge, Mass.: MIT Press.

Rebelo, Sergio. 1990. "Long Run Policy Analysis and Long Run Growth." *Journal of Political Economy*, 99: 500–521.

Ricardo, David. 1817. *On the Principles of Political Economy and Taxation*. In Piero Sraffa, ed., *The Works and Correspondence of David Ricardo*, vol. 1. Cambridge: Cambridge University Press. 1951.

Romer, Paul. 1986a. "Increasing Returns and Long-Run Growth." *Journal of Political Economy*, 94: 1002–1037.

Romer, Paul M. 1986b. "Cake Eating, Chattering, and Jumps: Existence Results for Variational Problems." *Econometrica*, 54: 897–908.

———— 1990. "Endogenous Technological Change." *Journal of Political Economy*, 98: S71–S102.

Rosen, Sherwin. 1976. "A Theory of Life Earnings." *Journal of Political Economy*, 84: 545–567.

Schultz, Theodore W. 1962. "Reflections on Investment in Man." *Journal of Political Economy*, 70: S1–S8.

———— 1963. *The Economic Value of Education*. New York: Columbia University Press.

Searle, Allan D. 1945. "Productivity Changes in Selected Wartime Shipbuilding Programs." *Monthly Labor Review*, 61: 1132–1147.

Shell, Karl. 1966. "Toward a Theory of Inventive Activity and Capital Accumulation." *American Economic Review*, 56: 62–68.

———— 1967. "A Model of Inventive Activity and Capital Accumulation." In Karl Shell, ed., *Essays on the Theory of Optimal Economic Growth*. Cambridge, Mass.: MIT Press.

Smith, Adam. 1976. *The Wealth of Nations*. Chicago: University of Chicago Press.

Solow, Robert M. 1956. "A Contribution to the Theory of Economic Growth." *Quarterly Journal of Economics*, 70: 65–94.

Stigler, George J. 1952. "The Ricardian Theory of Value and Distribution." *Journal of Political Economy*, 60: 187–207.

—— 1960. "The Influence of Events and Policies on Economic Theory." *American Economic Review*, 50: 36–45.

Stokey, Nancy L. 1988. "Learning by Doing and the Introduction of New Goods." *Journal of Political Economy*, 96: 701–717.

—— 1991a. "The Volume and Composition of Trade Between Rich and Poor Countries." *Review of Economic Studies*, 58: 63–80.

—— 1991b. "Human Capital, Product Quality, and Growth." *Quarterly Journal of Economics*, 106: 587–616.

Summers, Robert, and Alan Heston. 1984. "Improved International Comparisons of Real Product and Its Composition: 1950–1980." *Review of Income and Wealth*, Series 30.

—— 1988. "A New Set of International Comparisons of Real Product and Price Levels: Estimates for 130 Countries: 1950–1985." *Review of Income and Wealth*, Series 34, 1–25.

—— 1991. "The Penn World Table (Mark 5): An Expanded Set of International Comparisons, 1950–1988." *Quarterly Journal of Economics*, 106: 327–368.

Tamura, Robert. 1986. "On the Existence of Multiple Steady States in One Sector Growth Models with Intergenerational Altruism." University of Chicago working paper.

—— 1988. "Fertility, Human Capital, and the 'Wealth of Nations.'" University of Chicago doctoral dissertation.

—— 1991. "Income Convergence in an Endogenous Growth Model." *Journal of Political Economy*, 99: 522–540.

—— 1994. "Fertility, Human Capital, and the Wealth of Families." *Economic Theory*, 4: 593–603.

—— 1996. "From Decay to Growth: A Demographic Transition to Economic Growth." *Journal of Economic Dynamics and Control*, 20: 1237–1262.

Thompson, Peter. 2001. "How Much Did the Liberty Shipbuilders Learn?" *Journal of Political Economy*, 109: 103–137.

Townsend, Robert M. 1994. "Risk and Insurance in Village India." *Econometrica*, 62: 539–592.

Uzawa, Hirofumi. 1965. "Optimum Technical Change in an Aggregative Model of Economic Growth." *International Economic Review*, 6: 18–31.

Veloso, Fernando A. 1999. "Two Essays on Income Composition, Endogenous Fertility and the Dynamics of Income Inequality." University of Chicago doctoral dissertation.

Vernon, Raymond. 1966. "International Investment and International Trade in the Product Cycle." *Quarterly Journal of Economics*, 80: 190–207.

Willis, Robert J. 1973. "A New Approach to the Economic Theory of Fertility Behavior." *Journal of Political Economy*, 81: S14–S64.

The World Bank. 1984, 1986. *World Development Report*. Oxford: Oxford University Press.

Wrigley, E. A. 1988. *Continuity, Chance and Change*. Cambridge: Cambridge University Press.

Young, Allyn A. 1928. "Increasing Returns and Economic Progress." *Economic Journal*, 38: 527-542.

Young, Alwyn. 1991. "Learning by Doing and the Effects of International Trade." *Quarterly Journal of Economics*, 106: 369-406.

—— 1992. "A Tale of Two Cities: Factor Accumulation and Technological Change in Hong Kong and Singapore." *Macroeconomics Annual*. National Bureau of Economic Research.

—— 1993. "Invention and Bounded Learning by Doing." *Journal of Political Economy*, 101: 443–472.